P9-CKB-643

GUSTAVO GUTIÉRREZ

MODERN SPIRITUAL MASTERS
Robert Ellsberg, Series Editor

This series introduces the essential writing and vision of some of the great spiritual teachers of our time. While many of these figures are rooted in long-established traditions of spirituality, others have charted new, untested paths. In each case, however, they have engaged in a spiritual journey shaped by the challenges and concerns of our age. Together with the saints and witnesses of previous centuries, these modern spiritual masters may serve as guides and companions to a new generation of seekers.

A complete list of previously published titles in this series is available at www.orbisbooks.com

MODERN SPIRITUAL MASTERS SERIES

GUSTAVO GUTIÉRREZ

Spiritual Writings

Selected with an Introduction by

DANIEL G. GROODY

ORBIS BOOKS

Maryknoll, New York 10545

Founded in 1970, Orbis Books endeavors to publish works that enlighten the mind, nourish the spirit, and challenge the conscience. The publishing arm of the Maryknoll Fathers and Brothers, Orbis seeks to explore the global dimensions of the Christian faith and mission, to invite dialogue with diverse cultures and religious traditions, and to serve the cause of reconciliation and peace. The books published reflect the views of their authors and do not represent the official position of the Maryknoll Society. To learn more about Maryknoll and Orbis Books, please visit our website at www.maryknollsociety.org.

Copyright © 2011 by Daniel G. Groody.

Published by Orbis Books, Box 302, Maryknoll, NY 10545-0302.

All rights reserved.

No part of this publication may be reproduced or transmitted in any form or by any means, electronic or mechanical, including photocopying, recording, or any information storage or retrieval system, without prior permission in writing from the publisher.

Queries regarding rights and permissions should be addressed to:
Orbis Books, P.O. Box 302, Maryknoll, NY 10545-0302.

Manufactured in the United States of America.

Library of Congress Cataloging-in-Publication Data

Gutierrez, Gustavo, 1928–
    [Selections. English. 2011]
    Spiritual writings / Gustavo Gutierrez ; selected with an introduction by
Daniel G. Groody.
        p. cm.
    Includes bibliographical references and index.
    ISBN 978-1-57075-947-5 (pbk. : alk. paper)
    1. Liberation theology. 2. Theology, Doctrinal. 3. Poverty – Religious aspects –
Christianity. I. Groody, Daniel G., 1964– II. Title.
BT83.57.G86913 2011
230'.2–dc23   2011017220

Contents

Part Two
THE EYES OF FAITH:
UNDERSTANDING GOD'S MERCY

Part Three
THE CHALLENGE OF THE KINGDOM:
LIVING IN THE SPIRIT

Sources

A Theology of Liberation: History, Politics, and Salvation. Trans. and ed. Sister Caridad Inda and John Eagleson. Maryknoll, N.Y.: Orbis Books, 1973. Fifteenth Anniversary Edition with a new Introduction by the Author, 1988. Original title: *Teología de la liberación: Perspectivas,* Lima: CEP, 1971.

We Drink from Our Own Wells: The Spiritual Journey of a People. Trans. Matthew J. O'Connell. Maryknoll, N.Y.: Orbis Books, 1983; Twentieth Anniversary Edition, 2003. Original title: *Beber en su propio pozo: En el itinerario espiritual de un pueblo,* 2nd ed., revised. Lima: CEP, 1983.

On Job: God-Talk and the Suffering of the Innocent. Trans. Matthew J. O'Connell. Maryknoll, N.Y.: Orbis Books, 1987. Original title: *Hablar de Dios desde el sufrimiento del inocente.* Lima: CEP, 1985.

The God of Life. Trans. Matthew J. O'Connell. Maryknoll, N.Y.: Orbis Books, 1991. Original title: *El Dios de la vida.* Lima: CEP, 1989.

Las Casas: In Search of the Poor of Jesus Christ. Trans. Robert R. Barr. Maryknoll, N.Y.: Orbis Books, 1993. Original title: *En busca de los pobres de Jesucristo.* Lima: CEP, 1992.

Sharing the Word through the Liturgical Year. Trans. Colette Joly Dees. Maryknoll, N.Y.: Orbis Books, 1997; Eugene, Ore.: Wipf and Stock, 2009. Original title: *Compartir la palabra: A lo largo del año litúrgico.* Lima: CEP, 1995.

The Density of the Present: Selected Writings. Maryknoll, N.Y.: Orbis Books, 1999. Adapted from *Densidad del presente: Selección de artículos.* Lima: CEP, 1996.

All Rights reserved.

Additional selections from *Páginas* (Lima), *Signos,* and *Theological Studies* used with permission.

Foreword

In his beautiful book *We Drink from Our Own Wells: The Spiritual Journey of a People,* Gustavo Gutiérrez expresses his own sense of the importance of spirituality by quoting one of the most influential figures on his own spiritual-theological itinerary: Marie-Dominique Chenu:

> The fact is that in the final analysis theological systems are simply the expressions of a spirituality. It is this that gives them their interest and grandeur.... One does not get to the heart of a system via the logical coherence of its structure or the plausibility of its conclusions. One gets to that heart by grasping it in its origins via that fundamental intuition that serves to guide a spiritual life and provides the intellectual regimen proper to that life.[1]

We owe a debt of gratitude to Daniel Groody, C.S.C., for collecting these texts that help us approach, however haltingly and inadequately, the "fundamental intuition" that has served to guide the spiritual life of this figure who has so crucially shaped theology over the past fifty years and has provided the intellectual regimen out of which his many works were written. For it is surely true that Gutiérrez's work belongs among the theological systems of which Chenu wrote. Already with the publication of his *A Theology of Liberation* in 1971 he was speaking of "a great need for a spirituality of liberation."[2] Noting, with many others, the growing split, beginning in the

---

1. *We Drink from Our Own Wells* (Maryknoll, N.Y.: Orbis Books, 1984), 147 n. 2. The quoted passage is from Chenu's small, but at the time controversial, book on the proper study of Thomas Aquinas: Marie-Dominique Chenu, *Le Saulchoir: Une école de théologie* (Etiolles, France: Le Saulchoir, 1937).

2. *A Theology of Liberation,* 74.

11

late Middle Ages, between this genre of theology and those of magisterial statements and academic theology, he observed that "we are suffering from this dichotomy even today," and asserted that "the spiritual function of theology, so important in the early centuries and later regarded as parenthetical, constitutes, nevertheless, a permanent dimension of theology."[3] His next monograph, *We Drink from Our Own Wells,* was his own explicit response to this exigency, but spirituality was never for him a sphere separated from theology, to be developed in its own isolated book. Spirituality is, for Gutiérrez, at the heart of theology, but also needs theology. They must proceed together.

In his later work he speaks of this relationship increasingly in terms of a mutually enriching relationship between the silence of prayer and action, on the one hand, and theological speech on the other. In a beautiful essay, "Theological Language: Fullness of Silence,"[4] Gutiérrez describes theology as the mediating link between a primordial spiritual experience (fullness of silence) and the only appropriate response to that experience: to share it with others; to announce the good news of the Gospel.

> The mystery of God must be accepted in prayer and in human solidarity; it is the moment of silence and of practice. Within that moment — and only from within it — will there arise the language and the categories necessary for transmitting it to others and for entering into communication, in the strong sense of the term: in communion with those others; that is the moment of speaking.[5]

It is in the struggle both to be faithful to what one encounters in silence (spirituality) and to respect the exigency (rooted in gratitude) to share it as good news to others — in the concrete particularity of their joys and hopes [*Gaudium et Spes*],

---

3. Ibid., 4.
4. "Theological Language: Fullness of Silence," trans. James Nickoloff and Margaret Wilde, in *Density of the Present: Selected Writings* (Maryknoll, N.Y.: Orbis Books, 1999), 186–207.
5. Ibid., 187.

and to the poor above all — that one deploys all the tools
of rational analysis (the second permanent task of theology as
defined in *A Theology of Liberation*), and critical reflection on
praxis in the light of the Gospel (the third).[6] This dynamic inter-
play is found in every one of Gutiérrez's essays and books, and
if the texts below focus (rightfully and helpfully) on the first
"moment," the others should never be forgotten in Gutiérrez's
oeuvre: the engagement with economic and political structures
using the best conceptual and argumentative tools available;
painstaking attention to Scripture and tradition; scrupulous historical research into the past (as with the magisterial book on
Bartolomé de Las Casas, for instance). In this interweaving
of spiritual experience, intellectual labor, and proclamation (in
word and deed) of the Good News, Gutiérrez is a true son of
St. Dominic: *contemplata aliis tradere* — handing on to others
what one has been given in contemplation.

Yet, like all spiritual masters, Gutiérrez is appreciative of
the full breadth and depth of the Christian spiritual tradition.
His work equally reminds one of the Ignatian motto, *simul in
actione contemplativus.* He argued in his own way for what
the Jesuit Ignacio Ellacuría described as "contemplation in the
action of justice," first and foremost with his definition and
interweaving of the two necessary "languages" of theology: the
language of prophecy and the language of contemplation.[7] He
shows the presence of both "languages" in the mystical writings
of John of the Cross. His conviction that "there is nothing more
demanding than gratuity,"[8] the sense that the fulfilling experience of God's boundless and unconditional love unleashes the
most radical forms of discipleship, surely puts him in proximity
to Francis of Assisi. And so it goes. Teresa of Avila, Bernard of
Clairvaux, Irenaeus of Lyons, Thérèse of Lisieux: they all find

---

6. *A Theology of Liberation*, 4–11.
7. Gustavo Gutiérrez, *On Job* (Maryknoll, N.Y.: Orbis Books, 1987), 94–97.
See this volume, pages 136–40.
8. Gustavo Gutiérrez, *Páginas* 164 (August 2000): 28–36. See this volume, page
76.

a place. But also figures more marginal to (but not less fruitful for) the mainline traditions: the sixteenth-century Amerindian, Guamáan Poma or the twentieth-century Peruvian novelist and poet, José María Arguedas. And, perhaps most importantly of all, the many men and women in Latin America today who make up for him a people in search of God, in search of God precisely in the midst of conditions that appear to make it absurd to speak of God — especially a God of love. Their voices are lovingly allowed to speak, this time to us, in *We Drink from Our Own Wells*. They are just as much a part of the cloud of witnesses who give us the courage to continue running the race set before us, who proffer the greatest possible credibility to Arguedas's powerful statement: "Is not what we know far less than the great hope we feel?"[9]

However one ultimately construes the spirituality of liberation that nourishes the "fundamental intuition" behind Gutiérrez's work, one cannot but be struck by its roots in the tradition, its coherence, and its comprehensive scope. As Daniel Groody shows in his introduction, Gutiérrez's spirituality is christocentric, has a Trinitarian depth structure, is shaped by the Spirit, and is necessarily communal-ecclesial in expression. What I find most striking is how powerfully Gutiérrez brings home the fact that spirituality is permeated by grace (gratuitousness); indeed, one might go so far as to say that for Gutiérrez, as for Karl Rahner, the spiritual life, including its most sublime moments, is nothing other than the graced life of the "ordinary Christian." Resolutely anti-elitist in his approach (again, like Rahner), Gutiérrez goes further to challenge those of us who are not poor to attend carefully to the extraordinarily (although scandalously) ordinary lives of the poor:

> The Bartimaeuses of this world have stopped being at the side of the road; they have jumped up and come to the Lord, their lifelong friend. Their presence may upset the old followers of Jesus, who spontaneously, and with the

9. Quoted in *On Job*, x.

best reasons in the world, begin to defend their privileges. They have discovered — and it cost them an effort to do so — *one* way of being a Christian, and no doubt they think it is *the* way to be a Christian for everyone. . . . They frequently react to the eleventh-hour disciples (workers) with the "envy" the Gospel describes (Matt. 20:1–16, esp. 15). Clearly the gratuitousness of God's love challenges the patterns we have become used to.[10]

Speaking elsewhere, and autobiographically, Gutiérrez puts it this way:

Working in this world [of the poor] and becoming familiar with it, I came to realize, together with others, that the first thing to do is to listen. Listen endlessly to the human and religious experience of those who have made the sufferings, hopes, and struggles of this people their own. Listen, not condescendingly, but to learn about the people and to learn about God.[11]

We are all the beneficiaries of Gutiérrez's careful listening.

Gustavo Gutiérrez has said that "for me, to do theology is to write a love letter to the God in whom I believe, to the people to whom I belong, and to the church of which I am a part. It is a love that recognizes perplexity, even disgust, but that above all brings joy."[12] I close by expressing my own thanks to Gustavo for allowing us to share in some small way in this beautiful correspondence, and to Daniel Groody for making many of the most moving of its letters available in this volume.

MATTHEW ASHLEY
University of Notre Dame

---

10. Gustavo Gutiérrez, *The Density of the Present* (Maryknoll, N.Y.: Orbis Books, 1999), 162–65. See this volume, page 103.

11. "The Task of Theology and Ecclesial Experience," in *The Density of the Present: Selected Writings* (Maryknoll, N.Y.: Orbis Books, 1999), 171.

12. "Theological Language: Fullness of Silence," 207.

Preface

Shortly after graduating from college, my good friend Jim Phalan and I hiked the Grand Canyon. Few places in the world rival the splendor of its breathtaking beauty. Our meandering traverses through this nature-painted canyon were marked at times by silent amazement, meaningful discussions, and rich theological conversation. Though the problems of the world seemed far away, we began asking where we wanted to go with our lives and how the world and its needs affected the choices we were making. Some of my own interest in these questions was generated by having lived under military dictatorships in Uruguay and Argentina, which made a deep impression on me. But it took time to understand the implications of these experiences for my own life of faith. Inevitably we began talking about what it means to follow Christ in the context of poverty and injustice in the contemporary world. During this hike Jim introduced me to the thought of Gustavo Gutiérrez. Little did I realize how that initial conversation would open up for me a whole new set of perspectives that would unfold in the years that followed.

Sometime later I moved to Chile during the end of Augusto Pinochet's dictatorship, and I began reading the works of Gutiérrez in more depth. I also started working with different Christian base communities in the country and listened to people's stories of poverty and oppression in various ways. From these dark and difficult times emerged some shining examples of people who clamored for their rights and fought for justice and peace, even at the price of their own lives. I admired some of these people and the social movements that fought for a better world, but there were others in these same movements who left me troubled and unsettled. Beneath the theological words and the social analysis were attitudes of self-righteousness, judgmentalism, and aggressiveness that left me wanting to fight for liberation from a deeper place. I began to appreciate not only *that* one fights for liberation but *how* one does it. I was drawn particularly to those whose fight for justice emerged from a quality of soul and deep spirituality. For me spirituality and social concerns each flowed into the other, which was why Gutiérrez's vision of mysticism and justice together compelled me in many ways.

I met Gustavo first through his books, and I did not imagine that I would ever meet him in person. But as I was finishing up doctoral studies in 2000, Virgil Elizondo invited me to join him for a symposium in Paris, where Gustavo was living. During a lunch together Virgil asked Gustavo if he would like to come to the University of Notre Dame to teach. As events unfolded, Virgil, Gustavo, and I all began working together at Notre Dame that fall and were joined by Tim Matovina as well. Together with Matt Ashley, we formed a great team and grew not only as colleagues but as friends. We began teaching together, organizing conferences, working on publications, and talking about many of the themes presented in this volume. Each of us came to appreciate Gustavo not only through his writings but especially through his joy, simplicity of heart, humor, quick wit, and thoughtful concern for those around him.

More than a decade after we all started at Notre Dame, I began a conversation with Robert Ellsberg about the Spiritual Masters Series at Orbis books. Tim Matovina had recently completed an outstanding volume on the spiritual writings of Virgil Elizondo, and Robert and I began talking about creating a similar collection of Gustavo's writings. Preparing this volume provided a welcome opportunity to reread Gustavo's works and go over some of his central spiritual texts with him.

More than a collection of selected writings, which has been done most notably by Jim Nickoloff, I wanted to assemble a spiritual resource that included some of the most-up-to-date reflection from Gustavo, who turned eighty-three at the time of its completion. Most of the material contained in this volume is from previously published material, but some is new material, and other selections come from articles not previously translated or published in English. After various revisions, Gustavo read through the material numerous times, making additional suggestions throughout the process. Some refinements in translations, development of his ideas, and some slight editorial adaptations from the original versions have been made. All Scripture references are from the New Revised Standard Version of the Bible except where otherwise noted. In the end, this volume is not an exhaustive compendium of his spiritual writings, nor a digest of his theological ideas, but rather the core writings and most current revisions that are at the heart of Gustavo's spiritual vision.

As I reflected with Gustavo on his writings and his legacy, I recalled his influence not only on his peers and on my own life but also on a whole new generation of theologians. In 2002, we organized an international conference on the Option for the Poor in Christian Theology at Notre Dame. In addition to bringing together a senior generation of scholars who forged a way in this field, we also invited a new, emerging generation from different parts of the world who are carrying on this tradition. At the end of the conference, after each highlighted some areas where they are doing research in this field, Gustavo gave each one a cross, made by Edilberto Merida of Peru, whose passionate sculpture of the crucified Christ appears on the cover of *A Theology of Liberation*. Handing a cross to each one of this new generation, Gustavo then said the words, "Receive the cross of Christ. May it illumine and guide your theological reflection and your option for the poor."

Some of these theologians who are now carrying out this great reflection include Jacques Haers from Belgium; Carlos Mendoza and Eduardo Gonzalez from Mexico; Therese Tinkasiimire from Uganda; Clemens Sedmak from Austria; Renata Furst from Honduras; María José Caram from Perú; Gioacchino Campese from

Italy; Mary Doak, Paul Kollman, John Markey, Robert Lassalle-Klein, Michael Lee, Natalia Imperatori-Lee, Catherine Punsalan, Alex Nava, LaReine Marie Mosely, Maria Teresa Davila from the United States; Jude Lal Fernando from Sri Lanka; Elías López Pérez from Spain; and Ernesto Valiente from El Salvador. To this list must also be added newer scholars like Victor Carmona, Daniel Castillo, David Lantigua, and Mike Griffin, all of whom have been mentored by Gustavo. Since the conference ended, many in this group, and many others not named here, have continued to form a community of friends, interested in common themes, who are working on common projects together.

This volume is one such project, and because this book is shaped so profoundly by gratuity, I thank all those who helped bring it to completion, especially Claudia Ramirez, Timothy Matovina, Virgil Elizondo, Terry Garza, John Cavadini, Matt Ashley and our colleagues at the Institute for Latino Studies and the Department of Theology, the Kroc Institute for International Peace Studies, the Institute for Scholarship in the Liberal Arts, and the Kellogg Institute for International Studies at the University of Notre Dame. I also thank Mike and Liz LaFortune, Macrina and Ed Hjerpe, Fulata Moyo, Robert Ellsberg, and my brothers in the Congregation of Holy Cross, especially Richard Warner, Tim Scully, and Jim King. Lastly, but by no means least, I would like to thank Mary J. Miller, whose hard work, generous support, attention to detail, and dedicated assistance helped make this work possible.

Introduction

"The contemporary theologians who are most perceptive of the political, economic, and ecological crisis of this moment," writes Timothy Radcliffe, "are also those who are most deeply rooted in the mystical tradition."[1] Among the most notable and influential theologians of the twentieth century, Gustavo Gutiérrez holds a central place. A Dominican priest and Latin American scholar, he is known to most as the father of liberation theology and its central notion of the preferential option for the poor. Many are drawn to his social convictions, and some troubled by them, yet far fewer know the profound spirituality that has forged his theological vision. These writings explore the life of Jesus Christ, the desire to follow him as a disciple, and the commitment to live in solidarity with those the world ignores and rejects. The purpose of this book is to present the rich spirituality that nourishes this dedication to the poor and insignificant.

Formative Years

Gustavo Merino Gutiérrez was born in the Monserrat barrio of Lima, Peru, on June 8, 1928. Growing up with two sisters, he knew both the joys of a caring family and the struggles of their simple means and fragile livelihoods. When he was still young, Gutiérrez was afflicted with osteomyelitis and from age twelve to eighteen he was confined to bed and a wheelchair, which limited his early education to home-schooling. Prior to this time he

---

1. Timothy Radcliffe, cited in preface of Albert Nolan, *Jesus Today: A Spirituality of Radical Freedom* (Maryknoll, N.Y.: Orbis Books, 2006), x.

had a very active childhood. He loved sports and good conversations with his friends, with whom he would discuss a wide range of topics from Christian faith to literature to the political situation of Peru.

His own illness over time sensitized him to the physical, psychological, and spiritual suffering of others, and it would teach him much about hope and joy, as well as compassion and solidarity. Though his early illness imposed on him many personal limitations, it also opened up for him a life-long love of learning, as he began reading books from a wide variety of fields. His own ailments led him initially to study medicine, but midstream during his undergraduate years he felt called to pursue a priestly vocation and moved from the university to the seminary.

Soon after entering the seminary his friends and superiors encouraged him to expand his theological horizons even further by studying in Europe. From 1951 to 1959 he studied philosophy, psychology, and theology at the Catholic University of Louvain in Belgium, the University of Lyon in France, and the Gregorian University in Italy. In Lyon, the life and thought of Marie-Dominique Chenu had a great influence on him. Chenu was a Dominican priest who had been very active with the priest-worker movement and began doing theological reflection from within the social situation of the working classes. His articulation of the relationship between theology and spirituality particularly intrigued Gutiérrez. In his book *Le Saulchoir: Une école de théologie,* Chenu notes that if one wants to understand theology, then one has to look at the spirituality behind it. Though many see theology as the precursor to spirituality, Chenu understood spirituality as a way of life that engages not only the mind and the world of ideas but the heart and all its rich affectivity. Theology was a second act that reflected on that life and arises "at sundown." Gutiérrez would take this insight and later articulate the theological task as a reflection on faith in the light of praxis. In this sense Gutiérrez came to see theology not as religious metaphysics but as a reflection on Christian life under the light of faith, a *lumen fidei,* in order to live out the truth in love.

In addition to Chenu, Gutiérrez's spiritual trajectory was profoundly shaped by many other Dominicans, and their method of theology greatly attracted him. While in France he worked with other noted scholars such as Yves Congar, Edward Schillebeeckx, and Christian Ducoq. Gutiérrez was also drawn to the life of Dominican Bartolomé de Las Casas (1484–1566), whose defense of the poor, indigenous slaves during the Spanish conquest affirmed the close link between salvation and social justice.

Though initially ordained as a priest for the Diocese of Lima in 1959, Gutiérrez formally joined the Dominican order in 1998. But the influence of the Dominican charism on Gutiérrez predated his formal incorporation into the order. He was particularly taken by the Dominican integration of study, prayer, and preaching. St. Dominic believed that one studied theology in order to preach. This interrelationship between spirituality, theology, and the preaching of the Gospel would later influence Gutiérrez as he connected spirituality, evangelization, and theology. "Spirituality," Gutiérrez would say, "leads to evangelization, and reflection on that process is at the heart of theological reflection."

In addition to the Dominicans, Gutiérrez was influenced by many other notable thinkers of his time. His work on the editorial board of the international journal *Concilium* and other venues brought him into friendship with some of the leading theologians of the day, including Karl Rahner, Hans Küng, Virgil Elizondo, Cassiano Floristan, Jean-Baptist Metz, Henri de Lubac, Juan Alfaro (of Rome), and many others. In the Protestant world, the work of Karl Barth, Dietrich Bonhoeffer, and Paul Tillich shaped his thinking, as well as social scientists such as François Perroux and Paulo Freire. From the perspective of philosophy, Gutiérrez would bring his claims of faith into dialogue with thinkers such as Albert Camus, G. W. F. Hegel, Jean-Paul Sartre, and Gabriel Marcel; film directors such as Luis Buñuel and Ingmar Bergman; and writers such as Peruvians José María Arguedas, Felipe Guamán Poma de Ayala, and César Vallejo.

After almost a decade of studies in Europe, Gutiérrez returned to Lima in 1960 as a priest and teacher. Between 1960 and 1966 Gutiérrez's theological perspective continued to expand and deepen while the pastoral challenges he faced pushed him to examine the Christian tradition in new ways. Though Gustavo's studies abroad were valuable and formative, they left unanswered many pressing questions that stemmed from his native social context. He discovered many "classical" theological formulations were not adequate to deal with the needs of the poor and oppressed in Latin America, so he began to read the theological tradition from a new perspective. He started rereading and relearning his previous education, especially by rereading the Bible and rereading history.

Three things about the notion of poverty struck him at this time: (1) Material poverty is never good but an evil to be opposed. It is not simply an occasion for charity but a degrading force that denigrates human dignity and ought to be opposed and rejected. (2) Poverty is not a result of fate or laziness, but is due to structural injustices that privilege some while marginalizing others. Poverty is not inevitable; collectively the poor can organize and facilitate social change. (3) Poverty is a complex reality and is not limited to its economic dimension; poverty means early and unjust death, and to be poor, above all, means to be insignificant. As he began reading the Scriptures from the perspective of poverty, the text of Matthew 25:31–46 and the emphasis on the least of society became an acute focal point for his theological reflection. He began to react against some prevailing, religiously formulated notions about poverty that idealized its place in the life of faith. He negated superficial perspectives of poverty and spirituality that avoided the truth that poverty is ugly, with nothing romantic about it. He would say that Jesus said, "Blessed are the poor," not "blessed is poverty," and he would underscore that love of God and love of the poor are inseparable. Standing in solidarity *with* the poor also began to mean taking a stand *against* inhumane poverty.

As he addressed the problem of poverty, he saw how social sciences offered important instruments for understanding reality. Like other Latin Americans in the 1970s such as Henrique Cardoso and Enzo Faletto, he drew on the theory of dependence, which took some notions from Marxist analysis. Many have misunderstood and misinterpreted the connection between Gutiérrez, liberation theology, and Marxism, and some critics of Gutiérrez see liberation theology as some kind of "warmed-over" Marxism with a religious mask. But nothing could be further from Gutiérrez's own vision. While he did draw on certain tools of social analysis in order to understand reality, he did not, and has not, subscribed to Marxist philosophy or Marxist conclusions. Gutiérrez has affirmed consistently that the first and last line of liberation theology is against Marxism. For Marx, Christian religion was alienating. For Gutiérrez, it is liberating.

The church issued two documents on the subject of liberation theology, and the first highlighted the *abuses* of liberation theology while the second highlighted the *positive role* of liberation in salvation history. At no time was Gustavo or his writings ever reproved by the Vatican. "The theology of liberation," Gutiérrez states, "is about God. God's love and God's life are, ultimately, its only theme." Gutiérrez became a theologian and a priest because he believed evangelization is a more powerful response to poverty than violence, and his main concern is precisely how to be Christian in the context of global poverty.

Gutiérrez makes distinctions between material poverty, voluntary poverty, and spiritual poverty. Real poverty means privation, or the lack of goods necessary to meet basic human needs. It means inadequate access to education, health care, public services, living wages, and discrimination because of culture, race, or gender. Gutiérrez reiterates that such poverty is evil; it is a subhuman condition in which the majority of humanity lives today, and it poses a major challenge to every Christian conscience and therefore to spirituality and theological reflection.

Spiritual poverty is about a radical openness to the will of God, a radical faith in a providential God, and a radical trust in a loving God. It is also known as spiritual childhood, from which flows the renunciation of material goods. Relinquishing possessions comes from a desire to be more possessed by God alone and to love and serve God more completely. Spiritual poverty does not infer that there is something bad about material possessions, nor that real poverty in itself is good, or that it is a path to holiness. Rather spiritual poverty refers to those who have become more open to God's revelation, action, and guidance in their lives and who humbly recognize their place in the universe as children of God. Spiritual poverty is a grace that means I have trustingly put all of my life in the hands of God and express it through my commitment to the poor.

Voluntary poverty is a conscious protest against injustice by choosing to live together with those who are materially poor. Its inspiration comes from the life of Jesus, who entered into solidarity with the human condition in order to help human beings overcome the sin that enslaves and impoverishes them. Voluntary poverty affirms that Christ came to live as a poor person not because poverty itself has any intrinsic value but to criticize and challenge those people and systems that oppress the poor and compromise their God-given dignity. It involves more than detachment, because the point is not to love poverty but to love the poor.

Historical Context

In addition to pastoral and scholarly influences, Gutiérrez was profoundly shaped by the events of his time. The 1950s and 1960s gave rise to many different liberation movements throughout the world, as well as many waves of renewal across the globe. The foremost event within the church was the Second Vatican Council (1962–65). Gustavo was profoundly taken by John XXIII, particularly his challenge to read the Gospel in light of the signs of the times and his summons to serve the poor in the world. Vatican II opened the way for Gutiérrez to explore new theological horizons as well, and during the latter part of the Council, Gutiérrez attended the fourth session as a theological assistant to Bishop Manuel Larraín of Chile. Gutiérrez was grateful for what happened at the Council, but because of the work that needed to be done, he was not completely satisfied with its outcomes. The optimism of the Council compelled him, but the reality of poverty in Latin America continued to challenge him pastorally, theologically, and spiritually.

As the Council was ending, Gutiérrez went away on retreat to spend more time praying over some core issues stirring within him. He felt drawn particularly to the works of Dietrich Bonhoeffer and his attempt to speak about God in a contemporary, adult, and secularizing world. In a similar way Gutiérrez knew spiritual and theological reflection needed further reformulation in light of the poverty and injustice of Latin America. The question for Gutiérrez was more and more about how to speak to the poor about God's love for them, when so much of their lives pointed to the contrary.

After Vatican II subsequent church documents, such as Pope Paul VI's *Populorum Progressio* (1967), began clarifying the church's commitment to human development. The church started talking not only about the personal dimensions but also the social dimensions of morality, and it argued that poverty is not the inevitable fate of human civilization but a social reality that is contrary to the will of God. Soon after, in some of the courses he taught in Latin America, Gutiérrez began formulating the beginnings of what later became known as a theology of liberation. In June 1967, Fr. Theodore Hesburgh, C.S.C., invited Gutiérrez to come to the University of Notre Dame to further his theological research, and later that year, at a course in Montreal on "The Church and Poverty," he presented some reflections about the biblical meaning of poverty. He realized that poverty needed to be understood not simply as a socioeconomic issue but a theological issue as well.

The theme of poverty would be further explored as the Latin America bishops reflected on the significance of the Council and subsequent documents of Catholic social teaching. The second General Conference of the Latin American Episcopacy held in Medellín, Colombia, from August 26 to September 6, 1968, would begin exploring the integral link between the proclamation of the Gospel and action on behalf of justice. Subsequent conferences in Puebla, Mexico (1979), Santo Domingo, Dominican Republic (1992), and Aparecida, Brazil (2007), would take up the questions that Gutiérrez and others posed, offering the beginnings of a much-needed contextualized theological vision from Latin America.

The bishops at Medellín, directly or indirectly, were greatly influenced by Gutiérrez's works and in 1968 began to speak much more strongly in terms of liberation:

> The Latin American episcopate cannot remain indifferent in the face of tremendous social injustices existent in Latin America, which keep the majority of our peoples in dismal poverty, which in many cases becomes inhuman wretchedness. A deafening cry pours from the throats of millions of [our people], asking their pastors for a liberation that reaches them nowhere else.[2]

In 1979, the bishops further reiterated at Puebla that the current social situation in Latin America is a sin that cries out to heaven for remedy and calls society to conversion:

> The situation of inhuman poverty in which millions of Latin Americans live is the most devastating and humiliating kind of scourge. And the situation finds expression

---

2. Medellín document on the poverty of the church in *The Church in the Present-Day Transformation of Latin America in Light of the Council*, ed. Michael Colonnese (Bogotá: General Secretariat of CELAM, 1968), 1–2.

in such things as a high rate of infant mortality, lack of adequate housing, health problems, starvation wages, unemployment and underemployment, malnutrition, job uncertainty, compulsory mass migrations, etc. Analyzing this situation more deeply, we discover that this poverty is not a passing phase. Instead it is the product of economic, social, and political situations and structures, although there are also other causes for the state of misery.[3]

Moreover, at Puebla, the bishops repeated the challenge of liberation in light of the scandalous social situation of Latin America:

Viewing it in the light of faith, we see the growing gap between rich and poor as a scandal and a contradiction to Christian existence. The luxury of a few becomes an insult to the wretched poverty of the vast masses. This is contrary to the plan of the Creator and to the honor that is due Him. In this anxiety and sorrow the church sees a situation of social sinfulness, all the more serious because it exists in countries that call themselves Catholic.[4]

Such statements were bold and challenging, and they stirred up controversy inside and outside the church. Whether one agreed with them or not, the relationship between poverty and the church, and spirituality and justice, brought these questions to the forefront of the church's response to the modern world.

Within the larger global society at this time, there was much reflection about "development" and "revolution." Gutiérrez saw something of value in these notions, but he did not draw directly from them because he wanted to probe the evangelical and social dimensions of liberation. For these reasons he chose

---

3. Puebla Final Document in *Puebla and Beyond: Documentation and Commentary*, ed. John Eagleson and Philip Scharper, trans. John Drury (Maryknoll, N.Y.: Orbis Books, 1979), 29–30.
4. Ibid., 28.

not to name this theology "development theology," or "revolutionary theology" but "liberation theology." He tried to place social liberation in the framework of salvation in Jesus Christ.

eology gained
n   rious forms of
d   nmunities that
t   970s Gutiérrez
a   Mexican Amer-
i   where he not
(in the United
                                                                   gy with noted
                                                                   f San Antonio,
                                                                   nt milestone in
                                                                   logy of Libera-
                                                                   rst published in

For Gutierrez, spirituality and liberation th all-embracing terms that encompass the totality of life. The horizons of these words are not limited to life above or below the firmament by focusing either on the world to come or on this world alone. Spirituality is not simply about one's personal relationship with God, detached from contemporary problems, focused on other-worldly speculation, or only the rewards of a future life. At the same time liberation is not limited to social issues, related only to events in this world, to political changes, human timelines, or social ideology. Dualisms that divide the material and the spiritual, the temporal and the religious, the personal and the social, do not take into account the unity of salvation history, which will be discussed in more detail below. For Gutiérrez, spirituality and liberation unite both this world and the next by grounding a life of faith within history and human experience, one in which God's life and mercy take flesh amid the suffering of human beings and the redemptive promises of Christ's life-giving death and resurrection. For Gutiérrez, spirituality is about following Jesus, and liberation means giving life.

The role of spirituality in the process of liberation comes through in all of Gutiérrez's writings, but its first, explicit articulation is in five pages of *A Theology of Liberation.* From the very beginning he realized the relationship between sp   ty and   on, but to this theme needed fur   ns and other co   years before he expanded on it and pu   *Spiritual Jour-ney*   rs is a direct refe   hen it comes to s   m their own wel   the process of li   as disciples by a   rises out of it,"   mooths out any   same time supp   ruitful."[5]

In   y of living a spi   d entering into   paschal mystery for Gutiérrez entails living in solidarity with the poor and struggling for their liberation. *We Drink from Our Own Wells* outlines the contours of such a spirituality of the poor and their struggle for life. This spirituality has deeply personal dimensions, but it is not an individualistic enterprise. Spirituality is fundamentally about the journey of an entire people. As we commit to following Christ in this way, a new fellowship is created, a new life emerges, a new energy is born, and a new freedom to love is made possible. In the process God's reign irrupts into history, beginning with the poor and excluded. Those who experience poverty and exclusion start to become aware of the causes of

---

5. *We Drink from Our Own Wells*, 5.

their poverty and begin affirming their God-given rights as children of God and even find the capacity to trust in God and celebrate life amid tremendous trial and adversity.

Gutiérrez would develop these spiritual reflections even further in his book *On Job: God Talk and the Suffering of the Innocent,* offering biblical reflection from the perspective of the poor. The initial intuitions of this book emerged from Gutiérrez's own experience of suffering as a child, but they developed further in his work among the poor in Peru. "The people in Lima," Gutiérrez noted, "taught me volumes about hope in the midst of suffering... hope in the difficult moments." His ongoing work among the poor would initiate permanent dialogue with his theology, and like Job in his theological exchanges with friends, Gustavo's own experience amid the poor led him to question some of the theological notions that romanticized poverty and separated spirituality from history. In this work he reads the story of Job in light of pressing human issues like the transcendence of God, the problem of evil, human suffering, the question of retribution, friendship, and others. At their core these subjects lead us to questions such as, How are we to talk about God? What do the Scriptures have to say to the innocent who suffer? How are we to speak about God from the context of global poverty and injustice? What is God's call to us at this time of history? And how are we to respond to Christ amid the inequities of the world? These questions and others are central to Gutiérrez's spiritual writings.

Major Themes of Gutiérrez

Those who have studied with Gustavo or attended his public lectures know that he has certain stylistic conventions that shape his presentations. He frequently structures his talks around three central points, and so it seemed most fitting to organize this volume around three core points as well. Nothing seemed more appropriate to me or Gustavo than to give this work a Trinitarian structure. To bring out the core spiritual focus of his work, the first part is organized around the Son, the second around the

Father and the third around the Holy Spirit. Like the Trinity, these sections are all interconnected, but the table of contents itself summarizes the framework around which to understand these central spiritual writings. Each of the three sections has seven subsections.

The first part of this book begins on a christological note because an encounter with the Lord sets the spiritual journey in motion. This encounter is the "starting point for a route to be taken in the following of Jesus Christ."[6] It affects how we understand ourselves, how we live with others, and how we walk in the world. Some of the writings in this section highlight the person of Mary, who manifests in her life an openness to the gratuity of God and a spirit that trusts in his power to save and empower the lowly. This section ends on the connection between mysticism and politics and the role of the poor in a Christian spirituality. Without spirituality, the task of liberation takes on an entirely different trajectory. For Gutiérrez, Christ is at the heart of humanity's deepest searching for liberation, and without rooting life in him, liberation is just another ideology that leaves untouched the deeper needs for human redemption.

The second part of this volume organizes Gutiérrez's writings around the Father. Whatever we say about God must begin first of all with mystery. Consequently, spirituality begins in silence. Much of this section revolves around the question of contemplation. These writings highlight how listening is a prerequisite to speaking about God. In Gustavo's words, "Everything begins in silence; that is the first step in speaking of God; that is the moment of listening and prayer; later the language engendered in that quiet will come." Drawing from the beautiful words of Irenaeus of Lyon, he adds: "from the Father's silence comes the Word of the Son."[7] Yet it is from this silence, prayer, and contemplation that one begins to see the world in a new way. Without these, liberation can become clouded by frenetic

---

6. Ibid., 1.
7. Ibid., xviii.

activism or angry judgmentalism, from which people also need liberation. Entry into the holy ground of the Father involves purification, especially from false gods and selfish pride that enslaves, and the writings selected here bring out the call to choose life amid the darkness of human society, the idols of our own making, and the injustices of the modern world.

The selections in the third part of this volume deal with life "according to the Spirit." After encounter and contemplation comes one's response in faith expressed through following Jesus Christ. This response puts the reign of God at the heart of life, sharing the table, living the beatitudes, but also witnessing to life. Included in this section are brief selections about people whom Gustavo admires and values as notable examples of Christian life. As they witness to God's love for the world and express it through an undying love for each other, they have something to say about solidarity with the poor, the dignity of each person, and fraternity and equality of all before God.

While the Trinity is at the heart of these writings, I would like to highlight four additional themes that come through these texts, namely (1) the unity of gratuity and justice, (2) the unity of human history and salvation history, (3) the unity of contemplation and action, and (4) the unity of the universality of God's love and the preferential option for the poor.

The Unity of Gratuity and Justice

No theme shapes the writings of Gutiérrez from beginning to end more than the gratuity of God. This gift of gratuitous love, made known above all in the gift of Jesus Christ, is about God's total acceptance of every human being without regard for their moral or spiritual condition. For him God's unmerited and all-embracing love for all people is the most important message of the Bible and the central focus of the Scriptures. Without gratuity, the Gospel makes no sense, nor does the challenge of justice and a steadfast commitment to the poor. Certainly it is possible to serve the poor out of noble, humanitarian concern, but the focus of Gutiérrez is not volunteerism, altruism, or humanism. For him the faith that does justice is a response to the God who has first loved us. Gratuity reveals the love that makes human beings whole, and without love, there is no Christian spirituality, no genuinely human life. Though gratuity is unmerited, it is an invitation to a radical transformation. It begins with God's unconditional love, but it calls forth the response of loving others as God loves. For Gutiérrez this means that the gift is also a challenge. As faith puts one in right relationship with God though the grace of internal justice, it also calls a person to seek external justice through the promotion of good works, through changing structures that oppress, through empowering the lowly, in brief, through the work of liberation. In his teaching and his writings, Gutiérrez brings this out by noting that in German, the word *gabe* (grace, gift) is related to the word *aufgabe* (duty, obligation, commitment). He sees Christian faith as lived between *gabe* and *aufgabe,* between grace and duty, between the gift given from God for the believer and the gift given by the disciple for others. Throughout these spiritual writings, Gutiérrez notes that there is nothing more liberating, or demanding, than gratuity, which is expressed in the call to establish justice, to serve one another, to protect the rights and dignity of others by loving gratuitously, as God does.

Unity of Salvation History and Human History

Throughout Gutiérrez's spiritual writings, there is an underlying emphasis on the unity of salvation history and human history. On the one hand his writings are an implicit critique of other-worldly piety that separates this world from the next and does not realize that salvation history is about both what happens now *and* the life to come. Religious acts of devotion have some proximate value in our love of God, but they alone are not enough to constitute a Christian spirituality that leads us to love our neighbor. On the other hand Gutiérrez challenges those who reduce the kingdom of God to political changes and human timelines, and Christian theology to social ideology. Though social activism has immanent value in loving our neighbor, it does not take us beyond ourselves to places of gratuity and contemplation, without which we can never understand who we are before God. For Gutiérrez salvation is about both this world and the next, which makes the present task of liberation all the more urgent. This task will never be fully completed this side of heaven, for only God alone can bring it to its fulfillment, but through the person of Jesus and his life-giving death, eternal life begins now.

For Gutiérrez there is no dualism between salvation history and human history. Instead there is one history because there is one God and one life in God. God's grace meets us and acts in that history, and an essential task of living out the spiritual life is discerning God's Spirit within it. Salvation history is one history, which is why history figures prominently in these writings. The work of the church is to announce the Gospel in that history, but part of this challenge requires a faithful response to contemporary society by helping others with temporal needs, even as the church and state occupy different roles in the process. As Pope Benedict XVI noted in *Deus Caritas Est,* spirituality and justice are inseparable in this unified vision of history:

> The church cannot and must not take upon herself the political battle to bring about the most just society possible. She cannot and must not replace the state. Yet at the same time, she cannot and must not remain on the sidelines in the fight for justice. She has to play her part through rational argument and she has to reawaken the spiritual energy without which justice, which always demands sacrifice, cannot prevail and prosper. A just society must be the achievement of politics, not of the church. Yet the promotion of justice through efforts to bring about

openness of mind and will to the demands of the common good is something which concerns the church deeply. (*Deus Caritas Est* 28)

The central focus for Gutiérrez is not so much how to order society but how to ensure justice for all of God's children. As Benedict puts it, "Love of God and love of neighbor have become one: in the least of the brethren we find Jesus himself, and in Jesus we find God" (*Deus Caritas Est* 15).

The Unity of Contemplation and Action

Contemplation is about attentiveness to God's gratuitous action in the world, and it is both the motivation for and stimulus toward greater apostolic activity. In the economy of grace and freedom, there is always a circular motion between gift and response, being loved and loving others, between contemplation and action. Gutiérrez highlights that what we have contemplated we transmit, and the free love offered by and received from God is what allows us to offer it to others. Contemplation enables us to affirm life in the midst of death. It helps us grow in freedom to forget ourselves in such a way that we are free to love.

Animated by the Spirit of the risen Christ, followers are not forlorn and sad, gloomy and depressed by the world and its problems. They are not glum and do not brood at the unjust world and its evils and dispense to it pearls of false prophecy. The contemplative spirit does not put the rich on guilt trips even though it warns of the dangers of idolatry, the illusions of self-sufficiency, and the hollowness of an ego-minded material prosperity that does not know how to share. Such posture not only deprives the poor but also dehumanizes the rich, especially because part of the task of becoming human is recognizing our interconnectedness to others. Instead, contemplation and action partner together with fiesta and prophecy. As Virgil Elizondo observes in his book *Galilean Journey,* fiesta without prophecy easily degenerates into indulgence, escapism, and drunkenness. But prophecy without fiesta can degenerate into anger, cynicism, spiritual elitism, and a suffocating spiritual seriousness. Contemplation leads us into the life of God and helps us know ourselves as made in that same image and likeness.

Knowing ourselves before God and contemplating God's action in the world stimulates us to concerns greater than ourselves and to loving as we are loved. Love is what makes us human, and responding to that love is what leads to becoming more and more like God. Contemplation leads us into divine life and love and generates in us new capacities to love and promote life, and we express that love in our solidarity with any person in need. These desires are at the heart of human existence, and these spiritual writings bring out the human need to be loved and valued at the core of one's being, beyond one's physical characteristics, beyond one's usefulness, even beyond one's apostolic efficacy. There is a sense of liberation that comes from knowing that we are accepted for who we are in our absolute nakedness, as much as it attracts and frightens us at the same time. It is this love that God offers to all, but it must be accepted in order for it to transform. Love leads to action, but action without love, or service without Spirit, leads to a hollow activism rather than a genuine holiness. Through contemplation and action, prayer, worship, and service, we come to realize we are both "made in gratuity" and made to love gratuitously.

The Unity of God's Universal Love and Preference for the Poor

Finally, Gutiérrez's writings bring out God's universal love for everyone, especially the poor. Some see Gutiérrez's insistence on the preferential option for the poor as an exclusive option, a sectarian statement, a reductive theological perspective that gives primacy to one's social or economic status. But this is not Gutiérrez's focus. Gratuity is at the same time universal and particular, not because God has favorites but because, like any parent, love extends particularly to those who are in most need. Gutiérrez brings out that gratuity and particularity are not self-contradictory but two sides of the same spiritual coin. As Pope Benedict XVI put it, "Love of God and love of neighbor are thus inseparable; they form a single commandment. But both live from the love of God who has loved us first" (*Deus Caritas Est* 18).

The option for the poor, when borne as a spiritual commitment, is not simply about having fewer clothes and fewer things or clinging to an ego-centered, self-ordained sense of being a great prophet. It is generated first through a spiritual poverty, which is not primarily about detachment from material things. Spiritual poverty is about spiritual childhood, living out the trust that my life is in the hands of God. It also entails a divesting even of those images of the false self that keep us from relating to others in a more authentic way. The option for the poor flows as a consequence of spiritual poverty but not as a substitute for it. Spiritual poverty leads to service and otherness, and concern for the most vulnerable. It begins with material poverty, but above all, to opt for the poor means to be in solidarity with those the world regards as insignificant. For Gutiérrez the poor are much more than a social class; the poor are also a way of mediating our relationship with God. The poor mediate Christ, and Christ is the mediator of the poor. "To opt for the poor," says Gutiérrez, "is to make an option for Jesus Christ, who is salvation." Putting God and the poor first is a way of following Jesus, a way of living out spirituality.

The goal of the option for the poor is to foster equality and fraternity that lead to the creation of mutually enriching friendships. Without friendship, an option for the poor can easily become commitment to an abstraction (to a social class, a race, a culture, an idea), and in the process some who work on behalf of the poor may in fact not treat the poor well at all. In such cases the rivers of spirituality do not run very deeply. In John's Gospel, friendship is at the core of Christian spirituality. Christ says, "I do not call you servants, but friends." When we become friends with the poor, their presence leaves an indelible imprint on our lives, and through them we are much more likely to remain committed. For Gutiérrez, liberation theology provides a way of thinking about friendship with the poor and its integral link with spirituality, but for him whether one draws from the wells of liberation theology or another way is not most significant. For Gutiérrez, what matters in the end is not liberation theology but the message of the Gospel and liberation of people.

Gutiérrez's Contribution to Christian Spirituality

Gustavo Gutiérrez is not only one of the most influential theologians of the twentieth century, but also one of the century's most important spiritual voices as well. Biblical scholar John Donahue noted that " 'the option for the poor' may be as controversial and important for our generation as was 'justification by faith' for previous ones."[8] Though some might see in this spirituality something that is distinctively new, in many ways it is a contemporary articulation of issues of faith and justice at the heart of the Christian tradition.

As one begins to assess the mark Gutiérrez has made on the church, the academy and the world, one might begin with a litany of his numerous degrees, awards, and honors. Such an approach would be a good start. Based on the permanent mark he has left on theological scholarship the twentieth century, he received a doctorate in theology from the Catholic University of Lyon in 1985. Subsequently he received some twenty-five honorary doctorates from universities such as Nijmegen, Tübingen, Freiburg (Germany), Fribourg (Switzerland), Brown, Yale, Holy Cross, Notre Dame, and many others. He was elected as a member of the Peruvian Academy of Language and awarded the Legion of Honor by the French government in 1993. In 2002

---

8. Cited by Norbert Lohfink, *Option for the Poor: The Basic Principle of Liberation Theology in the Light of the Bible* (Berkeley: Bibal Press, 1995), viii.

he became a member of the American Academy of Arts and Sciences, and in 2003 he received the distinguished Prince of Asturias award in Spain.

It is indeed hard to measure the significant influence he has had on the church's social teaching. John Paul II made explicit reference to the preferential option for the poor in some of his writings, and Archbishop Oscar Romero, who took a class from Gustavo Gutiérrez in August 1972, was also shaped by his theology. In Romero's own journal reflections, he noted that liberation theology as presented by Gutiérrez was not, in fact, what others had told him about it.[9] The religious, theological, and above all spiritual approach to liberation theology attracted Romero and made a positive impression on him. It filled out in many ways some of the core insights initially articulated by Paul VI in *Populorum Progressio* and no doubt shaped Romero's own commitment to the poor until the end of his life. At the Latin American Episcopal Conference in Aparecida, Brazil, in 2007, many of the perspectives that Gutiérrez and others had been writing about for years were incorporated into the final document, especially the importance of the preferential option for the poor in the life of the church. Gutiérrez's own goal was not to make ecclesial headlines or the footnotes of papal teaching but above all to assist the church in living out the spirituality that it teaches.

On November 7, 2009, the master general of the Dominicans, the Most Reverend Carlos Aspiroz-Costa, conferred on Gutiérrez the order's Degree of Master in Sacred Theology. He thus joined the ranks of honor conferred to only a select company of distinguished Dominican theologians such as Albert the Great and Thomas Aquinas. This degree is given to those considered "eminent in promoting sacred sciences through sustained doctrinal reflection and research and the publication of

---

9. Roberto Morozzo della Rocca, *Primero Dios: Vita di Oscar Romero* (Milan: Mondadori, 2005), 101.

works of exceptional theology." In his letter of conferral the master general wrote:

> A fundamental quality of Gustavo Gutiérrez's theological perspective is the importance that he gives to the poor as a critical lens for understanding the Gospel. The theologian as a believer touched by God's mercy is open, like the Good Samaritan, to the suffering of the poor. This leads to passionate concern for their liberation from suffering linked to a liberating praxis — a praxis that in its own way radically nourishes theological reflection about God's role in a context shadowed by the unjust and premature deaths of the poor.

Beyond his widespread influence, his notable accomplishments, and the litany of achievements on his curriculum vitae, however, lies perhaps a far greater grandeur, and one that finds its glories not in the spotlight of prestige but under divine standards of the Gospel, which itself is the longtime spiritual fruit of a faith seeking understanding that produces knowledge born of love. In some ways his mark on "living texts" of human beings far outweighs the "written texts" of his books, articles, and numerous awards. The lives he has touched during decades of service as a parish priest in the Church of the Holy Redeemer in Rimac, Peru, and work at the Institute of Bartolomé de Las Casas in Lima since 1974 have given countless people a sense of their own value and significance and helped them discover the priceless gift of their worth and treasured place in the reign of God.

In the face of the great challenge of poverty in the modern world, Gutiérrez's contribution to understanding the Gospel today consists in living out a spirituality expressed in following Jesus and realized in a commitment of solidarity to those who are poor and insignificant. He has made people aware of the role of poverty in a life of faith and has given people a great social conscience as they try to discern what it means to be faithful to the Gospel message, especially in a globalized consumer society that increasingly leaves out the concerns of the poor and quickly calculates financial costs, often at the expense of significant human costs. In the end, this spirituality is connected to love, and beyond love of neighbor and love of the poor, it is also connected to love of those who oppress, and even to the love of one's enemies.

As we finished up this volume, I asked Gustavo, now at eighty-three, how he would like to be remembered when the last chapter of his life is written. He said he did not think much about that question, as if to suggest that what matters is not so much him but the message he has tried to proclaim. As I asked him to clarify that further, he said "I hope my life in the end tries to give testimony to the message of the Gospel, above all that God loves the world and loves those who are poorest within it." Perhaps these words best capture the spirit of a man who may be small in stature and humble in heart but magnanimous in his soul. At the core of this man is an effort to follow Jesus, whose words in the fourth chapter of Luke best summarize Gustavo Gutiérrez and the message of his spiritual writings:

> The Spirit of the Lord is upon me, because he has anointed me to bring glad tidings to the poor. He has sent me to proclaim liberty to captives and recovery of sight to the blind, to let the oppressed go free, and to proclaim a year acceptable to the Lord. (Luke 4:18–19)

Part One

The Gift of Life:
Meeting Jesus Christ

1

Liberating Spirituality

Spirituality is about following Jesus. It is a way of life that animates and transforms our way of being in the world and orients us to the centrality of the reign of God and God's in-breaking into human history. From the very outset of his writings, Gutiérrez lays out the relationship between salvation and the historical process of human liberation in light of a faith that seeks justice. The selections in this section come from one of his earliest and best-known works, A Theology of Liberation, *which was first published in Spanish in 1971. He articulates the significance of spirituality in the process of human liberation, the challenge of conversion, and the promises of joy and life. These writings combine a profound sense of the unmerited, gratuitous gift of God's love and the urgency of solidarity with those that society considers the least important.*

A WAY OF BEING CHRISTIAN

Spirituality, in the strict and profound sense of the word, is the dominion of the Spirit that informs every detail of our lives. If "the truth will make you free" (John 8:32), the Spirit "will guide you into all the truth" (John 16:13) and will lead us to complete freedom, the freedom from everything that hinders us from fulfilling ourselves as humans beings and children of God, and the freedom to love and to enter into communion with God and with others. The Spirit will lead us along the path of liberation because "where the Spirit of the Lord is, there is freedom" (2 Cor. 3:17).

A spirituality is a concrete way, inspired by the Spirit, of living the Gospel; it is a definite way of living "before the Lord," in solidarity with all human beings. It arises from an intense spiritual experience, which is later explicated and witnessed to. Some Christians are beginning to live this experience as a result of their commitment to the process of liberation. The experiences of previous generations are there to support it, but above all, to remind them that they must discover their own way. Not only is there a contemporary history and a contemporary Gospel, there is also a contemporary spiritual experience which cannot be overlooked. Spirituality involves reordering the great axes of the Christian life in terms of this contemporary experience. The synthesis of this reordering stimulates a new, deepened understanding of various ideas, bringing to the surface unknown or forgotten aspects of the Christian life, converting them into life, prayer, commitment, and action.

The truth is that a Christianity lived in commitment to the process of liberation presents its own problems that cannot be ignored and meets obstacles that must be overcome. Encountering the Lord and his love nourishes and strengthens us, but this love does not know its full potential. This is a real difficulty, but the solution must come from the heart of the problem itself. This is the challenge confronting a spirituality of liberation. Where oppression and human liberation seem to make God irrelevant — a God filtered by our longtime indifference to these problems — there must blossom faith and hope in him who came to root out injustice and to offer, in an unforeseen way, total liberation. This is a spirituality that dares to sink roots in the soil of oppression and germinate the seeds of liberation.

CONVERSION TO THE NEIGHBOR
AND TO THE LORD

A spirituality of liberation will center on a *conversion* to the neighbor, the oppressed person, the exploited social class, the despised ethnic group, the dominated country. Our conversion to the Lord implies this conversion to the neighbor. Evangelical conversion is indeed the touchstone of all spirituality. Conversion means a radical transformation of ourselves; it means thinking, feeling, and living as Christ — present in exploited and alienated persons. To be converted is to commit oneself lucidly, realistically, and concretely to the process of the liberation of the poor and oppressed. It means to commit oneself not only generously, but also with an analysis of the situation and a strategy of action. To be converted is to know and experience the fact that, contrary to the laws of physics, we can stand straight, according to the Gospel, only when our center of gravity is outside ourselves.

Conversion is a permanent process in which very often the obstacles we meet make us lose all we had gained and start anew. The fruitfulness of our conversion depends on our openness to doing this, our spiritual childhood. All conversion implies a break: "Whoever loves father or mother more than me is not worthy of me" (Matt. 10:37). To wish to accomplish it without conflict is to deceive oneself and others. But it is not a question of a withdrawn and pious attitude. Our conversion process is affected by the socioeconomic, political, cultural, and human environment in which it occurs. Without a change in these structures, there is no authentic conversion. We have to break with our mental categories, with the way we relate to others, with our way of identifying with the Lord, with our cultural milieu, with our social class, in other words, with all that can stand in the way of a real, profound solidarity with those who suffer, in the first place, from misery and injustice. Only through this, and not through purely interior and spiritual attitudes, will the "new person" arise from the ashes of the "old."

Christians have not done enough in this area of conversion to the neighbor, to social justice, to history. They have not perceived clearly enough yet that to know God is to do justice. They still do not live in one sole action with both God and all humans. They still do not situate themselves in Christ without attempting to avoid concrete human history. They have yet to tread the path that will lead them to seek effectively the peace of the Lord in the heart of social struggle.

COMMUNION WITH GOD AS A GIFT

A spirituality of liberation must be filled with a living sense of *gratuitousness*. Communion with the Lord and with all humans is more than anything else a gift. Hence the universality and the radicalness of the liberation that it affords. This gift, far from being a call to passivity, demands a vigilant attitude. This is one of the most constant biblical themes: the encounter with the Lord presupposes attention, active disposition, work, fidelity to God's will, the good use of talents received. But the knowledge that at the root of our personal and community existence lies the gift of the self-communication of God, the grace of God's friendship, fills our life with gratitude. It allows us to see our encounters with others, our loves, everything that happens in our life as a gift. There is a real love only when there is free giving — without conditions or coercion. Only gratuitous love goes to our very roots and elicits true love.

Prayer is an experience of gratuitousness. This "leisure" activity, this "wasted" time, reminds us that the Lord is beyond the categories of useful and useless.[1] God is not of this world. The gratuitousness of God's gift, creating profound needs, frees us from all religious alienation and, in the last instance, from all alienation. The Christian committed to the Latin American revolutionary process has to find the way to real prayer, not evasion.

---

1. See José María González Ruiz, *Dios es gratuito, pero no superfluo* (Madrid: Ediciones Marova, 1970).

New experiences, new demands have made heretofore familiar
and comfortable paths impassable and have made us undertake
new itineraries on which we hope it might be possible to say with
Job to the Lord, "I had heard of you by the hearing of the ear,
but now my eye sees you" (42:5). Bonhoeffer was right when
he said that the only credible God is the God of the mystics. But
this is not a God unrelated to human history. On the contrary, if
it is true that one must go through humankind to reach God, it
is equally certain that the "passing through" to that gratuitous
God strips me, leaves me naked, universalizes my love for others,
and makes it gratuitous. Both movements need each other dialec-
tically and move toward a synthesis. This synthesis is found in
Christ; in the God-Man we encounter God and humankind. In
Christ humankind gives God a human countenance and God
gives it a divine countenance. Only in this perspective will we
be able to understand that the "union with the Lord," which all
spirituality proclaims, is not a separation from others; to attain
this union, I must go through others, and the union, in turn,
enables me to encounter others more fully.

LIBERATION AND JOY

Conversion to one's neighbors, and in them to the Lord, the
gratuitousness that allows me to encounter others fully, is the
source of Christian joy. This joy is born of the gift already
received yet still awaited and is expressed in the present despite
the difficulties and tensions of the struggle for the construc-
tion of a just society. Every prophetic proclamation of total
liberation is accompanied by an invitation to participate in
eschatological joy: "I will rejoice in Jerusalem and delight in
my people" (Isa. 65:19). This joy ought to fill our entire existence, making us attentive both to the gift of integral human
liberation and history as well as to the detail of our life and the
lives of others. This joy ought not to lessen our commitment
to those who live in an unjust world, nor should it lead us to a

facile, low-cost conciliation. On the contrary, our joy is paschal, guaranteed by the Spirit (Gal. 5:22; 1 Tim. 1:6; Rom. 14:17); it passes through the conflict with the great ones of this world and through the cross in order to enter into life. This is why we celebrate our joy in the present by recalling the Passover of the Lord. To recall Christ is to believe in him. And this celebration is a feast (Rev. 19:9), a feast of the Christian community, those who explicitly confess Christ to be the Lord of history, the liberator of the oppressed. This community has been referred to as the small temple in contradistinction to the large temple of human history. Without community support neither the emergence nor the continued existence of a new spirituality is possible.

The Magnificat expresses well this spirituality of liberation. A song of thanksgiving for the gifts of the Lord, it expresses humbly the joy of being loved by him: "...my spirit rejoices in God my Savior, for he has looked with favor on the lowliness of his servant...for the Mighty One has done great things for me" (Luke 1:47–49). But at the same time it is one of the New Testament texts that contains great implications both as regards liberation and the political sphere. This thanksgiving and joy are closely linked to the action of God, who "has brought down the powerful from their thrones, and lifted up the lowly; he has filled the hungry with good things, and sent the rich empty away" (1:52–53). The future of history belongs to the poor and exploited. True liberation will be the work of the oppressed themselves; in them, the Lord saves history. The spirituality of liberation will have as its basis the spirituality of the *anawim*.

— *A Theology of Liberation*, 117–20

2

Encountering Jesus

Though Gustavo's writings deal in a profound way with social, political, and economic issues, the inspiration, motivation, and foundation for human liberation is rooted in a profound christology. Christ reveals God's undying love for the world, from which flows the response in faith manifested by a commitment to the reign of God. Such a faith is not simply a rational assent to propositional truths but the meeting of the Lord in history, through which one experiences the gift of friendship with God and a call to universal fellowship with others. Drawn from his first major work on spirituality, We Drink from Our Own Wells, *these selections speak of the God who first loved us and the Lord who invites us into a spiritual journey that manifests his saving presence in all dimensions of human existence.*

SEARCHING FOR LIFE

To encounter the Lord is first of all to be encountered by the Lord. "You did not choose me, but I chose you. And I appointed you to go and bear fruit" (John 15:16). In this encounter we discover where the Lord lives and what the mission is that has been entrusted to us. The Gospels contain various stories about encounters with Jesus. Among these there is one in John that is especially penetrating and rich in meaning:

The next day John again was standing with two of his disciples, and as he watched Jesus walk by, he exclaimed, "Look, here is the Lamb of God!" The two disciples heard him say this, and they followed Jesus. When Jesus turned and saw them following, he said to them, "What are you looking for?" They said to him, "Rabbi" (which translated means Teacher), "where are you staying?" He said to them, "Come and see." They came and saw where he was staying, and they remained with him that day. It was about four o'clock in the afternoon. One of the two who heard John speak and followed him was Andrew, Simon Peter's brother. He first found his brother Simon and said to him, "We have found the Messiah" (which is translated Anointed). He brought Simon to Jesus, whom looked at him and said, "You are Simon son of John. You are to be called Cephas" (which is translated Peter). (John 1:35–42)

This simple sketch of an encounter with the Lord becomes a paradigm for the many others that would take place in the lives of Christians of every age.

According to the fourth Gospel, when John saw Jesus coming toward him he said: "After me comes a man who ranks ahead of me, because he was before me" (1:30). The forerunner steps aside and invites his disciples to follow the one whose way he had been preparing. The first disciples of Jesus come from the school of the Baptist. John acknowledges Jesus as "the Lamb of God." The echoes of the exodus that are so strong in the Gospel of John, especially in its early chapters, justify us in interpreting this original expression in the light of the Passover lamb "whose blood freed the people from death." The Lamb of God is the sacrificial victim of the new covenant; his blood will be shed as that of the lambs of the old covenant had been.

The two disciples follow Jesus. Before they do so they have been advised of the difficulties and conflicts they will face in taking the path of the Lamb of God. It is not an easy road, but one that leads through persecution and ends in a martyr's

death. The master does not hide this from them: "If they persecuted me, they will persecute you" (John 15:20). But the
journey is also accompanied by the promise of final victory and
the sovereign rule of the Lamb.

The verb "to follow" is used in the Gospels for the progres-
sion of disciples as they walk in the footsteps of the master.
It signifies both the obedient acceptance of the Lord's call and
the creativity required by the new way they are to travel. Jesus
says to Philip: "Follow me" (John 1:43; see also 8:12; 10:4;
12:26; 13:36; 21:19). The disciples here follow Jesus in silence,
but it is a silence with profound meaning, for their following is
already an adherence of faith and an acceptance of the consequences the following entails. They have taken the first step in
their "staying with" Jesus (John 1:39).

Jesus breaks the silence of his followers and asks: "What are
you looking for?" (John 1:38). This formal question, direct and
unavoidable, is meant to sound out the quality of the initial
adherence that the disciples of John have just given to following
Jesus. Jesus puts them in the critical position of defining themselves from the outset. It is not enough simply to follow him,
for there are forms of adherence that are not reliable (John
2:23–25) and others that break down at the first demands of
discipleship (Luke 9:61; 18:18–23). Jesus' question is directed
to all who claim to follow him, whatever the period of history
to which they belong.

The term "Rabbi" occurs eight times in the Gospel of John;
it is used seven times of Jesus and once (3:26) of John the
Baptist. The word was then applied to anyone regarded as a
teacher, as a man learned in some area; it was applied chiefly,
however, to anyone who taught by the witness he gave, by his
manner of life. The question that the disciples ask in response
to the question of Jesus takes that fact into account: "Where
are you staying?" (John 1:39). The disciples are here "invit-
ing themselves" to intimacy with Jesus. Their question expresses
their desire and intention to be taught through sharing the life
of Jesus.

Jesus invites the disciples to enter his own sphere, to come and see where he is staying, and to accept the consequences of such coming and seeing. The text, however, makes no reference to any dwelling of Jesus, and there is nothing to keep us from thinking that this Galilean, this itinerant preacher, has no permanent abode. This is, in fact, what he himself says in the Gospel of Matthew: "Foxes have holes, and birds of the air have nests; but the Son of Man has nowhere to lay his head" (8:20). His mission causes him to extend the boundaries of his dwelling and family; it is in that light that he sets down the condition for belonging to the community he is assembling: "For whoever does the will of my Father in heaven is my brother and sister and mother" (Matt. 12:50).

John himself, nonetheless, gives us a clue as to the dwelling of Jesus. He tells us in the Prologue of his Gospel: "And the Word became flesh and lived among us" (1:14). This is the place where Jesus dwells: the tent he has pitched in the midst of us, at the center of history. Jesus lives in his task of proclaiming the Gospel, for that is where his Father's business is located (Luke 2:49).

This is what the disciples saw and, because they decided to enlist for this work, they stayed with him from that day forward. This passage in its bare simplicity tells us of the birth of a Christian community. Jesus and the two disciples, with others soon following, share a life. For all of them following Jesus entails a commitment to a mission that requires them, like their master, to pitch camp in the midst of human history and there give witness to the Father's love.

John did not forget the hour when he met Jesus: "It was about four o'clock in the afternoon." Like every event that leaves its mark on a human life, this encounter remained a detailed memory and made an indelible impression. The exact moment in time does not as such seem to have any significance for us today; after all, it would make no difference to us whether this encounter took place at ten in the morning or two in the afternoon. In its very insignificance this mention of four o'clock in the afternoon conveys a profound personal message, for we all have these "four o'clocks" in our lives, intense moments of encounter with the Lord in which our spiritual lives are nourished. They are the well from which we drink every so often.

MEETING THE MESSIAH

Encounter with the Lord is not restricted to the disciples, for the very nature of the event leads to communication, to witness. The former disciples of John the Baptist are fully conscious of the kind of encounter that has just taken place. This is why they jointly recognize Jesus, whom they have called Rabbi, as the Messiah. That is, they recognize in him the only-begotten Son of God who has come in order to proclaim the good news of his reign. The community now beginning to take shape will be a messianic community whose task is to offer a specific witness in the midst of human history. Following Jesus is not, purely or primarily, an individual matter but a collective adventure. The journey of the people of God is set in motion by a direct encounter with the Lord but an encounter in community: "*We* have found the Messiah."

Matthew and Luke also enable us to penetrate more deeply into the meaning of encounter with the Lord that results in following him. In Matthew we read:

> When John heard in prison what the Messiah was doing, he sent word by his disciples [var.: by two of his disciples] and said to him, "Are you the one who is to come, or are we to wait for another?" Jesus answered them, "Go and tell John what you hear and see: the blind receive their sight, the lame walk, the lepers are cleansed, the deaf hear, the dead are raised, and the poor have good news brought to them. And blessed is anyone who takes no offense at me." (11:2–6)

As in the passage from the fourth Gospel, here again John sends two disciples to meet Jesus to inquire whether Jesus is the Messiah or whether they must still wait for someone else. The reports the Baptist has heard have perplexed him to some extent, but they have also stirred up hope.

Again as in John, Jesus' answer takes the form of concrete witness. This time he bids the disciples, not to come after him and see, but to return to John the Baptist and tell him what they have seen and heard. Jesus' works are to provide the answer to the question of his identity. They are works that match those foretold by Isaiah (61:1–2) in a passage that plays an important role in the Gospels in defining the mission of the Messiah. Luke 4:16–20 makes use of the same passage in order to elicit from Jesus what has been called his "first messianic declaration."[1] Works done to benefit the poor and needy identify Jesus as the Messiah, the same Messiah whom (in the passage from John) the disciples claim to have met. Perhaps these disciples had witnessed such works when they accepted the invitation to live with the Rabbi. The Son of Man who has no place to lay his head lives in these actions that manifest the breakthrough of the reign of God into the present age. That reign is meant first and foremost for the poor and then, through them, for every human being.

The cures of which the parallel passages in Matthew and Luke speak are an anticipation and pledge of that reign. The alleviation of the suffering of *some* of the poor in the time of Jesus is a sure promise that the good news of the reign of God is being proclaimed to *all* the poor of history. It is a proclamation through liberating words and liberating actions. The Gospel is proclaimed to the poor by means of concrete deeds. When Jesus made human beings see and walk and hear and, in short, gave them life, he was giving an example for that time and a mandate to the Christian community throughout history. This is what is meant by "remembering the poor," and it is something

---

1. John Paul II, encyclical *Rich in Mercy*, no. 3.

we should be "eager to do" (Gal. 2:10). There is no authentic evangelization that is not accompanied by action in behalf of the poor.

The cures reported give full meaning to the good news for the poor that is promised in Isaiah and that becomes a reality through the messianic activity of Jesus. But this method of revealing his messiahship will not be readily understood, and this is why the passage ends in a beatitude: "Blessed is he who takes no offense at me." It is in this messianic work that Jesus has his dwelling. It is in this work that worship "in spirit and truth" is to be offered (John 4:23). Happy they who do not take offense but instead accept the invitation to follow Jesus and live with him.

The meeting of the Baptist's disciples with Jesus also comes from the Johannine writings and deals with the necessity of sharing with others the experience of the Lord:

> We declare to you what was from the beginning, what we have heard, what we have seen with our eyes, what we have looked at and touched with our hands, concerning the word of life — this life was revealed, and we have seen it and testify to it, and declare to you the eternal life that was with the Father and was revealed to us — we declare to you what we have seen and heard so that you also may have fellowship with us; and truly our fellowship is with the Father and with his Son Jesus Christ. We are writing these things so that our joy may be complete.
> (1 John 1:1–4)

This text presents to us the experience that the disciples had of Jesus, and they do so with all the intimacy implied in the verbs "see," "hear," and "touch." These are direct, unmediated experiences that are communicated in order that others too may have the joy of encountering the Lord. The Gospels are full of such testimonies (Luke 2:16–17, 38; John 4:28–30; 20:17–18). What is manifested in this way is life. That is the content of the reign of the Father, the living God who raises Jesus to life and thus overcomes death once and for all.

A follower of Jesus is a witness to life. This statement takes on a special meaning in Latin America, where the forces of death have created a social system that marginalizes the very poor who have a privileged place in the kingdom of life. The passage from 1 John gives us a better understanding of what we call nowadays the spiritual life: life according to the Spirit, life lived in love. In this same Letter John speaks to us the final word about God: "God is love" (1 John 4:8). The follower of Jesus must therefore not live in fear: fear, according to John, is the opposite of the love that sets us free (1 John 4:18). Anyone who has met the Lord "has the Son" and "has life" (1 John 5:12). Witness must be borne to this life.

ACKNOWLEDGING THE MESSIAH

To give witness to life implies passage through death. This experience, which marks the present Latin American situation, is an ineluctable consequence of the encounter with and acknowledgment of Jesus as the Messiah, of whom the texts of John and Matthew speak. This is not something easy for a follower to accept. A text from Mark will help us to understand this point:

> Jesus went on with his disciples to the villages of Caesarea Philippi; and on the way he asked his disciples, "Who do people say that I am?" And they answered him, "John the Baptist; and others, Elijah; and still others, one of the prophets." He asked them, "But who do you say that I am?" Peter answered him, "You are the Messiah." And he sternly ordered them not to tell anyone about him.
>
> Then he began to teach them that the Son of Man must undergo great suffering, and be rejected by the elders, the chief priests, and the scribes, and be killed, and after three days rise again. He said all this quite openly. And Peter

took him aside and began to rebuke him. But turning and looking at his disciples, he rebuked Peter and said, "Get behind me, Satan! For you are setting your mind not on divine things but on human things."

He called the crowd with his disciples, and said to them, "If any want to become my followers, let them deny themselves and take up their cross and follow me." (Mark 8:27–34)

This passage occupies a central place in the evangelist's narrative. It is the culminating moment of what is called the "messianic secret" in Mark: when someone recognizes that Jesus is the Messiah, he orders that person not to speak about it.

The affirmation that Jesus of Nazareth is the Messiah, the Christ, is the nucleus of christological faith. The first sentence in Mark's Gospel reads: "The beginning of the good news of Jesus Christ, the Son of God" (1:1); John's Gospel ends with: "But these are written so that you may come to believe that Jesus is the Messiah, the Son of God, and that through believing you may have life in his name" (20:31). According to Luke this affirmation is a summation of Peter's preaching to the Jews among the newer members of the community of believers: "Therefore let the entire house of Israel know with certainty that God has made him both Lord and Messiah, this Jesus whom you crucified" (Acts 2:36).

To profess "this Jesus," to acknowledge "Jesus the Messiah," is to express a conviction. It is not simply putting a name and a title together; it is an authentic confession of faith. It is the assertion of an identity: the Jesus of history, the son of Mary, the carpenter of Nazareth, the preacher of Galilee, the crucified, *is* the Only Begotten of God, the Christ, the Son of God.

In Mark's text, the question "Who do you say that I am?" does not come from the crowd or from Jesus' disciples (as in John 1:38 and Matt. 11:3); it comes from Jesus himself. It is directed to those who have accompanied him for some time and have been witnesses of his words and deeds. The question is not, therefore, directed to persons who do not know him or who have had little contact with him. It is directed to those who have reason to know something about him because they have followed him. They are his disciples.

It is a question that looks for a profession of faith, though, in other contexts, it sometimes elicits an answer that includes an element of doubt or perplexity. The language is direct and leaves no room for evasion. And it is not directed to one person, but to the disciples conjointly. Profession of faith will be communal, as will also the expression of doubt or perplexity.

The interrogation is twofold, looking for two answers. The first question asks what others say about Jesus. His mission has been public; the crowds have some ideas about him. What is asked, then, is how the disciples interpret what they have heard; what impact it has had on them. This is a question, then, about the faith of the disciples themselves: what others have learned in the faith is an aspect of our own faith. Knowledge of Jesus, then and now, does not rely only on what believers have seen for themselves, but also on what they perceive in those who say they are his followers. Since Mark 6 has already narrated sending the disciples on an evangelical mission (6:6–13), the question becomes: What testimony have you given of me?

This first question is a question about the lived faith of the members of Jesus' immediate circle of companions. When we refer to what others think, we always show what *we* think: we accept an opinion, or take distance from it, or refute it.

The answer to this question about Jesus is not something that pertains to us in a private capacity. Nor does it pertain only to the church. Christ stands beyond its frontiers and questions all humankind, as Vatican II clearly reminded us. "Who do they say that I am?" is a question that, precisely because it escapes private or ecclesiastical confines, retains its validity for the community of yesterday and today. It is important for ecclesial faith to know what others think about Jesus and how our testimony as disciples is received. To know how to listen will help us to make a better and more efficacious proclamation of our faith in the Lord vis-à-vis the world.

The text continues: "They told him, 'John the Baptist... Elijah... one of the prophets.' " It is significant that the crowds, at least from what the disciples here report, did not think that Jesus was the Messiah. In this text it does not seem that political messianism played a major role among the populace.

Matthew, in a parallel text, adds the name of Jeremiah to that of Elijah. All three mentioned are important in the religious history of the Jewish people. John the Baptist, Elijah, and Jeremiah were prophets. If Jesus is not sketched in all his singularity, what is implied is something freighted with consequences; Jesus is perceived as within the prophetic line, that which speaks "in the name of God." Jesus is given a high place in having his preaching associated with the great prophetic perspective of Israel. But this does not tell everything.

The second question has more of a bite to it and goes much deeper: Who do *you* say that I am? You; not the others. What is asked refers to an objective reality, the presence, of the Lord. The question pulls us out of our subjective world and, "turning us inside out," locates the point of reference of our faith, and of our life, beyond ourselves, in the person of Jesus. The answer will have to have the seal of objectivity. But the question is directed to them and its answer will be made by them and consequently will be shaped by their way of viewing Jesus. The answer depends on what is asked and who is being asked. Knowing Jesus has an impact on all the aspects of our existence, and they will all be present in the response that we give.

The text continues with the clear confession of Peter in the name of the other apostles: "You are the Messiah." Not simply a prophet, as the crowds thought, but the Only Begotten of God, the Christ, he in whom God's promises are realized. Mark writes his Gospel in the light of this acknowledgment and synthesizes the faith of the disciples, yet insists once more: "he sternly ordered them not to tell anyone about him."

FOLLOWING THE MESSIAH

What follows is decisive. Jesus reveals something new: "the Son of Man must undergo great suffering, and be rejected by the elders, the chief priests, and the scribes, and be killed, and after three days rise again." This was something he had not revealed until that moment: that his mission would be rejected by those held in respect (the elders, chief priests, and scribes — that is, the Sanhedrin), and this rejection will lead to his death. Peter, who had just acknowledged Jesus to be the Messiah, refuses to accept the conflictual part of Jesus' mission. What disturbs Peter is not the failure of his mission — given that Jesus speaks also of his resurrection "after three days" — but the conflict and suffering that had to be endured.

Jesus' reply is radical: "Get behind me, Satan." The expression could mean "take up again your post as a disciple and do not be an obstacle (Satan) in my way." The place for the disciple of Jesus is behind him, behind the Master. So interpreted, what seems a harsh reprimand is really a call to return to the path of discipleship. So taken, it implies confidence in Peter's capacity to realign himself with the followers of the Master. Peter's reluctance to accept the consequences that accrue to messiahship for Jesus and his followers is flatly rejected. Peter, even though he had made himself worthy of being compared to Satan, receives a call that includes a pardon. Jesus' reprimand comports the admixture of mitigation.

Here we touch on a central point in belief in Jesus. This text has often been interpreted to mean that Peter's resistance stems from a political conceptualization of the Messiah. Jesus, by contrast, here reveals that his mission is spiritual. The disciples were given a progressive enlightenment on this truth (Mark 10:35–45). It must also be seen in a broader and deeper perspective, that of the rejection of the nationalist and zealot conceptualization of the Messiah. Mark writes from this perspective. But he and the other evangelists also make clear that the reasons for Jesus' confrontation with the powerful of his

day are to be found in the proclamation of the good news of the
Father's love of all humankind, especially the poor. This marks
the character of Jesus' messiahship. What was rejected in him,
and led to his death on the cross, was the same nucleus of his
teaching: the kingdom of God.

Jesus' concrete form of proclaiming the gratuitous love of
God and the kingdom had inevitable consequences for the religious, social, and economic order prevailing in his time. "They
watched him" and planned his execution (Mark 3:1–6). At bottom, the conflict and suffering that Peter reacted to (and all of
us with him!) were provoked by that same mission. Hostility
did not arise because the teaching of the Messiah was political (which it clearly was not, particularly in the strict sense of
the term), but precisely because it was a religious teaching that
affected all human existence.

What prompted Peter's rejection was his reluctance to accept
the consequences and requirements of acknowledging that Jesus
is the Christ. This is what Peter balked at. It is not enough
to recognize that Jesus is the Christ; it is necessary to accept
all that that implies. To believe in Christ is also to assume
his practice. A profession of faith without practice is incomplete, as stated in Matthew, "Not everyone who says to me,
'Lord, Lord,' will enter the kingdom of heaven, but only the one
who does the will of my Father in heaven" (7:21). Orthodoxy,
correct opinion, demands orthopraxis: comportment in accord
with the opinion expressed.

The practice of following Jesus will show what lies behind
acknowledging the Messiah. It will show whether our thoughts
are those of God or only our own (Mark 8:33) — the ideas
we have of Jesus and of our discipleship. It is in our historical
following — in our walking the path of Jesus — that the final
judgment on our faith in Christ will be made. Following Jesus
is the solid ground on which can be built a reflection on Jesus
as the Christ, a christology; otherwise it will be built on sand.
In theology, as in all intellectual elaboration, critical thought
is required. In our undertaking, the critique that comes from

practice — following Jesus — cannot be left out. To the question "Who do you say that I am?" we cannot give a merely theoretical or theological answer. What answers it, in the final analysis, is our life, our personal history, our manner of living the Gospel.

Peter's affirmation "You are the Messiah" is fundamental, but accepting all the consequences demanded must be the guiding thought of our lives. Only then is our response valid, as honest and sincere as it may be without it. Our response to the question, "Who do you say that I am?" does not end with a profession of faith or a theological systemization. It is a question addressed to our life that permanently tests the faith of the entire church, since the consequences of following Jesus mean "taking up the cross." The experience of martyrdom lived in Latin America heightens and sharpens this meaning of the text.

The true disciple must, therefore, be prepared to confront a like situation. Such preparation is not an easy matter. Peter's reaction — measured by our profession of the faith — is an abiding possibility. It expresses itself in subtle and cunning ways. The testimony of numerous Latin Americans makes this possibility manifest, but it also makes us realize that there are some who have determined to put themselves behind Jesus and follow him, paying the price of rejection, of calumny, or even of the surrender of their own lives. Those who lose their life for the Lord and the Gospel will save it. Following Jesus is oriented to the horizon of resurrection, definitive life.

— *We Drink from Our Own Wells,* 38–51

3

Drinking from the Well of Gratuity

"Spirituality," Gutiérrez notes, "is like living water that springs up in the very depths of the experience of faith." It is not so much our love for God that sets in motion the process of human liberation, but above all God's love for us, calling us to drink and grow from the well of the spiritual experience of the poor. The contemplative dimension names that reality of God deeply encountered only in prayer and worship. Many of Gutiérrez's writings emphasize that faith is a gift and a demand that flows from the gratuity of God and leads to a response of committed discipleship lived in solidarity with other persons. Christian faith is lived between the gift of being justified by grace and doing justice in the world, between the gift given from God for the believer and the gift given by the disciple for others.

EVERYTHING IS GRACE

The experience and idea of the gratuitousness of God's love are fundamental in the Christian life. The gratuitous initiative of the Lord is a dominant theme in Pauline theology (Rom. 5:15–17; 2 Cor. 8:9) and later in Augustinian theology. 1 John says God "first loved us" (4:19). Everything starts from there. The gift of God's love is the source of our being and puts its imprint on our lives. We have been made by love and for love. Only by loving, then, can we fulfill ourselves as persons; that is, how we respond to the initiative taken by God's love.[1] God's love for us is gratuitous; we do not merit it. It is a gift we receive before we exist, or, to be more accurate, a gift in view of which we have been created. Election to adoptive filiation comes first:

> Blessed be the God and Father of our Lord Jesus Christ, who has blessed us in Christ with every spiritual blessing in the heavenly places, just as he chose us in Christ before the foundation of the world, to be holy and blameless before him in love. He destined us for adoption as his children through Jesus Christ, according to the good pleasure of his will. (Eph. 1:3–5)

Gratuitousness thus marks our lives so that we are led to love gratuitously and to want to be loved gratuitously. It is a profoundly human characteristic and part of how we are made. True love is always a gift, something that transcends motives and merits. As is said so beautifully in the Song of Solomon, "Many waters cannot quench love, neither can floods drown it. If one offered for love all the wealth of one's house, it would be utterly scorned" (8:7). Gratitude is the space of that radical self-giving and that presence of beauty in our lives without which even the struggle for justice would be crippled.

The experience of gratuitousness is the space of encounter with the Lord. Unless we understand the meaning of gratuitousness, there will be no contemplative dimension in our life. Contemplation is not a state of paralysis but of radical self-giving. In the final analysis, to believe in God means to live our life as a gift from God and to look upon everything that happens in it as a manifestation of this gift.

My intention is to penetrate to the deepest meaning of history and, in the words of Ignatius of Loyola, to "find God in

---

1. See Hugo Echegaray, "Conocer a Dios es practicar la justicia," in *Anunciar el Reino* (Lima: CEP, 1981), 31. "The measure of our fidelity depends not on the native capacities of our own hearts but on the abundant gifts that the Lord bestows on us. The word of God awakens profound and unforeseeable energies."

all things." But the fact is that the attitude of finding God in all things can be acquired only if we can activate a contemplative dimension in our lives. Contemplation disposes us to recognize that everything is grace. Prayer is an expression of faith and trust in the Lord; it is an act that is peculiar to and characteristic of the believer. It takes place in the context of the love that we know to be marked in its very source by gratuitousness. Prayer is in fact a loving dialogue, to use the description given by Teresa of Avila. It arises as a humble and trusting response to the Father's gratuitous gift of love and expresses our desire to share that gift in an unaffected way with our brothers and sisters.

Like every dialogue of love, prayer runs the risk of being interpreted as a "useless activity," whereas in point of fact it is precisely an experience of a gratuitousness that creates new forms of communication. It is expressed, for example, in the silence proper to prayer, as indeed to every loving encounter. A moment comes when words can no longer communicate the depth of what is experienced. Simple and silent presence is a touchstone of love.

Some sectors of the Latin American church are passing through a time of prayer. It is surprising to see a people becoming increasingly better organized and more effective in the struggle to assert its rights of life and justice and at the same time giving evidence of a profound sense of prayer and of a conviction that in the final analysis love and peace are an unmerited gift of God.

In their religious celebrations, whether at especially important moments or in the circumstances of everyday life, the poor turn to the Lord with the trustfulness and spontaneity of a child who speaks to its father and tells him of its suffering and hopes.[2] One Christian community that had suffered a harsh

---

2. I offer as an example the following prayer in which Bishop José Dammert sums up the feelings of his people: "Lord, the men and women of the Andes cry to you because of the utter poverty in which we live, subject to the vagaries of nature and even more to oppression by other human beings. The fruit of our labor

trial writes with simplicity: "We tell all our Christian brothers and sisters that we have the courage to continue to celebrate our faith in groups as often as we can."[3] "As often as we can": the harsh situation in which a people lives forces it to pray "in the catacombs." — *We Drink from Our Own Wells,* 109–12

EFFICACIOUS LOVE

Our fidelity to the Lord must find expression at the present time. The encounter with God results from divine initiative that creates an impact of gratitude, which should permeate the entire Christian life. Authentic love tries to start with the concrete needs of the other and not with the "duty" of practicing love. Love is respectful of others and therefore feels obliged to base its action on an analysis of their situation and needs. Works in behalf of the neighbor are not done in order to channel idle energies or to give available personnel something to do; they are done because the other has needs and it is urgent that we attend to them. In Latin America today, many of these needs are found at the most elementary levels of physical survival.

This desire for effectiveness gives a new force to the experience of gratuitousness. This experience is not meant to serve as a refuge for historical powerlessness (which is to be rejected as an unchristian attitude), but rather sets up a demand for real and effective commitment. As Archbishop Romero acutely

---

in fields and mines is appropriated by others who leave us but a few crumbs. Necessity compels us men and women of the Andes to toil from childhood on, and the harshness of our life leaves us no respite. We know, nonetheless, that you are a God of mercy and that you take pity on the needy. Therefore we renew our cries — often in silence like Mary at the foot of the cross — from the depths of our hearts. We adore your providence and we intensify our hope of the human fellowship that your Christ teaches us and that we practice with generous hospitality" (*Veinticinco años al servicio de la Iglesia* [Lima: CEP, 1983], 248–49).

3. Letter from the communities of El Quiché, January 1981, after the massacre in that part of Guatemala and the forced withdrawal of the bishop and pastoral ministers, in *Morir y despertar en Guatemala* (Lima: CEP, 1981), 144.

remarked: "The world of the poor teaches us the form Christian love must take . . . that it must indeed be gratuitous but that it must also seek to be effective in history."[4]

Concern for effective action is a way of expressing love for the other. The gratuitousness of the gift of the kingdom does not do away with effective action but rather calls for it all the more. "In the presence of this God who acts gratuitously we must show society a reign that is not reducible to energy expended in the service of human development, but that has its source in an encounter with a personal God with whom intimacy is bestowed as a *gift* and who, once given to us, neither suppresses nor competes with the human *effort* to build a better world."[5]

Gratuitousness is an atmosphere in which the entire quest for effectiveness is bathed. It is something both subtler and richer than a balance maintained between two important aspects. This alternative perspective does not represent an abandonment of efficacy but rather seeks to locate efficacy in a comprehensive and fully human context that is in accord with the Gospel. That context is the space of freely bestowed encounter with the Lord. A gratuitous encounter is mysterious and it draws us into itself. Many Latin American Christians are attempting to live the gratuitous love of God by committing themselves to a liberative undertaking.   — *We Drink from Our Own Wells*, 107–9

GRATUITY AND FRATERNITY

Matthew 25:31–46 plays an important role in the Latin American spiritual experience. The passage is a great help in grasping the requirement of effective action in the service of the other

4. Oscar Romero, address at Louvain University (February 2, 1980), in *Signos de vida y fidelidad: Testimonio de la Iglesia in América Latina, 1978–1982* (Lima: CEP, 1978), 372b.

5. CLAR, *Documento de la IV Asamblea General* (December 1969), in *Signos de liberación: Testimonio de la Iglesia in América Latina, 1969–1973* (Lima: CEP, 1973), 279a.

and also the "earthiness" of Christian love, in contrast to a spiritualistic interpretation of that love. The Matthean text makes it easier to understand that encounter with the poor through concrete works is a necessary step in view of encounter with Christ himself.

But a true and full encounter with our neighbor requires that we first experience the gratuitousness of God's love. Once we have experienced it, our approach to others is purified of any tendency to impose an alien will on them; it is disinterested and respectful of their personalities, their needs, and their aspirations. The other is our way for reaching God, but our relationship with God is a precondition for encounter and true communion with the other. It is not possible to separate these two movements, which are perhaps really only a single movement: Jesus Christ, who is God and man, is our way to the Father but he is also our way to recognition of others as brothers and sisters. The experience of the gratuitousness of God's love — which is a basic datum of the Christian faith — is not simply a kind of historical parenthesis as it were; rather it is about becoming authentically human. A realization of this is gradually becoming a basic element in the spiritual experience now emerging in Latin America.

The experience is not universal, nor is it always explicit, nor is it entirely new. Nonetheless a significant dynamism is clearly forming. The experience of gratuitousness is not a form of evasion but rather the locus of life and the reality that envelops and permeates the endeavor to achieve historical efficacy. This efficacy will be sought with ever increasing fervor in the measure that it reveals to us the gratuitous love of God: God's preference for the poor and, inversely, contemplation of God within that history.   — *We Drink from Our Own Wells*, 112–13

4

Forming Christian Community

The spirituality of liberation is rooted not only in a rich chris-
tology but a profound ecclesiology as well. Though a gratuitous
encounter with the Lord is deeply personal, it is not individual-
istic, and in the end it must lead to forming new relationships.
These writings emphasize the importance of the practice of
Christian faith in forming Christian community. Spirituality
deepens these relationships as it invites us to enter into soli-
darity with the poor in history and to love all people as God
loves, even one's enemies. Spirituality lived as friendship with
God and others seeks to address the suffering and hopes of
people's lives.

GRATUITY AND THE CHURCH

Life in community cannot be understood without the immense
gratuity of God's love and the consequent demands that flow
from its reception. Outside of this gratuitous love and its demands, life in the church can be lost in laws of purely formal
conduct and distorted in abuses of power, according to the
worldly categories that privilege the powerful. Not living fra-
ternally, not loving our brothers and sisters in the liberation of
forgiveness, is to ignore in practice Jesus' presence. It means not

being a sign of the kingdom, which is a gift; to embrace it is to change perspective.

The ethics of the kingdom has its source in the initiative of God's love. To see history from the perspective of the smallest of the world, to receive the poor and excluded, to be in solidarity with them, means embracing Jesus and placing him in the center of our prayer and our commitment. With him we must walk, like the pilgrim church that goes forth, with its stumbling and deficiencies, toward the loving God, the God of life. The so-called "community discourse" of Matthew 18 — which expresses a rich and complex ecclesial experience — highlights the gratuity of God's love as the foundation of ecclesial life and of Christian behavior. This central affirmation, placed at the beginning and at the end of the chapter (18:1–5; 23–35), provides the framework for the instruction on forgiveness and other aspects of life in a Christian community (18:6–22).

God's free and gratuitous love, the heart of biblical revelation, is the foundation and the ultimate meaning of community of Jesus' disciples, whose calling is to be a sign of that love in history. The parable of the unmerciful servant at the end of the chapter (18:23–35) gives us an important clue to its overall meaning. In this parable the forgiveness of monetary debt signifies the forgiveness of offenses, and in both cases God's gratuity and goodness are manifest.

The parable has two distinct sections and a very important conclusion. The first section deals with a debt of ten thousand talents, a spectacular quantity that makes us realize we too owe a balance impossible to repay (similar to the external debt of some poor countries today). The servant does not ask for relief from his debt but only an extension with assurance to the king that he will one day repay it all. It is obvious that he will not be able to accomplish that. The king's pardon is not based on this false promise, but rather on the compassion that he feels for the anguish of the servant and his impassioned plea that the king not lose patience. Furthermore, the king grants him more than he wished for. The foundation for this initiative of forgiveness is based on the king's free will, his gratuity expressed and underscored by the impossible objective of paying back the enormous debt.

The king's generous behavior is contrasted with the stinginess and stubbornness of the servant who has just been pardoned and now encounters a fellow servant who owes him a hundred denarii.[1] The ridiculous disparity between the two debts is intentional and instructive. A merciless legal penalty would result in the servant's imprisonment, although in this case repayment was possible. Nevertheless the plea to lengthen the terms of the debt was ignored. The debtor who had been shown mercy now became a ruthless creditor.

The conclusion is evident. In accord with a frequent theme in the Gospels, the forgiven servant should have conducted himself like the merciful king. Being forgiven entails knowing how to forgive and with the same gratuity as the king. This is the demand that accompanies the gift of God's gratuitous love, a love based not on the merits of the people who receive it but on the merciful behavior of the giver. In the case of the unmerciful servant it is a love that should have been rooted in the grace of which he had been the recipient. The last verse (18:35) refers to the fraternity that must first exist among members of the same community and then surpass those boundaries and become a sign of God's love in history.

TRUE GREATNESS

Matthew 18:1–5 also speaks of the kingdom, thus providing the framework of gratuity that gives consistency and foundation to the chapter. The passage begins with the question: "Who is the greatest in the kingdom of heaven?" In answering the question we notice Matthew's constant preoccupation (also treated

---

1. A denarius was the usual day's wage for a laborer. A talent was worth more than fifteen years' wages of a laborer. –NRSV

in Mark 9:33–37) with the disciple's status. Jesus answers the question with a symbolic and prophetic gesture: "Truly I tell you, unless you change and become like children, you will never enter the kingdom of heaven" (Matt. 18:3). In the next verse he calls us to be humble, like a child, who "is the greatest in the kingdom of heaven" (18:4).

This status requires more than an internal disposition. Beyond the child's moral quality or innocence, the words and gestures of this episode point clearly to a social inferiority. In Jesus' time the child was seen as an incomplete being, or at most a being in a transitional stage. Children could offer little to society; their status, far from serving as a model for an older person, was of one who must obey orders from those who considered themselves as important and in charge. The promise to enter the kingdom is not based on merits acquired for acting meekly like a child to receive the grace of the kingdom. It resides, instead, in God's fondness toward that which is not valued in this world, for the least in history, for those without any social standing. This is the situation of the poor people and the children in Jesus' time. To be childlike does not mean to go back chronologically or psychologically to infancy; it is to identify and enter into solidarity with those who are seen as inferior. And it is equally important for us to emulate the humility that many of them demonstrate.

In fact, "child" and "humiliate" have in this and other biblical passages a rich significance. These terms refer to a situation of physical and social inferiority. We have seen this regarding the child but we can also relate "to humiliate" with the term *tapeinós,* meaning "weak," "insignificant," "poor," and "humiliated," more than "humble." In dealing with concrete human social conditions, these terms are equally apt for expressing realities of interior order, spiritual dispositions, and the humility of a child as a virtue.

Identifying with those considered insignificant and the change of attitude required by Jesus are demonstrated in the welcoming of the child as representative of the social categories of "helpless" and "despicable." Here we see what is at stake for a disciple of Jesus: "Whoever welcomes one such child in my name welcomes me" (18:5). "In my name" is to say, "in my place," "according to my wish," "my will." The Lord himself is present in our encounter with the other. Again we are faced with God's gratuitous love, and we are likewise faced with cardinal norms for the believer's conduct. Whatever is done to a child is also done to the person of Jesus. This refers to a deeply biblical insight of Matthew, expressed in its definitive form in the scene of the final judgment (25:31–46).

For Matthew, to accept the gift of a loving God entails a welcoming of and solidarity with our brothers and sisters. These actions are not a prerequisite for a love that saves but rather a consequence that flows from one who has received it. There is nothing more demanding than gratuity. Matthew, who often insists on the performance of good works, refers to this gratuity on numerous occasions.

LIFE IN COMMUNITY

Jesus' followers should live their faith in the God of life in community. Matthew provides specific norms to guide communal sharing. Matthew 18:4 indicates a first requirement for life in community: leave aside personal and social privileges. The greatest in the kingdom is the smallest in this world, the rejected and despised. Those who follow that norm of life must not worry about who is "the greatest one" in the Christian community.

Those who reject and scandalize the most insignificant ones, instead of entering the kingdom, will definitively be separated from it (18:6). Matthew's use of the term "little ones" refers to the simple people who "the wise and the intelligent" look down upon and categorize as ignorant; but to them God reveals himself (Matt. 11:25). These are the important figures in Matthew 18:6–14; they are believers characterized by their smallness and frailty in society. Welcoming the little ones is not predicated on the moral merits of simple people but rather on the fact that they are defenseless, without social significance. It is because we must love as God loves, gratuitously. A well-known illustration is the parable of the lost sheep. The fragile, lost animal, needing help, must be the first concern of the shepherd, who is obligated to go and look for it — the text highlights the initiative — leaving momentarily the other sheep. It is not a matter of numbers or majority but of necessity and urgency. The one in danger and isolated goes before the ninety-nine who are safe and sheltered. The term here is not "little ones" in the plural; one is enough to motivate remedial action by the shepherd. Each person has intrinsic value. Another expression of gratuity, promulgated in this parable, is leaving sure and familiar territory to take up an eager search.

The parable indicates what the ecclesial priority should be: care for the weak and the least. We must not simply avoid scandalizing the little ones but also go in search of the lost one (18:14). The parable also has a missionary focus. The church must protect its members and, equally important, go beyond its borders. Jesus is the universal shepherd, and the church is mission. Leaving the well-traveled path implies trust and courage, and there is no authentic mission without risk.

LOVING EACH OTHER

Matthew's Gospel also reminds us that the church is formed by the just and by sinners or, more precisely, by people who are both at the same time. We learn that interaction with each other has its demanding moments. Matthew 18:15–17 deals with fraternal correction. Because of a mutual concern for each other, Christian love rejects friendships that are based on a shallow, peaceful coexistence. If a member of the church commits a transgression, for example, rejecting or ignoring the insignificant ones, he or she must be confronted about distancing himself or herself from the Gospel of Jesus. Therefore it is appropriate to proceed in stages. The first is a discreet but effective face-to-face dialogue, which seeks to "regain that one" (18:15). This personal encounter must be sought. If this does bring about reconciliation, the person must engage additional members of the community in the confrontation (18:16) because it is the community that is in difficulty. If the new admonition is ignored the text makes it explicitly necessary to call the entire community, the *ekklēsia* (church; 18:17).

After this, the only thing left is to separate the member who refuses to accept the good news from the community. The allusion to the "gentile or tax collector" points to those who are distant from the faithful community. Verse 18 suggests the procedure of what to do in these types of situations that grow in severity and gives the foundation for the disciplinary rules: that which the community binds and loosens on earth will also be done in heaven. The attitude before the sinning member is not simply a matter of opportunity, nor is it limited to a human opinion; it is a demand from afar; it expresses the vocation and the role of the church in human history. It refers to an authority agreed upon by the whole church, but which can be used only with diplomacy, persuasion, and fraternal dialogue.

In Matthew 18:19–20 we learn of a vital element regarding life in community: Jesus' presence in the midst of it. That presence assures the value of prayer in community: it will reach the Father. This will occur when we behave as authentic brothers and sisters, in the fraternity that these disciplines seek to assure. God's presence in history reaches its pinnacle in the incarnation and is sustained in the church as a visible sign of the kingdom. Prayer is always an experience of gratitude that emphasizes the love of God. Without the practice of prayer there is no Christian life. Christ is the heart of the assembly of the faithful.

Confronting one another means knowing how to forgive. The always impulsive Peter asks a question of a quantitative nature: "How often should I forgive?" (18:21) and suggests a generous response: "As many as seven times?" — generous because the number seven symbolizes a certain completeness.

The Lord deepens this symbolism and broadens the suggestion, playing with the number seven and eliminating all the limitations of forgiveness: always. His answer is, "seventy-seven times" (18:22). The question was asked in name of the faithful community by him who is often portrayed as its spokesperson. The response is therefore directed toward the community.

Forgiveness is liberating. Those who are forgiven are liberated from their fault and their anguish, and those who forgive are liberated from all resentment and bitterness. To forgive is to give life, which must characterize the assembly of Jesus' followers. Refusing to forgive or forgiving with limitations is to refuse to believe in the God of life, who pardons and forgets sin. The terrible and frequently used phrase "I forgive, but I don't forget" cannot be farther from the mind of Christ. Forgiveness brings us back to the parable of the unforgiving creditor. In effect, the increase in forgiveness ("seventy-seven times) is about God's gratuitous love, which we are all called to practice.

— Páginas 164 (August 2000): 28–36

5

Living with Christ in the World

Gutiérrez was profoundly shaped by the historical currents of the day, most notably the Second Vatican Council (1962–65). He was particularly influenced by Pope John XXIII and his challenge to read the Gospel in light of the signs of the times and to engage the poor in the life of the church. This opened up new vistas in theology, which led Gutiérrez to explore the meaning of evangelization from the context of the poor and marginalized. The situation in Latin America prompted Gutiérrez to ask: "How do we speak about a personal God in a world that regards the poor as non-persons?" And, "How do we say to the poor that God loves them, when so much of their lives seems to suggest otherwise?" These writings reflect a larger shift in the church, as well as in spirituality. As they name the temptations of elitism, perfectionism, and individualism, they also articulate a spiritual vision based on building a more just and human society. In this light the mission is no longer about the church against *the world or the church* in *the world but the church* for *the world.*

The situation created by the process of liberation — a process that in its varied embodiments is attacking the age-old wretchedness and exploitation that have characterized Latin America — is raising serious questions about a certain approach to Christian life. Familiar reference points are being obscured;

confusion, frustration, and defensive withdrawal are experienced on a wide scale. But a process of reevaluation is also in evidence and new paths are being opened. All this is a judgment being passed by God and by history: a history in this case that the poor and the dispossessed — those who are the privileged ones in God's kingdom — have begun to create.

HISTORICAL MOVEMENTS AND FOLLOWING JESUS

Every great spirituality is connected with the great historical movement of the age in which it was formulated. This linkage is not to be understood in the sense of mechanical dependence, but following Jesus is something that penetrates deeply into the course of human history. This is true, for example, of the mendicant spirituality that was born at a time when, despite apparent good health, the first germs of a crisis for Christianity were incubating. The new spiritual way was closely linked to those movements of the poor that represented a social and evangelical reaction to the wealth and power that the church had attained at that time.[1] The time of the pontificate of Innocent III (1198–1216) showed clearly the heights that the political power and affluence of the church had reached. Without attention to the historical context in which Francis of Assisi and Dominic Guzmán developed their apostolate and bore their evangelical witness, it is impossible to understand either the full significance of the mendicant orders or the reception and resistance they encountered.[2]

The same holds true for Ignatius of Loyola. His spirituality had for its context the transition to the so-called modern age.

---

1. See the historical study by Michel Mollat, *Les pauvres au moyen âge* (Paris: Etudes Sociales, 1979).

2. See Miguel Gelabert and José María Milagro, *Santo Domingo de Guzmán, visto por sus contemporáneos* (Madrid: Biblioteca de Autores Cristianos, 1947), and the beautiful book of Leonardo Boff, *Francis of Assisi: A Model for Human Liberation* (Maryknoll, N.Y.: Orbis Books, 2006).

The broadening of the known world by geographical discoveries, the assertion of human reason that found expression in the birth of experimental science, the extension of the scope of human subjectivity in religious matters as evidenced by the Protestant Reformation — these were converging phenomena that led to a new way of understanding the role of human freedom. It was not a mere coincidence that freedom, a freedom directed to the service of God and others, should be a central theme in Ignatian spirituality.

Examples might be multiplied (John of the Cross and Teresa of Avila and their relationship to the reform within the Catholic Church, and many others). They would only confirm what I have already said: the concrete forms of following Jesus are connected with the great historical movements of an age.

A grasp of that constant enables us to understand what is happening in Latin America. Perhaps we lack the perspective required for realizing what is happening, inasmuch as the immediacy of events makes impossible the distance needed. The breakthrough of the poor is finding expression in the consciousness of the identity and the organization of the oppressed and marginalized of Latin America. In the future, Latin American society will be judged, and transformed, in terms of the poor. These are the ones who in this foreign land of death that is Latin America seek what Gabriel García Márquez, in his beautiful address upon receiving the Nobel Prize, called the utopia of life: "Faced with oppression, pillage, and abandonment, our response is life.... It is a new and splendid utopia of life, where no one can decide for others how they will die, where love will be certain and happiness possible, and where those condemned to a hundred years of solitary confinement find, finally and forever, a second chance on this earth."[3]

In search of this utopia, an entire people — with all its traditional values and the wealth of its recent experience — has taken to the path of building a world in which persons are more

---

3. "La soledad de América Latina," *Páginas* 51 (February 1983): 28.

important than things and in which all can live with dignity, a society that respects human freedom when it is in the service of a genuine common good, and exercises no kind of coercion, from any source. — *We Drink from Our Own Wells, 26–27*

THE RISK OF ELITISM AND PERFECTIONISM

Christian spirituality has long been presented as geared to elite minorities. It seems to be the peculiar possession of select and, to some extent, closed groups; it is linked for the most part to the existence of religious orders and congregations. Religious life, in the narrow sense of this term, encompassed a "state of perfection"; it implicitly supposed, therefore, that there were other, imperfect states of Christian life. Religious life was marked by a full and structured quest for holiness; in the other states there were found, at best, only the less demanding elements of this spirituality. The way proper to religious life supposed some kind of separation from the world and its everyday activities (one form of the well-known *fuga mundi,* "flight from the world"). The second way did not call for that kind of effort and could be traveled without fanfare in the midst of occupations that had little or nothing religious about them.

The "spirituality of the laity" that accompanied the rise of the lay apostolic movements in the first decades of our century was a reaction against the more rigid aspects of that perfect/imperfect outlook that represented a narrowing and impoverishment of Christian life. The counterclaim was provocative but inadequate, because the spirituality of the laity was still strongly characterized by important elements taken from the way of Christian perfection that had been canonized by the experiences of monastic and religious life.

In reality, that approach implied a distinction that resulted in two classes of Christians or two ways of Christian life. The distinction was already admitted in the theological schools

of earlier centuries and has continued to reappear throughout
the history of the church and even today, although in more
subtle forms. Any spirituality limited to minorities is today under heavy
crossfire. It is challenged on the one side by the spiritual experience of the dispossessed and marginalized — and those who
side with them — in their commitment to the struggle for liberation. Out of this experience has come the inspiration for a
popular and community quest of the Lord that is incompatible
with elitist models. It is challenged by the questioning of those
who live a life focused on concerns of the spiritual order and
who are now beginning to realize that such a life is made possible for them, at least in part, by their freedom from material
worries (food, lodging, health needs). These, of course, are concerns that fill the daily lives of the poor masses of the human
race. The minorities to whom this spirituality is directed are
also privileged minorities from the social, cultural, and, to some
extent, economic standpoint. We are dealing with a matter that
calls for radical treatment: a return to the sources, a salvaging of
the values contained therein, and a rejection of the inertia and
sense of established position that inevitably mark such a situation. Only thus is it possible to prevent the cancerous growth of
aspects of spirituality that are legitimate in themselves.
                          — We Drink from Our Own Wells, 9, 13–14

THE RISK OF
AN INDIVIDUALISTIC SPIRITUALITY

A second characteristic of the spirituality in question, and one
that is also being challenged today, is its individualistic bent.
The spiritual journey has often been presented as a cultivation of individualistic values as a way to personal perfection.
The relationship with God seemed to obscure the presence of
others and encouraged individual Christians to be absorbed in

their own interiority in order to understand and develop it better. For this reason the spiritual life was called the interior life, which many understood as a life lived exclusively within the individual. The important thing in it was the deployment of the virtues as potentialities that had to do with the individual and had little or no connection with the outside world. In this outlook the important thing is one's intention. It is this that gives value to human actions; the external effects of these actions are less important. Actions without any apparent human significance thus acquired spiritual and sanctifying value if done for important and legitimate motives.

When only a few authentic dimensions of Christian life are thus developed, the result may be a dangerous privatization of spirituality. As certain spiritual traditions moved away from their sources, they began to flow in the limited channels of the manuals and the spiritual treatises until finally they went astray — and in the process began to dry up — as increasingly shallow streams representing only an individualistic outlook. The community dimensions inherent in all Christian life became formalities; they were unable to alter the perspective that turned the journey to God into a purely individual venture. It is not surprising, then, that in such a context charity should be regarded as simply another Christian virtue to be cultivated.

This way of understanding the following of Jesus is usually characterized as "overly spiritualized." It is based on the fact that it shows little interest in temporal tasks and a great deal of insensitivity to the presence and needs of the real, concrete persons who surround Christians as they follow this spiritual way.

An important source of the "spirituality of evasion," as Puebla calls it (no. 826), is this individualism. Individualism operates, in fact, as a filter that makes it possible to "spiritualize" and even volatilize what in the Bible are nuanced statements of a social and historical nature. For example, the poor/rich opposition (a social fact) is reduced to the humble/proud opposition (something within the individual). "Passage"

through the individual interiorizes, and robs of their historical
bite, categories reflective of the objective realities in which individuals and peoples live and die, struggle, and assert their faith.
This kind of reduction has often taken place. Individualism
and spiritualism thus combine to impoverish and even distort
following Jesus. An individualistic spirituality is incapable of
offering guidance in this following to those who have embarked
on a collective enterprise of liberation. Nor does it do justice
to the different dimensions of the human person, including the
material aspects of human life.

— *We Drink from Our Own Wells,* 14–16

SEPARATING SPIRITUALITY
FROM DAILY LIFE

When spirituality is separated from daily life, people begin to
live a somewhat dichotomized existence. On the one hand, they
feel the need of a sure spiritual way; this is especially the case
perhaps in those who have had a more systematic formation in
this area. On the other hand, daily life with its demands for
commitment seems to run on a tangential track; it does not initially conflict with the spirituality one has acquired, but neither
does it enrich it. In the long run, this kind of dual existence
is highly unsatisfactory. Upon the disappearance of the fixed
points that should give unity to everyday activity, persons live
at the mercy of events, unable to establish fruitful links between
them and forced simply to jump from one to another. They are
convinced that they have learned a great deal from solidarity
with the poor and from carrying out their work of evangelization among them, but when they try to express this perception
they fall back on categories that begin to seem increasingly alien
and remote. The problem results from the fact that they have
not reexamined these categories in the light of their new experiences or, more exactly, that they do not have another path that
can replace the one that no longer seems to lead to the goal.

An important and painful example of the lack of vital unity (which every spirituality demands) is the separation that takes place between prayer and action. Both are accepted as necessary, and in fact they are. The problem is to establish a connection between them. But unity is not to be recovered by eliminating one of the two poles that are in tension. The recovery must rather be the result of an effort to be faithful, in both prayer and concrete commitments, to the will of the Lord in the midst of the poor. An authentic unity is based on a synthesis of elements that are seemingly disparate but that in fact enrich one another.   — *We Drink from Our Own Wells,* 17–18

6

Walking with Mary

The themes of gratuity and justice come together in Gutiérrez's writings on the person of Mary, who embodies the model of authentic discipleship and solidarity. She does not presume or assume any titles or privileges for herself, but she opens herself up to the power of divine life and becomes a model of the spiritual life. Her Magnificat expresses the truth that all is grace, and the reception of grace leads us to walk together with the lowly.

MARY: DAUGHTER OF A PEOPLE

Mary is not an isolated individual, but a daughter of a people. Luke calls attention to this relationship and even goes so far as to identify Mary with Israel. In his infancy Gospel he announces the great themes of the kingdom, which are at the heart of Jesus' preaching. This approach achieves a sublime intensity in the song known as the Magnificat, which Luke places on the lips of the Mother of the Lord. Up to this point, Mary has said little; now Luke has her speak for ten verses. Various attempts have been made to subdivide the text; no consensus has been reached. In my opinion, however, there is greater agreement on the deeper unity of the song and on seeing as its central point the assertion of the holiness of God: "holy is his name"

(1:49). This is the essential message conveyed by Mary's way of speaking about God.

GRATUITY AND THE LOWLY

It is often said that in the first verses (Luke 1:46–50) of the Magnificat, Mary speaks as an individual. That is why we find the expressions "my soul" and "my spirit," which are Semitic expressions for the pronoun "I."

The fact of these expressions should not, however, make us forget that throughout the entire song, Mary expresses herself as a daughter of a people; in some sense, she represents this people:

And Mary said:
"My soul magnifies the Lord,
  and my spirit rejoices in God my Savior,
for he has looked with favor on the lowliness of his servant.
  Surely, from now on all generations will call me blessed;
for the Mighty One has done great things for me."
(Luke 1:46–49a)

Mary and her people sing of the greatness of God. God is the Lord, the Mighty One, who acts with power. The power of God is revealed in history through saving actions. Yahweh, the God who is and is with us, will become the liberator of Israel. The Book of Exodus tells us that God said: "I have observed the misery of my people who are in Egypt" (Exod. 3:7). Deuteronomy is more specific: "the Lord ... saw our affliction, our toil, and our oppression" (Deut. 26:7). Therefore, because he had witnessed this situation, Yahweh brought the people out of Egypt "by a mighty hand and an outstretched arm" (Deut. 4:34) and established a covenant with them. One must refer back to Israel's experience if one is to understand

an event of the magnitude of the Messiah's coming. This coming is also a manifestation of the power of God and of God's
intervention in history. Mary tells us that God saw "the lowliness of his servant."
The Greek word for humility or lowliness, *tapeinōsis*, has a definite connotation of affliction and oppression, as we saw in the
passage from Deuteronomy. The Greek *tapeinōsis* often translates the Hebrew word '*oni*, which signifies affliction caused by
servitude and despoliation (or by sterility in the case of women;
see Gen. 16:11). Mary, then, who is a servant and, in addition,
a woman, who has placed her life in the Lord's hands, is in a
"situation of humiliation."

God has "looked upon" the situation of Mary. The expression "look upon" is often used with reference to the concern
God has for those who suffer injustice and humiliation. It is a
gaze of love that makes Mary happy. God will act in history and
renew the covenant on her behalf; God has the power to do so.
Contemplation of God's liberating power brings joy for those
who benefit from God's action. Various expressions of this joy
are evident in the first chapters of Luke. Mary rejoices (1:47) in
response to the exhortation of the angel Gabriel (1:28). This is
an attitude of great depth and fullness. "God my Savior" is the
source of her happiness; all will admit that she is happy, and
will declare her blessed. The statement is a reminder of what
Isaiah says in 61:9–10; the nations will acknowledge those
whom the Lord has liberated.

The joy is Mary's but it is also the joy of the entire people.
At the birth of Jesus the shepherds are told: "Do not be afraid;
for see — I am bringing you good news of great joy for all the
people" (2:10). This joy is the subject of the angel's proclamation, for it is in fact a central element of the Gospel. Joy enables
Mary to proclaim the good news. The feeling of joy expands her
heart and makes her even more disposed to receive the presence
of God. In this way she becomes more a servant, more a person
who places her entire trust in the Lord. It is out of a complete adherence to God, symbolized by her virginity, that Mary

speaks of God and helps us to place ourselves in the presence of God's gratuitous love.

The second part of verse 49 contains the central statement of the Magnificat:

> ...and holy is his name.
> His mercy is for those who fear him
> from generation to generation.
> (Luke 1:49b–50)

The Magnificat is a hymn of praise to the holy God. Psalm 111 praises God for the work of liberation and does so in words close to those of the Magnificat: "He has sent redemption to his people; he has commanded his covenant forever. Holy and awesome is his name" (Ps. 111:9). God's holiness gives meaning to the work of liberation. This mighty God is also merciful. Might and mercy are two aspects of God's greatness; God is a loving power, an efficacious love. God's mercy makes God receptive and tender.

The exercise of God's power and mercy makes known to us God's greatness and holiness. "Holy is his name" is a statement that recurs throughout the Bible and one that Mary makes her own. Everything comes from God and from God's freely given unmerited love. This idea is at the heart of biblical revelation and therefore also of the preaching of Jesus. At the Annunciation Mary was told: "the child to be born will be holy; he will be called the son of God" (Luke 1:35). The literary form of the text makes us think that Luke's intention here is clearly to say that the holy one, the wholly other, is not a distant God. God becomes flesh, one of us, in the womb of Mary. The incarnation does not deprive God of transcendence but reveals to us what kind of holiness is God's.

God's holiness is that of one who fulfills promises (see Luke 1:55); who enters into our history in order to bring it into the sphere of the divine; who transforms the present world. God is the God who does justice. To this end God makes an agreement with the people. It is as a member of this people that Mary speaks. Her contemplation of God's holiness is not an evasion of history; her joy at the gratuitous love of the Lord does not make her forget the demands of justice. Engaging history and building a just world would lack real depth for Christians apart from the acceptance of God as the one absolute in our lives and as the ultimate foundation of our hope and our joy.

A DIFFERENT HISTORY

God's ways are not our ways (Isa. 55:8–9). In God's plan, the least of history becomes the first (see Isa. 58). God's preference for the weak and oppressed runs throughout the Bible. The people of Israel have an obligation to bear witness to this predilection; the Messiah comes to proclaim it by his actions and words. Luke is especially alert to this point. He shows God being revealed to the unimportant folk of history such as Zechariah, Elizabeth, Simeon, Anna, and, above all, Mary. This revelation also speaks to us of the radical change of values and situations that is wrought by the coming of the Messiah. Mary's song expresses this in a forceful way:

> He has shown strength with his arm;
>   he has scattered the proud in the thoughts of their
>   hearts.
> He has brought down the powerful from their thrones,
>   and lifted up the lowly;
> he has filled the hungry with good things,
>   and sent the rich away empty. (Luke 1:51–53)

These verses are an abiding challenge and reason for hope and joy among the Christian people. These three verses tell us how God (who is the subject of all six verbs) manifests power and mercy in history and makes the divine holiness present.

First of all, God disperses the arrogant. "The strength of his arm" is an expression that occurs frequently in the context of the exodus. It signifies the power by which Yahweh delivers the people. The verb used for "scattered" is a strong one; it means to put an enemy to flight. The thought is an echo (such as is found in, for example, Ps. 89:10b, which may be one of the sources of the Magnificat) of what happened to the armies of the pharaoh. The power of God is exercised against the arrogant, those who make a show of being more than they are, the proud and insolent. These people are blusterers at heart. A literal translation of the text would be: "scattered the proud in the thoughts of their heart." This is why some translate: "scattered the plans of the proud." Among these plans is the intention to humiliate the poor. These people feel that they were born to be in control and to be respected. Pride makes them enemies of God.

This verse does not say who they are who are contrasted with the proud; the next two verses will do this. But the preceding verse does speak of "those who fear him [God]" (Luke 1:50). "Fear" of God is an important theme in the Bible, but the fear is not a fear of a powerful and even angry being. The idea here is different and reaches deeper: "fear" of God means respect for the plans, and trust in the person, of one who loves us faithfully. His servants (Mary, 1:48, and Israel, 1:54) are those who commit their lives to him. The proud are those who reject God's will, God's purpose, which is life, peace, and justice for all and especially for the poor and the unimportant people.

God's second action is described in the form of an antithesis in which rulers are contrasted with the lowly. By "powerful" is meant here those who use their rule to dominate and oppress. Such people are brought low. God loathes those who take advantage of their power to mistreat and rob others. Jesus rejects this kind of power and offers himself as the model servant (see Luke 22:24–27).

The lowly will be lifted up. The reference is to the humiliated, the poor, the oppressed. Mary has already spoken of her own "lowliness." Here she is speaking of the "lowliness" of the poor in Israel and indeed throughout all of human history. The parallelism is intentional and meaningful. The holy God (who is powerful and merciful) is on the side of the weak and abused, not of the powerful. Paul says to the Christians of Corinth:

Consider your own call, brothers and sisters: not many of you were wise by human standards, not many were powerful, not many were of noble birth. But God chose what is foolish in the world to shame the wise; God chose what is weak in the world to shame the strong; God chose what is low and despised in the world, things that are not, to reduce to nothing things that are. (1 Cor. 1:26–28)

A passage from Albert the Great, centuries ago, is clear on the social and historical implications of the verse on which I am commenting:

The rulers whom God throws down are those who glory in their power and misuse it by using it to oppress the poor. ... They are the rulers we call "tyrants." Power worthy of the name is power exercised within the limits set by justice and equity. But the rulers of whom the Magnificat is speaking use their power tyrannically, that is, not according to reason but arbitrarily. It is these whom God throws down from their thrones.[1]

The common sense and evangelical inspiration of these words of the great Dominican make them fully applicable to our own day. If we attempt to strip Mary's song of its historical sting, then we overlook the promises made in the Old Testament. More importantly, we take the wrong path to discovery of the spiritual meaning of a song that is so full of the presence of God that it requires no great efforts on our part to raise us up to contemplation and hope.

The third action of God displays the same inversion of situations. Here the hungry are contrasted with the rich. The ones who will go away empty are those who have "gotten rich":

---

1. Albert the Great, *In Lucam*, in his *Opera Omnia* 22 (Paris, 1904), 138, cited in E. Hamel, "Le Magnificat et le renversement des situations," *Gregorianum* 60 (1979): 56.

gotten rich, that is, at the expense of the poor and defenseless. The poor are described in terms of a cruel and very basic deprivation — namely, hunger. "The hungry" is more accurately translated as "the starving," meaning those for whom hunger is like a sickness. The starving will be satisfied. Psalm 107 said long ago: "For he satisfies the thirsty, and the hungry he fills with good things" (107:9). The contrast between rich and hungry is reinforced by the contrast between empty and full. The reference to concrete or material situations is clear. It calls us to commitments concerned with bringing into existence a history that differs from that of our experience.

In Latin America we are convinced that without commitment to the poor and those who count for nothing there is no authentic Christian life. We are also convinced that without contemplation and acknowledgment of God's gratuitous love there is likewise no authentic Christian life. The spiritual meaning of the Magnificat is to be found precisely in this combination, which also finds expression in the structure of the song.

Paul VI sums this up accurately in his Apostolic Exhortation *Marialis Cultus* (37):

> The figure of the Blessed Virgin does not disappoint modern men and women; rather she offers them the perfect model of the Lord's disciple: the disciple who builds up the earthly, temporal city while being a diligent pilgrim toward the heavenly, eternal city; who works for that justice which frees the oppressed and that charity which assists the needy; but above all, the disciple who is an active witness to that love which builds up Christ in people's hearts.[2]

Mary's song tells us about the preferential love of God for the lowly and the abused and about the transformation of history that God's loving will implies. Consequently, the text is not rendered more spiritual by emptying it of the God whom Jesus

---

2. Translated in *The Pope Speaks* 19 (1974–75): 75.

Christ came to reveal to us and making it insubstantial and inoffensive to those who enjoy unjust privileges in this world. The spiritual power of Mary's words consists in their ability to make us see that the quest of uprightness and justice must be located within the parameters of God's gratuitous love, or it loses its deeper meaning. Her words help us to understand that this free and unmerited love, which inspires our prayer and thanksgiving, requires of us a solidarity with those who live in circumstances contrary to the purpose of the God of Jesus Christ — namely, that all should have life.

— The God of Life, 179–85

7

Becoming a Disciple

Though honored around the world for his scholarly work,
Gutiérrez has never forgotten the primacy of his pastoral work
among the poor and insignificant. In the process he has high-
lighted the political implications of a genuine spiritual commit-
ment. Gutiérrez's writings explore how one lives as a Christian
when so much of the world lives in destitution. Though origi-
nally written in 1984, his words take on even more relevance
today, with 19 percent of the world struggling to survive on
$1 or less a day, 48 percent on $2 or less a day, and two-
thirds of the planet living in poverty. In view of these statistics,
Gutiérrez's writings highlight not only the financial costs but
also the human costs that must be accounted for as one seeks to
be faithful to the Gospel message in a globalized world.

MYSTICISM AND POLITICS

Mysticism clearly has something to do with an experience of
God in a key of love, peace, and joy. In contrast, oppression
refers to a situation of poverty, injustice, and exclusion, with
its resultant suffering, rejection, and rebellion. Are these then
incompatible human experiences?

Those who find themselves in these situations are human
beings with all the personal dimensions this implies; they also

belong to peoples with a history, culture, and vision of the universe. In exploring this subject we meet people in whom poverty and dispossession mark their faith in God and leave a mark on the condition of oppression and discrimination. There is certainly a close relationship between mysticism and politics. Without contemplation, prayer, thanksgiving to God, there is no Christian life, any more than there is without commitment, solidarity, and love of neighbor. Can we talk of a mystical dimension in the faith life of a person who suffers exclusion and injustice and eventually embarks on a path of liberation from these conditions?

An attempt to answer this question presupposes a move from the realm of the individual to a position within sociocultural contexts and a historical perspective and to viewpoints from different geographical points on the planet. Above all, however, it requires us to be sensitive to one of the facts most pregnant with consequences for present-day Christianity: the Christian faith has not just begun to spring up, but has also grown and matured in non-Western peoples who have been poor and oppressed for centuries.

Today in the church certain conflicts of interpretation about the times we live in and the challenges they present to us frequently provoke tension, difficulties, and misunderstandings that prevent us from seeing that something much more important than these differences of opinion is taking place among us. In a famous article, a sort of balance-sheet of Vatican II, Karl Rahner said that the Council's main significance was that it marked the beginning of a third stage in the life of the church, a period in which it could begin to be genuinely universal.

The vigorous existence of local churches in places geographically and culturally far removed from Europe, the force of their voices, containing accents of pain and hope, the contribution of their theological reflection, and the new challenges this brings represent a most important event for the Christian faith. This is the context in which we must discuss the subject of mysticism and oppression. The presence of those who are different from Western culture is now established but not always recognized; it will lead us to reexamine central texts of the Christian revelation that can throw light on the process under way and finally indicate the pattern of spirituality represented by the preferential option for the poor.

— The Density of the Present, 157–59

SPIRITUALITY AND OTHERNESS

Recognizing otherness is still an unfinished task. This was one of the earliest intuitions of liberation theology. The perspective of the "underside of history" is an obligation still in full force. The perception of the otherness of the poor and oppressed (in social, racial, cultural, and gender terms) enables us to understand how they can enjoy a keen sense of God, which does not disdain celebration and joy, in the midst of a situation of expropriation and a struggle for justice. By unknown paths the experience of oppression has turned out to be fruitful ground for the mystical dimension of Christian life.

What seems contradictory or, at best, suspect, to a modern mentality becomes real and full of promise in a different socio-cultural context. I am not talking about the practice of prayer as a protection against daily sufferings or religious observance as a shock absorber to deaden the reaction of rejection provoked by exploitation and contempt. Such situations exist, of course, and not just as exceptions, but they do not account for or explain the whole situation. There are many cases in which the mystical and spiritual perspective is, on the contrary, the best antidote to the use of Christianity as a search for a refuge or a justification of the status quo and one of the main factors in generating and developing human and Christian solidarity.

Moreover, this complex experience provides criteria for discernment with results that seem simple, but are nonetheless unexpected. For example, I can never forget the distinction I heard made by a woman belonging to a Christian base community: a Christian can live joy in a situation of suffering, but not of sadness. Sadness, she explained, turns you in on yourself and can make you bitter. The Easter perspective of this approach to the experience of the poor is clear, but not everyone achieves it.

In other words, the subject of the mystical dimension in the existence of those who suffer oppression directs us to the situation of the Christian communities that have grown up in what until recently was called the Third World. Their experience of faith is not a simple reflection of what happens where Christianity has been rooted for many centuries. Forced to adapt to the climate of a different environment and feed on a sap produced by other soil, faith has produced rich fruits with a taste slightly different from that which many people are used to, but does that mean that these fruits are less authentic and nourishing?

The establishment of "winter gardens" to reproduce the European climate in other environments — a practice in which some persist — only leads to artificial situations with no future. The demands of inculturation go beyond adaptation and call for a revision of mental categories. This will not come about without cases of hesitation and misunderstanding, but also not without determination and courage on the part of those who see this change as essential if the Christian faith is to have a vital presence in the world of today.

— The Density of the Present, 160–62

SPIRITUALITY FROM BELOW

From their being second-class members even of the Christian churches, the oppressed are becoming full disciples of Jesus. From having their experience of God and their theological reflection underestimated, they are now beginning to enrich the universal Christian community, and this is also happening with the mystical dimension of their faith in a world of poverty, which some mistakenly think leaves no room for gratuitousness or at most summons us to the struggle for justice. The process has been and is long and costly, like that which John describes for us in the supremely important and beautiful ninth chapter of his Gospel.

The story in John 9 introduces us to a person who is clearly, for the evangelist, the model of the disciple. A blind beggar (and so doubly poor) recovers his sight through the action of Jesus. In the sharp dialogues, the former blind man repeats that Jesus gave him his sight. What John is doing is insisting on the experience that is at the start of the faith of a person taking the road toward discipleship.

Those who had been accustomed to see the man blind sitting, begging, doubt his identity. It can't be the same person: How can this reject possibly now be someone able to see and fend for himself? Those who are insignificant should stay that way; that's how the world is, and any change overturns an order in which everything is in its proper place. There now begins a series of dialogues in which, in a move that is extremely significant and unique in his Gospel, John makes Jesus disappear for twenty-eight verses. In his place is none other than the man he has cured and who gradually adopts the status of disciple: the evangelist even puts into his mouth an expression he usually keeps for the Lord: "I am the man" (literally, "I am," 9:9). His experience leads him to a simple affirmation, to a first step in his journey as a disciple: he received his sight from "the man called Jesus" (9:11).

However, the doubts of the man's neighbors are nothing to the aggressiveness the incident provoked in the powerful. The Pharisees believe he was never blind, and that they are faced, not with mistaken identity, but with a deliberate lie: Jesus cannot have done this. The former blind man does not stop at describing what happened: without fear he goes up another rung and tells the élite of his people that the person who did this "is a prophet" (9:17).

The dialogue — the dispute — begins to take on a theological flavor. Arguing from their abstract principles, the experts in the

Law insist that this Jesus is a sinner and cannot have done what
the accused — as he increasingly is — claims. The man starts
from his experience and grows in his convictions: "Do you also
want to become his disciples?" he asks ironically (9:27). He is
now arguing equal to equal with those who claimed a religious
and theological superiority, with those who assumed they knew
all about God, and refutes them when he maintains — to the
surprise and opposition of the great of his world — that if Jesus
"were not from God, he could do nothing" (9:33).

The author of the Gospel now brings Jesus back. With the
experience not just of being healed, but also of meeting Jesus,
the new disciple realizes what he now can see and confess without fear, "Lord, I believe" (9:38). The light of faith has opened
his eyes a second time and radically changed his life. From being
excluded, insignificant, and despised, he has come to be a disciple, to take Christ's place in the story, to confound those who
prided themselves on their knowledge.

This maturation of faith ought to overcome the skepticism
of those accustomed to a particular social or religious system,
enable them to resist the onslaught of the powerful, to stand
up to the pride of those who think they have nothing to learn,
to talk on an equal footing to those who boast of an alleged
superiority. In a sense the poor and oppressed peoples who have
made the Christian faith their own are represented by this beggar blind from birth. Many would have preferred to see them
always subject to charity, unable to stand up for themselves and
to think out in original ways their path as disciples of Jesus. Of
all the Lord's disciples — John likes to call them friends — the
man blind from birth is the evangelist's favorite, who, like the
poor of this world, has no name. His passage through history
and his becoming a disciple is bringing them out of anonymity.
Their experience of God, the mystical dimension of their lives,
does not appear at the end of the road; it grows little by little
out of their state of exclusion and oppression.

The Synoptic Gospels, in accounts that are less detailed but
no less significant, give us a similar message in the story of the

blind man of Jericho. At the exit from the city a sightless beggar (doubly poor, once more) is sitting by the edge of the road. As Jesus comes by, this man who sees what others are unable to see, shouts out "Son of David" and asks him for help (Mark 10:47).

The God of Jesus is none other than the God of the forgotten and excluded, of those whom people want to silence, which in this case was the action of the people around the Lord (see Mark 10:48). But Jesus has come for these first, and the prospect of the death he will face very soon in Jerusalem does not prevent him from having time for the suffering and the hope of this poor man. He asks him to come near, and the blind man does so; according to the text, "he sprang up," perhaps over the heads of those who were demanding that he be silent, and went to Jesus (10:50).

Jesus does not impose his power on him, does not claim to know what he wants, does not overwhelm him with his help; he asks, "What do you want me to do for you?" (10:51). Listening is an important element of dialogue, and in this case the Lord makes a space for the beggar to take an initiative and assert himself as a person. The poor are not objects of favor; they are subjects of rights and desires. When the man asks Jesus to make him see, Jesus observes that the blind man has taken an active part in this event: "Your faith has made you well" (10:52). At that moment Bartimaeus — this time we know his name — gets up, leaves the side of the road, and sets foot on it, following Jesus as a disciple.

The call to discipleship is permanent and includes in a special way the forgotten and oppressed. The Bartimaeuses of this world have stopped being at the side of the road; they have jumped up and come to the Lord, their lifelong friend. Their presence may upset the old followers of Jesus, who spontaneously, and with the best reasons in the world, begin to defend their privileges. They have discovered — and it cost them an effort to do so — *one* way of being a Christian, and no doubt they think it is *the* way to be a Christian for everyone. This sometimes throws up novel demands for proper conduct in life and in Christian thinking that are not confined to the offices of some church authorities; they are also the result of the exegesis and theology done in the North Atlantic world and even extend to ordinary Christians in those latitudes. They frequently react to the eleventh-hour disciples (workers) with the "envy" the Gospel describes (Matt. 20:1–16, esp. 15). Clearly the gratuitousness of God's love challenges the patterns we have become used to.   — *The Density of the Present*, 162–65

SPIRITUALITY AND POVERTY

Fundamental to the theological experience and reflection that has taken place in Latin America in recent decades is summed up in what we call the preferential option for the poor. The idea — and the phrase — has succeeded in piercing layers of initial resistance and hostility until it finally penetrated the universal magisterium of the church.

The preferential option came into being in the context of a historical event of vast proportions that we know as the entry of the poor onto the stage of history. This situation has forced before our eyes with stark clarity the ancient and cruel poverty of the great majority of the world's population, which has come onto the stage of society — as Las Casas said of the Indian nations of his time — with their poverty on their backs. But this situation has also brought into play the energies and qualities of this people. It is a phenomenon not without ambivalences, but challenging and in many respects full of promise, as it has enabled the poor and oppressed to begin to feel in control of their own history, like people at last holding the reins of their own destiny.

These events revived discussion about poverty in the church, and sent it in new directions. So in Latin America, since July 1967, a distinction has been made between three senses of poverty: real (or material) poverty, which is an evil; spiritual poverty in the sense of spiritual childhood, surrender of our lives to God's will; and poverty as solidarity with the poor and protest against the situation in which they live. This emphasis implies a particular analysis of poverty and its causes and also presupposes biblical basis both for the rejection of this inhuman situation and of the way spiritual poverty is understood. Finally it clarifies the reasons for Christian commitment in this field.

This impulse was welcomed a year later at the Latin American bishops' conference at Medellín (1968) and gave clarity to a commitment that many were beginning to make. Then, between Medellín and the next conference at Puebla (1979), this distinction gave rise, within the Christian communities, to the expression "preferential (spiritual poverty), option (solidarity and protest) for the poor (real poverty)." This option became a cornerstone for the church's pastoral action and an important standard for a way of being Christian, that is, for what we call a spirituality.

The ultimate reason for preferring the poor and oppressed does not lie in the social analysis we employ, in our human compassion, or in the direct contact we may have with the world of poverty. All these are valid motives, important factors in this commitment, but this option has its real roots in the experience of the gratuitousness of God's love, in faith in the God of life who rejects the unjust and early death which is what poverty means. It is a theocentric option, based on the practice of solidarity and the practice of prayer among us. It is a gift and a task.

The preferential option for the poor is much more than a way of showing our concern about poverty and the establishment of justice. At its very heart, it contains a spiritual, mystical element, an experience of gratuitousness that gives it depth and fruitfulness. This is not to deny the social concern expressed in this solidarity, the rejection of injustice and oppression that it implies, but to see that in the last resort it is anchored in our faith in the God of Jesus Christ. It is therefore not surprising that this option has been adorned by the martyr's witness of so many, as it has by the daily generous self-sacrifice of so many more who by coming close to the poor set foot on the path to holiness.

The answer to the question about the nature of the mystical dimension in the faith-life of an oppressed person involves understanding the meaning of the preferential option for the poor. And this is turn cannot be seen in its full scope until we become aware of the inculturation of the Christian faith in nations that are poor but rich through a cultural and historical journey different and distant from those of the North Atlantic world.

Faith in the risen Christ is nourished by the experience of suffering, of death, and also of hope among the poor and oppressed, by their way of relating to each other and to nature, by their cultural and religious expressions. Asserting one's own characteristics does not mean refusing to learn, to be enriched by, to open oneself to, other perspectives. It means rather staying alive to be able to receive and grow. Going to the roots ensures creativity, renews the tree. At the heart of a situation that excludes them and strips them of everything, and from which they seek to free themselves, the poor and oppressed believe in the God of life.

— *The Density of the Present*, 165–68

THE GIFT OF GRATUITOUS LOVE
AND OUR RESPONSE

We distort the Gospel when we pretend to choose between gratuitous love and what has been called a noble fight for justice or when we want to separate prayer from commitment. This means not being able to see the richness of the demands of these two dimensions of Christian life. The person who pretends to preserve one of these dimensions while neglecting the other will end up with not even half of one; he or she will lose it all. This is not the path toward following Jesus.

Solidarity with the poor is expressed in a preoccupation with their necessities: food, health care, housing. This is not all that is needed; also required is a commitment to eliminate what John Paul II and the Latin American episcopal conferences call the socioeconomic mechanisms that cause poverty and marginalization. The poor also require respect, equal treatment, love, friendship, a welcoming smile. We all really need these. We live out of justice, but also love and tenderness, and we must not fear saying this truth.

I am convinced that without gratuity, without love, without prayer, without joy there is no Christian life. But without solidarity, without those who are most poor, without making ours their sufferings and their hope, their right to life, there is also no genuine Christian life. There is nothing more demanding than gratuitous love. — *Páginas* 152 (August 1998): 82–83

MAKING OUR OWN
THE SPIRITUAL EXPERIENCE OF THE POOR

For many Latin American Christians at the present time the possibility of following Jesus depends on their ability to make their own the spiritual experience of the poor. This requires of them a deep-going conversion; they are being asked to make their own the experience that the poor have of God and of God's will that every human being have life.

In the past, Christians, formed in one or another spiritual school — missionaries, for example — may have felt that it was for them to communicate their own experiences to the people and to point out to the people the path of a suitable Christian life. Today they are called upon to turn that past attitude around. The "evangelizing potential" that Puebla (no. 1147) recognizes in the poor and oppressed points implicitly to one source of that power and ability to proclaim the Christian message. That source is precisely the spiritual experience to which the revelation of God's preference for "little children" (Matt.

11:25, NIV) gives rise. It is this encounter with the Lord that Christians must make their own.

The need is not simply to recognize that the experience of the people raises questions and challenges for the spirituality of these Christians. Many of those bound by religious vows, for example, have felt challenged by the real poverty of the dispossessed and marginalized. They asked themselves what meaning their own promise of living a poor life had in the face of such a situation. The questions were legitimate ones and showed a sensitivity entirely deserving of respect. However, the situation is a more inclusive one and reaches deeper. We are no longer faced with isolated questions, however penetrating. Something more systematic is making its appearance; its parts resist separation: they form an organic whole. In this framework the religious vows are recovering their full meaning.

This new reality invites Christians to leave the familiar world they have long inhabited and leads many of them to reread their own spiritual tradition. Above all, it is a question of making our own the world of the poor and their manner of living out their relationship with the Lord and taking over the historical practice of Jesus. Otherwise we shall be traveling a road that simply parallels that taken by oppressed believers. Then we shall have to try to build bridges that connect these different roads: bridges of commitment to the exploited, friendly relationships with some of them, celebration of the Eucharist with them, and so on. All these would be meritorious efforts no doubt, but they are inadequate because such connections do not change the fact that the roads are only parallel. The spiritual experience of the poor is too radical and too comprehensive in scope to merit only that kind of attention. The issue is making that experience our own. Any other response will be a halfway response.

For those who are located within a particular spiritual tradition, entry into the experience of the poor means taking that tradition with them. A rich variety has marked the ways in which throughout its history the Christian community has undertaken to follow Jesus; these ways represent experiences that we cannot simply leave behind. Advantage must rather be taken of that tradition in order to enrich the contemporary spiritual experience of the poor. The refusal thus to enrich the poor would betray a kind of avarice in the area of spirituality. Such avarice turns against the distrustful owners; their spiritual riches spoil and lose their value when kept "under the mattress." It is appropriate here to recall the parable of the buried talents.

Faith and hope in the God of life provides a shelter in the situation of death and struggle for life in which the poor and oppressed of Latin America are now living — they are the well from which we must drink if we want to be faithful to Jesus. This is the water of which Archbishop Oscar Romero had drunk when he said he had been converted to Christ by his own people.[1] Once this change had taken place, he could not but view his following of Jesus as closely bound up with the life (and death) of the Salvadoran people whose sufferings and hopes we all carry in our hearts. His spiritual life abandoned the ways of individualism and began instead to draw its nourishment from the experience of an entire people. This is why he could say two weeks before he was murdered:

> My life has been threatened many times. I have to confess that, as a Christian, I don't believe in death without resurrection. If they kill me, *I will rise again in the Salvadoran people.* I'm not boasting, or saying this out of pride, but rather as humbly as I can.[2]

---

1. "I am going to speak to you simply as a pastor who, along with his people, has been learning a beautiful and harsh truth: that the Christian faith does not separate us from the world but immerses us in it; that the church, therefore, is not a fortress set apart from the city, but a follower of the Jesus who lived, worked, struggled, and died in the midst of the city" (address at Louvain, in *Signos de vida y fidelidad: Testimonio de la Iglesia in América Latina, 1978–1982* [Lima: CEP, 1978], 367b).

2. Statement to José Calderón Salazar, correspondent for the daily *Excelsior* of Mexico City, published in *Orientación* (San Salvador), April 13, 1980. English translation from Plácido Erdozaín, *Archbishop Romero: Martyr of Salvador* (Maryknoll, N.Y.: Orbis Books, 1981), 75.

We all have the same vocation: to rise to life with the people in its spirituality. This implies a death to the alleged "spiritual ways" that individualisms of one or another kind create but that in fact lead only to an impasse. It also supposes a birth into new ways of being disciples of Jesus, the risen Christ. The newness draws its strength from the Bible and from the best in the history of spirituality and in this respect is profoundly traditional. Such is the experience of the poor of Latin America. Theirs is an authentic spiritual experience and encounter with the Lord who points out a road for them to follow.

— *We Drink from Our Own Wells*, 30–32

Part Two

The Eyes of Faith: Understanding God's Mercy

8

Rooting Theology in Spirituality

Spirituality is the key unifying force of theology. Drawing on the work of Marie-Dominique Chenu, Gutiérrez brings out that behind all theological reflection is an operative spirituality. Spiritual experience comes first, followed by reflection about it. Only then can a proposal be made to the whole community about how to be Christian. Theological reflection is a second step: "It rises only at sundown," Gutiérrez notes. Rooted in the experiences of praxis, prayer, and a pledge of commitment to the "least of these," spirituality for Gutiérrez means following Jesus in history and doing as he did.

SPIRITUALITY AND THEOLOGY

The peak of the spire of theological reflection is the classic *sequela Christi,* or following Jesus, which, especially since the seventeenth century, we often call spirituality. M.-D. Chenu proposed an inspiring view in one of his first works, saying: "Clearly, theological systems are nothing but the expression of spiritualities. That constitutes both their interest and their greatness." And he added, with precision: "A theology worthy of the

112

name is a spirituality that has found the appropriate rational instruments for its religious experience."[1]

Those words are especially useful for a discourse on the faith that defines itself as a reflection on practice in the light of faith. It is precisely on the terrain of a Christian's daily life that spirituality is situated. To be a disciple is to insert oneself into the practice of Jesus. Spirituality is the backbone of the discourse on faith; it gives this discourse its deepest significance and its most intensely questioning reach and locates spirituality in a primary place in liberation theology. Attention to the testimonies of Christian people and communities present in the world of the poor of Latin America and the Caribbean constitute this reflection's point of departure and nourish its progress.

In theology, our methodology is our spirituality. Methodology refers to an intellectual route; in this case of theological reflection, method is situated along the path on which we move toward God through spirituality. Silence is the first step in speaking of God; that is the moment of listening and prayer; later the language engendered in that quiet will come. The beautiful words of Irenaeus of Lyon are particularly inspiring: "From the Father's silence comes the Word of the Son."

This spirituality does not constitute a kind of parenthesis between daily commitments, nor is it an escape or refuge for difficult times. It is the spiritual trajectory of those who live their faith and keep their hope in the midst of a daily life experience permeated with poverty and exclusion, but also consisting of projects and a growing awareness of their rights and the social and cultural causes of the situation in which they live. Following the footsteps of Jesus without departing from reality, without distancing ourselves from the paths followed by our contemporaries, helps us keep our sense of hope and preserve our serenity when the tempest rages.

---

1. Marie-Dominique Chenu, *Le Saulchoir: Une école de théologie* (Etiolles, France: Le Saulchoir, 1937).

The experience of many Christians on this continent, on the many paths of solidarity with society's marginalized and insignificant, has led them to see that, in the end, what we call the irruption of the poor — their new presence in history — means a genuine irruption of God in their lives. That is how they have experienced it, with the suffering, the joys, the doubts, and the demands that this implies. The deepest sense of an encounter with the poor is an encounter with Christ. Which does not mean that the presence of the poor should mean the disappearance of their historic and social — and even their political, cultural, and gender-bound — reality; this is not a shortsighted spiritualization, forgetful of these human dimensions. Rather, it makes us see clearly what is involved in genuine solidarity with one's neighbor.

Precisely because we value and respect faith's human dimension, we find ourselves able, when we read it grounded in faith, to comprehend this new presence in history as a sign of the times in which God, who pitches his tent among us, questions us. This irruption is the source of a spirituality, of a collective — or communitarian — journey toward God. This happens in conditions that reveal to us the inhuman situation of the poor, in all its harshness. As Bernard of Clairvaux has expressed it, in the area of spirituality it is necessary to "drink from our own wells," from our own experience, not only as individuals, but also as members of a community. This position comes from the conviction that in the world of Latin America, marked by poverty and insignificance (a complex situation that cannot be reduced to the economic dimensions alone), by the ins and outs of the process through which a people becomes conscious of its human dignity and its value as daughters and sons of God, a way is being found — full of questions, trials, and joys — to follow in the footsteps of the Lord. A spirituality is developing.

GOD IN THE ROOTS

At the very core of the preferential option for the poor there is an experience of God's gift of love, which helps us enter into the mystery of his presence in our lives. The poor people of Latin America have taken the path of affirming their human dignity and their condition of being sons and daughters of God. The rejection of injustice and oppression that this implies is anchored in our faith in the God of life. Thus, it is not surprising that this option has been stamped with the blood of those who, as Archbishop Romero said, have died bearing "the martyr's sign." In addition to the archbishop of San Salvador himself, this is the situation suffered by great numbers of Christians in the social and cultural context that also calls itself Christian. No reflection on spirituality in Latin America can ignore this cruel contradiction. There are varied ways in which the experience of the cross marks the daily life of this continent's Christians. But it is also marked by the affirmation of life and by witness to the resurrection of Jesus.

Being aware of that spiritual experience, gathering the oral statements and written texts through which it is narrated, listening to its silences: these become the primordial duties of our theological reflection. The transparency and quality of the waters we need to drink refresh us in our travels following Jesus and confer upon our journey the special quality that comes from the way believers with their own history and culture live their faith.

The spiritual experience of the poor people of Latin America and the Caribbean, in the midst of a history replete with achievements and with obstacles, has affirmed itself and matured as a spirituality of liberation. There is no doubt of this being a process that invites us to take into account new aspects of the topic, to deepen old intuitions, to pay special attention to what indigenous cultures can offer in terms of concrete ways of following Jesus, to reread the current situation in light of the biblical message.

An interest in these topics does not in any way mean retreating from social options that are expressed as solidarity with the poor and oppressed. To say that would be a grave error. This would imply a lack of understanding of the intention of the theology of liberation and of the radical result of the decision to go to the root of Christian life, to the place where the love of God is daily intertwined with the love for our neighbor. The knot they tie is where spirituality is situated. Far from being an evasion of the challenges of the present, this gives firm resolve to the options. Rilke was right when he said that God is to be found in our roots. And there is no end to our going deeper into these roots.   — *We Drink from Our Own Wells*, xvii–xxi

9

Speaking and Listening to God

Becoming a neighbor to another is the result of an action, a commitment, of approaching another and going out of one's way. Gutiérrez encourages us to learn that the neighbor is not someone whom we find in our road, but rather our neighbor is someone in whose road we place ourselves. The poor are not usually nearby; they are usually distant. They become neighbor when we enter into relationship with them. Experience teaches us that it is possible to give from almost nothing, which, as Gustavo reminds us, is something everyone can do, even the poor. We can always offer companionship, support, and friendship, regardless of what we have. When our spirituality is formed out of these experiences we can begin to speak theologically. Without spirituality, theology answers questions that few people are asking and speaks before it really has anything to say.

A TIME TO BE SILENT, A TIME TO SPEAK

Theology is a language. It attempts to speak a word about the mysterious reality that believers call God. It is a *logos* about *theos*.

When I speak of "mysterious reality" I am using the word "mystery" in its biblical sense. The French philosopher Gabriel

Marcel helped us to understand the matter by drawing a distinction between "problem," "enigma," and "mystery." God is not a problem before which we stand impersonally and which we treat as an object. Nor is God an enigma, something utterly unknown and incomprehensible. In the Bible God is a mystery to the extent that God is an all-enveloping love. In Marcel's terminology, God is the mystery of the Thou that we can only acknowledge and invoke. From a biblical standpoint mystery is not ineffable in the literal meaning of the word; it must be spoken and communicated. To conceal it, to keep it withdrawn to a private sphere, or to limit it to a few initiates is to ignore its very essence. The mystery of God's love must be proclaimed. Doing so presupposes a language, a means of communication, a way of speaking located more in the disturbing certainty of hope than in the serenity brought about by an innocuous knowledge.

Believing is an experience that is both interior and shared in community. Faith is a relationship between persons; it is a gift. The mystery of God must be accepted in prayer and in human solidarity; it is the moment of silence and of practice. Within that moment — and only from within it — will there arise the language and the categories necessary for transmitting it to others and for entering into communication with them.

The Book of Ecclesiastes tells us that throughout human life everything has its moment and season: "a time to keep silence, and a time to speak" (3:7). One depends on the other, and they nourish one another. Without silence there is no true speaking. In listening and meditation, what is to be spoken begins to be sketched faintly and hesitatingly. Likewise, expressing our inner world will lead us to gain new and fruitful areas of personal silence and encounter. That is what happens in theology.

There is a connection between theological language and the human condition. In Latin America and beyond it, a way of speaking of God is stammeringly coming to birth, a way of speaking marked by the cultural diversity of humankind and the conditions created by poverty and marginalization. The questions that arise from the historical use of that theological language, its simultaneous particularity and universality, and finally the narrative dimension of the life and teachings of Jesus of Nazareth, will help us to approach this connection.

It is not enough to say that the word about God is born of the need to formulate and communicate an experience of belief. Belief comes in the context of living human experience, with all its challenging complexity. A whole social and cultural world is involved in the development of theological language. The questions that arise from situations of human extremity cut deep; the appeal cuts through anecdotal and passing experience to the essence. These questions leave us naked before the basic inquiry of all human beings. If we do not go down or rather up into the world of everyday suffering, of consuming anguish, of ever-burning hope, the theological task has no substance. Two writers (Felipe Guamán Poma de Ayala and José María Arguedas Altamirano) will help give flesh — wounded flesh — to this challenge as we see it today.

— *The Density of the Present,* 186–88

10

Walking with the Poor

Felipe Guamán Poma de Ayala (ca. 1535–1616) was an indigenous Peruvian who protested, as a Christian, the Spanish treatment of the native peoples of the Andes after the conquest of 1533. The son of a noble family from the southern province of Lucanas, near modern-day Ayacucho, he is best known as a Christian and for his illustrated chronicle, Nueva Corónica y Buen Gobierno.

ABANDONMENT AND HOPE

Felipe Guamán Poma lives in his own mental universe; this sometimes makes it difficult for unwary readers, especially if they are excessively marked by a Western perspective and logic. He writes his long report to the king of Spain as an Indian, a member of a people whose tribulations he seeks to denounce and whose rights he seeks to defend. He also writes as a new Christian, making the life of Jesus with his preferential love for the poor the fundamental criterion by which to discern justice and injustice in the Peruvian Andes.

Having walked nameless for thirty years in the midst of the abused and neglected Indians, he can speak firsthand about the abuses they suffer. His denunciation is anchored in painful experiences. The old cliché with which he ends his agonizing descriptions, "nothing can be done," shows dramatically that what he has seen and heard has carried him to the edge of despair. His cry and his call come from there. He writes in faltering and apparently disordered Spanish "the poor ones of Christ are canceled out and used," he exclaims, "and so my God, where are you? Can't you hear me to remedy your poor ones, because I am full to remedy."[1] Reproachfulness struggles to be heard in his cry, just as when Job says, after a heartrending depiction of the situation of the poor, "yet God pays no attention to their prayer" (Job 24:12). God's silence is even more unbearable for those who believe that the God of their faith is the God of life and love.

From the heights of the Andes Guamán Poma sketches out a language about God that he sees as valid "for all the world and Christendom."[2] The suffering of the poor helps him rediscover, and explain in his way, a profound Christian insight: "the rich and proud for them devalue the poor, thinking that where the poor are, there is no God and justice. So with faith they must know clearly that where the poor are, there is Jesus Christ himself, where God is, there is justice."[3] Behind that affirmation, upholding it, is the message of the biblical prophets and Jesus himself (see Matt. 25:31–46).

The theological language of Guamán Poma stands in the paradox, almost the contradiction, between the anguished question: "My God, where are you? Can't you hear me?" and the nonetheless hoped-for recognition of God's presence in the abandoned and mistreated people of this world. His God-talk does not drown its voice in the intimacy of a painful experience; still less is it limited to declarations of principle. It conveys demands for everyday behavior. Our author understands and writes his texts to stop the devaluation and persecution of "the

---

1. Felipe Guamán Poma de Ayala, *Primer nueva corónica y buen gobierno* (Mexico City: Siglo XXI, 1980), 1104.
2. Ibid., 1168.
3. Ibid.

poor ones of Jesus Christ."[4] For him, "to serve God as our Lord and to favor the poor ones of Jesus Christ" are inseparable dimensions of Christian practice.[5]

— *The Density of the Present*, 188–89

José María Arguedas Altamirano (1911–69) was a Peruvian novelist, poet, and anthropologist who wrote mainly in Spanish and Quechua. Brought up in poverty among Quechua Indians, he is generally considered one of the foremost figures of twentieth-century Peruvian literature. His works often explore themes related to the clash between white "civilization" and the indigenous "traditional" way of life, particularly in his books Los ríos profundos, Todas las sangres, *and* El zorro de arriba y el zorro de abajo.

THE LIBERATING GOD

Centuries after Guamán, José María Arguedas called attention to the persistent and increasing suffering of a marginalized people. This time religion was apparently aggravating that unjust pain. In the cathedral of Cusco the young Ernesto, Arguedas's alter ego, says in consternation about the Lord of the earthquakes: "raging, sorrowing, the Lord had a silence that did not calm, that caused suffering.... The face of Christ created suffering, spread it out to the walls, to the vaults and columns. I expected tears to fall from them."[6] These are tears that provoke and seek to justify other tears that are shed by those who see their human dignity trampled upon. Christ suffered, and he caused suffering. The beauty of that expression underlines an ancient, cruel, and profound reality.

---

4. Ibid., 903.
5. Ibid., 1105.
6. José María Arguedas, *Los ríos profundos*, in *Obras completas* (Lima: Editorial Horizonte, 1983), 3:24.

A religion that saddens and does not try, as it should, to help the heart grow in joy and hope plunges the poor back into their misery and their needs. What most exasperates Arguedas is that it makes others suffer; nothing is dirtier than that. The categories of purity and dirtiness were important to Arguedas. None of us have described with such empathy and mastery the everyday pain and the inexhaustible energy of a historically neglected people. But more than that, in the face of the suffering Christ, Arguedas sees the features of the houseboy, the Indian humiliated and abused by the sinister character called El Viejo, who represents the Antichrist. The resemblance between the crucified one and the houseboy reinforces a theme commonly found in the theology that is being developed today in Latin America: the poor are a crucified people.[7]

Because some religious interpretations justify and others reject the oppression of the poor, a character in *Todas las sangres* asks in annoyance: "How many Jesus Christs are there?" More than an expression of skepticism and detachment, this is a natural demand for explanation and clarification. A few lines later comes the terrible discovery: "The God of the nobility is different. He causes suffering without consolation." This line is at the heart of a dialogue between a priest and a mestizo sacristan who speaks for Arguedas. The fine and tender poet Gonzalo Rose once said of the God who causes suffering, "That's not our God, is it, Mamá?"[8]

Once more a heartbreakingly unjust condition and perplexity in the face of human sorrow takes us to the depths without diversion or mitigation, reopening a possibility and a method of God-talk. But Arguedas was not only able to depict the piercing sorrow of a people; he was also attentive to their simple hopes and everyday joys. Thus shortly before his own tragic death, he wrote to a friend saying, "My faith in the future, which has

---

7. See Ignacio Ellacuría, "El pueblo crucificado," in *Cruz y Resurrección* (Mexico City: CRT, 1978), 48.
8. Gonzalo Rose, "La pregunta" in *Hallazgos y extravíos* (Mexico City: FCE, 1968), 30.

never failed me, has been strengthened. How well we understand each other, and together see the light that no one can darken!"[9] The life that breathes in this text stands in apparent, or real, opposition to what was about to happen. Falteringly, with uncertain steps, from an experience that weaves together anguish and hope, sorrow and joy, tribulations and assurance, Arguedas goes more and more deeply into the enormous and complex reality that he wants to express and transform. At times he seems to feel that something has come back into the experience of the people with whom he has cast his lot and into his own experience. He calls it the liberating God, the One whom the mestizo sacristan declares absent wherever injustice rules.[10]

—The Density of the Present, 190–92

GOD'S ABSENCE AND PRESENCE

Attention to human suffering at the personal and social levels, to poverty and marginalization, keeps us, as Arguedas puts it, from "swimming in the rubble of this nation."[11] There is no greater challenge to our language about God than the suffering of the innocent. How can we understand a God of love in a world that bears the stamp of poverty, genocide, terrorist violence, disregard for the most elemental human rights? It is that simple and urgent. This question is surely broader than any answer theology can give. But it is an inescapable question. After the Holocaust, Emmanuel Lévinas insightfully developed an ethic of the other, holding up the face of someone who says "Don't kill me!" and thinking of God as Otherness.[12] Poverty

---

9. Quoted in Gustavo Gutiérrez, *Entre las calandrias* (Lima: CEP-IBC, 1990), 24.

10. See José María Arguedas, *¿Ultimo diario?* In *Obras completas* (Lima: Editorial Horizonte, 1983), 5:198.

11. José María Arguedas, *El zorro de arriba y el zorro de abajo* in *Obras completas* (Lima: Editorial Horizonte, 1983), 5:178.

12. E. Lévinas, *Totalité et infini* (The Hague: Martinus Nijhoff, 1968).

and its consequences are the great challenge of our time. Poverty, which in the last analysis means early and unjust death, is destroying persons, families, and nations. Indeed poverty cannot be reduced to the social and economic sphere; it is a global human problem.

Our discourse on God cannot be separated from the everyday life of the poor of this world, a life infused with sorrow and hope. The experience of hunger and oppression changes our God-talk. Indeed all that is truly human must be reflected in that language. Karl Rahner has said that in our time reality is struggling for a chance to speak. Theology should be in the midst of that struggle; it cannot stand off at a dead point of history and watch it pass. Language about God is about the complex goings and comings of human existence.

A theological language that does not reject unjust suffering, that does not speak out loud about the right of all to be happy, betrays the God of whom we speak. The creation story in Genesis tells us that at the end of the first week "God saw everything that he had made, and indeed, it was very good" (Gen. 1:31). The word used here for good also means beautiful. Theology is about the good and the beautiful in the work of God, in human life. For that reason theology cannot overlook that which breaks the beauty of this world and strangles the expression of human joy and happiness. If we approach human suffering, poverty, and injustice in solidarity with those who experience it, it is because the word about God is always a word about life and happiness. It is language about the One whom the Bible calls "you who love the living" (Wisd. 11:26).

Genuine theological language requires sinking roots into what André Malraux called "the human condition." To the extent that language about God takes on the human condition with its doubts and certainties, generosity and self-seeking, insecurity and constancy, laughter and tears, it passes through the density of the social, of gender, of the ethnic, and of the cultural so as to reach the deepest dimensions of the human.

— The Density of the Present, 186–94, 200

The Suffering of the Innocent

Jesus came to proclaim the in-breaking of God's reign into the world and the love of God for all humankind. Though God is a mystery, poverty is not. Poverty is a condition, not a destiny; the result of human causes, not God's will. In these sections from Gutiérrez's book On Job, he explores pressing questions like the transcendence of God, the problem of evil, human suffering, and the question of retribution. Gutiérrez reminds us that though God's providence is beyond our comprehension, God loves everyone, especially those who must endure inhuman conditions. Above all, he explores the question of how to speak about God from the context of global poverty and how to say to the poor "God loves you" when so much of their life speaks to the contrary.

Theology is talk about God. According to the Bible, however, God is a mystery. At the beginning of his *Summa Theologiae* Thomas Aquinas states as a basic principle governing all theological reflection that "we cannot know what God is but only what God is not."[1] We might think that theology sets itself an impossible task, but the task is not impossible. It is important to keep in mind that theological thought about God is *thought*

---

1. Thomas Aquinas, *Summa Theologiae*, I, 9, 3: "De Deo scire non possumus quid sit, sed quid non sit."

about a mystery. This influences an attitude to be adopted in the
effort to talk about God, an attitude of respect that is incompatible with the kind of God-talk that is sure, at times arrogantly
sure, that it knows everything there is to know about God. José
María Arguedas poses the question: "Is not what we know far
less than the great hope we feel?"[2] This question will bring an
unhesitating, humble yes from those who believe in the God of
Jesus Christ.

When we talk of mystery we do not mean something that
is hidden and must remain hidden. The mystery in this case
must rather be expressed, not concealed, communicated, not
kept to itself. According to Paul, revelation in this case is "the
revelation of the mystery that was kept secret for long ages
but is now disclosed, and through the prophetic writings is
made known to all the Gentiles, according to the command of
the eternal God, to bring about the obedience of faith" (Rom.
16:25–26). The revelation of the mystery of God leads to its
proclamation to every human being; this is the special characteristic of the biblical message regarding mystery. Reflection
on the mystery of God must therefore begin with God's resolve
of self-communication to "all nations" (Matt. 28:19). The setting and requirements of the proclamation are fundamental
presuppositions of any theologizing.

REVELATION AND
THEOLOGICAL METHOD

When we speak about God it is important to make two
connections.

1. The first is the relationship between revelation and gratuitousness. Christ reveals that the Father who sent him on a
universal mission is a God of love. This revelation assigns a

---

2. José María Arguedas, "¿Ultimo Diario?" In *Obras completas* (Lima: Editorial Horizonte, 1983), 5:197.

privileged place to the simple and the despised, as Jesus made clear: "I give praise to you, Father, Lord of heaven and earth, for although you have hidden these things from the wise and the learned you have revealed them to the childlike" (Matt. 11:25, NAB).

The words "wise and learned" refer to a social and religious minority in Israel: the teachers, or doctors, of the law, the high priests, and the scribes. These were the men who sat "on Moses' seat" (Matt. 23:2) and had taken possession of "the key of knowledge" (Luke 11:52). They were the ones who attributed the works of Jesus to the power of Beelzebul (see Matt. 12:24). They were important and religious persons. When Jesus said that the revelation given by the Father was hidden from the teachers, he was directly opposing the accepted and usual view of his day. He was challenging the religious and social authority of the experts in the law and saying that, because of the Father's predilection for them, the ignorant had a greater capacity for understanding revelation. This statement is one more sign of the originality of Jesus' teaching. He was here attacking the very foundation of the religious world of his time — namely, the identification of the primary addressees of God's word.

Over against the "wise and the learned" are the "childlike," (Gk., *nēpioi*), a term which carries a clear connotation of ignorance; they are the ones who must be led along the right path because they do not know how to guide themselves.[3] It does not refer to moral or spiritual dispositions; rather the word has a certain pejorative overtone. This is the point of the contrast with the "wise and learned."

The "little children" are related to the poor, the hungry, and those who weep (Luke 6:20–23); to sinners and the sick, who are despised on this account (Matt. 9:12–13); to sheep without a shepherd (Matt. 9:36); to the little ones (Matt. 10:42; 18:1–4); to those not invited to the banquet (Luke 14:16–24).

---

3. On this subject see, Jacques DuPont, *Les Béatitudes* (Paris: Gabalda, 1969), 2:198–204.

All these categories form a bloc, a sector of the people; they are "the poor of the land."

The ignorance in question is not in itself a virtue or a merit that explains the divine preference. It is simply a situation of need. Wisdom is not a demerit or something that provokes divine rejection. The wise are not necessarily proud in the moral sense; they may be, and indeed that is a danger for them. So too the ignorant may be humble, but they are not always such; humility is simply a possibility for them. It follows that the condition of being privileged addressees of revelation is the result not primarily of moral or spiritual dispositions but of a human situation in which God undertakes self-revelation by acting and overturning values and criteria. The scorned of this world are those whom the God of love prefers. This is a very simple matter, but for a mind that judges everything by merits and demerits, worthiness and unworthiness, it is difficult to grasp.

The reason for Jesus' gratitude is not primarily the fact that revelation has been hidden from some and granted to others. The structure of the sentence might suggest this interpretation, but the interpretation is wrong, as can be shown by a comparison with other passages that use contrast in a distinctively Semitic way to emphasize a point. The fact that God hides "these things" from the wise and reveals them to the simple is the concrete occasion for grasping what is behind this behavior and gives it its meaning — namely, the free and unmerited love of God for every human being and especially for the poor and forgotten. This interpretation of Jesus' words is supported by the undeniable fact that the Gospel treats this truth as a key element in the message of Jesus.

The real reason for Jesus' gratitude is his contemplation (in the full sense of the term as a form of prayer) of the Father's goodness and love that reach out to the simple and the unimportant, and give them preference. This predilection, which does not imply exclusivity, is underscored by hiding revelation from the wise and important. An entire social and religious order is hereby turned upside down.

The dominant element in the text as a whole is the gratuitous character of God's love. Puebla puts the matter very clearly:

The poor merit preferential attention, whatever may be the moral or spiritual situation in which they find themselves. Made in the image and likeness of God to be his children, this image is dimmed and even defiled. That is why God takes on their defense and loves them. (No. 1142)[4]

The ultimate basis of God's preference for the poor is to be found in God's own goodness and not in any analysis of society or in human compassion, however pertinent these reasons may be.

2. The second connection has to do with the way or method of speaking about God. God is first contemplated when we do God's will and allow God to reign; only after that do we think about God. To use familiar categories: contemplation and practice together make up a first act; theologizing is a second act. We must first establish ourselves on the terrain of spirituality and practice; only subsequently is it possible to formulate discourse on God in an authentic and respectful way. Theologizing done without the mediation of contemplation and practice does not meet the requirements of the God of the Bible. The mystery of God comes to life in contemplation and in the practice of God's plan for human history; only in a second phase can this life inspire appropriate reasoning and relevant speech. (Given the two meanings of the Greek word *logos* — "reason" and "word" — theology is a reasoned word or reason put into words.) In view of all this we can say that the first stage is silence, the second is speech.

Contemplation and practice feed each other; the two together make up the stage of silence before God. In prayer we remain speechless; we simply place ourselves before the Lord. To a degree, we remain silent in our practice as well, for in our

---

4. As is well known, this idea was expressed in the *Aporte de la conferencia episcopal peruana al documento de consulta del CELAM para la tercera conferencia general del episcopado latinoamericano* (Lima, 1978), n. 4. 2. 1.

involvements, in our daily work, we do not talk about God all the time; we do indeed live in God, but not by discoursing on God. Silence, the time of quiet, is a first act and the necessary mediation for the time of speaking about the Lord or doing theology, which is the second act.

The time of silence is the time of loving encounter with God and of prayer and commitment; it is a time of "staying with him" (see John 1:38–39). As the experience of human love shows us, in this kind of encounter we enter depths and regions that are ineffable. When words do not suffice, when they are incapable of communicating what is experienced at the affective level, then we are fully engaged in loving. And when words are incapable of showing forth our experience, we fall back on symbols, which are another way of remaining silent. When we use a symbol, we do not speak; we let an object or gesture speak for us. This is precisely how we proceed in the liturgy; symbolic language is the language of a love that transcends words.

This is why images of human love are so often used in the Bible in speaking of the relations between God and the people of God. When two lovers fall silent and simply remain in each other's presence, they know that they are experiencing love of each other at a deeper level. Silence, contemplation, and practice are all necessary mediations in thinking about God and doing theology. Theology will then be speech that has been enriched by silence. This reflective discourse will in turn feed the silence of contemplation and practice, and give it new dimensions.

Gratuitousness and revelation, silence and speech: these are two presuppositions of the effort at understanding our faith.

— On Job, xi–xiv

SPEAKING OF GOD IN LATIN AMERICA

How are we to talk about a God who is revealed as love in a situation characterized by poverty and oppression? How are we to proclaim the God of life to men and women who die prematurely and unjustly? How are we to acknowledge that God makes us a free gift of love and justice when we have before us the suffering of the innocent? What words are we to use in telling those who are not even regarded as persons that they are the daughters and sons of God? These are key questions being asked in the theology that has been forming in Latin America and in other places throughout the world where the situation is the same.

Bishop Desmond Tutu of Africa has spoken eloquently on this point:

> Liberation theology more than any other kind of theology issues out of the crucible of human suffering and anguish. It happens because people cry out, "Oh, God, how long?" "Oh, God, but why?..." All liberation theology stems from trying to make sense of human suffering when those who suffer are the victims of organized oppression and exploitation, when they are emasculated and treated as less than what they are: human persons created in the image of the Triune God, redeemed by the one Savior Jesus Christ and sanctified by the Holy Paraklete. This is the genesis of all liberation theology and so also of black theology, which is theology of liberation in Africa.[5]

Human suffering, involvement with it, and the questions it raises about God are in fact one point of departure and one central theme in the theology of liberation. But the first concern in this context is not with the "evil of guilt" but rather with the "evil of misfortune," the evil suffered by the innocent. I am here using a distinction made by Adolphe Gesché, who remarks:

> The West has not had a theology of the evil of misfortune, the evil suffered by the innocent. In my view, the

---

5. Desmond Tutu, "The Theology of Liberation in Africa," in *African Theology en Route: Papers from the Pan-African Conference of Third World Theologians, December 17–23, 1977, Accra, Ghana,* ed. Kofi Appiah-Kubi and Sergio Torres (Maryknoll, N.Y.: Orbis, 1979), 163.

basic importance of the theology of liberation, that which gives it a major importance that I hope it will not lose, is that it takes into account the widespread, objective evil that entails no fault in the sufferer.[6]

I myself believe that we must not forget the responsibility of those who may be the cause of the evil suffered by the innocent. The suffering of the innocent and the questions it leads them to ask are indeed key problems for theology — that is, for discourse about God. The theology of liberation tries to meet the challenge. The center of the world — so called because the crucified Jesus dwells there, and with him all who suffer unjustly, all the poor and despised of the earth — is the place from which we must proclaim the risen Lord.   — *On Job,* xiv–xv, xvii

---

6. Adolphe Gesché, "Le problème du mal, problème de société," in *Théologie de la libération* (Louvain-la-Neuve: Annales Cardijn, 1985), 33.

12

Believing in the Midst of Suffering

According to Gutiérrez, the two languages about which to speak of God are contemplative language and prophetic language. Contemplation is prayer and the language of gratuitous love while prophecy is commitment and the language of justice. As brought out in Gutiérrez's treatment of Job, the two are inextricably intertwined; contemplation and justice are two sides of the same spiritual coin. Gutiérrez reminds us that we cannot announce the Gospel without denouncing injustice, but justice and gratuitous love must also be inextricably bound. Liberation theology has tried to avoid being an empty theological language to the poor. To keep the two languages of justice and gratuitous love intertwined is an attempt to say to the poor, "God loves you."

THE MESSAGE OF JOB

The movement of the Book of Job is twofold: a forward, linear movement, and a circling movement of deepening insight into the answer to the opening question: Is it possible to believe in God without expectation of reward, or "for nothing"? In an effort to answer this question the poet comes upon the doctrine of temporal retribution. This, he finds, does not take into account his own experience or the experience of so

many others. He therefore looks for a correct way of talking
about God within the most strained and knotty of all human
situations: the suffering of the innocent.

The Book of Job does not claim to have found a rational
or definitive explanation of suffering; the poet is quite aware
that the subject is a complex one. His faith prompts him to
inquire into the possibility of finding an appropriate language
about God that does justice to the situation of suffering. Not to
make the effort is to risk succumbing to impotent resignation, a
religion of calculated self-interest, a cynical outlook that forgets
the suffering of others, and even despair.

Perhaps the author knew these attitudes from experience,
but his profound sense of God and his keen sensitivity to the
misfortunes of others kept him from yielding to these temptations; despite everything, he remained resolutely disposed to
look for and find a way of talking about God. He remains a
deeply human and religious man who takes seriously the reality of unjust suffering and does not play down the difficulty of
understanding it. His determination to seek and find is already
a gift from the Lord and he hopes to find a correct way of talking about God. His personal courage and his trust in God impel
him to follow paths that are a challenge to the theology of his
day. At once more traditional than those who boast of being
such, and more innovative than the standards of the mediocre
allow them to be, the poet of the Book of Job is guided by God's
hand to discover ways of talking about God.

As his experience of unjust suffering broadened, he acquired
a moving realization of the suffering of others. The ethical perspective inspired by consideration of the needs of others and
especially of the poor made him abandon a morality of rewards
and punishments and caused a reversal in his way of speaking
about God. After accepting adversity he rebelled and struggled with God but meanwhile kept hoping in God and, despite
everything, finally surrendered to God's presence and unmerited
love. But these two paths should not be thought of as simply

parallel; in fact, they cross and enrich each other and finally converge to yield a correct way of talking about God.

— *On Job*, 93–94

PROPHETIC LANGUAGE
AND MYSTICAL LANGUAGE

For Job to leave his own world and enter into that of the poor already meant taking the path of gratuitousness and not simply that of concern for justice. All prophecy has as its starting point an encounter with the Lord and the Lord's unmerited love (see the theme of the prophetic vocation in Isa. 6; Jer. 1:4–10; Ezek. 2 and 3). The result is that two languages — the prophetic and the contemplative — are required; but they must also be combined and become increasingly integrated into a single language.

Prophetic language makes it possible to draw near to a God who has a predilection for the poor precisely because divine love refuses to be confined by the categories of human justice. God has a preferential love for the poor not because they are necessarily better than others, morally or religiously, but simply because they are poor and living in an inhuman situation that is contrary to God's will. The ultimate basis for the privileged position of the poor is not in the poor themselves but in God, in the gratuitousness and universality of God's *agapeic love*. Nothing can limit or contain this love, as Yahweh makes clear to Job in the revelation of what Yahweh has established as the fulcrum of the world. Belief in God and God's gratuitous love leads to a preferential option for the poor and to solidarity with those who suffer wretched conditions, contempt, and oppression, those whom the social order ignores and exploits. The God of utter freedom and gratuitousness who has been revealed to Job can alone explain the privileged place of those whom the powerful and the self-righteous of society treat unjustly and make outcasts. In the God of Christian revelation, gratuitousness and preferential love for the poor go hand in hand; they are therefore also inseparable in our contemplation of God and our concern for the disinherited of this world. The doctrine of retribution contained a valid principle: that being a believer requires certain ethical behavior. But even this idea became distorted when inserted into a narrow framework of rewards and punishments. The language of the prophets took a different approach in emphasizing the connection between God and the poor. It acknowledged the demands of ethics, but it transformed their meaning, because the fulfillment of these demands was not regarded as a form of personal insurance or as a way of gaining a hold on God. Obedience was rather a matter of freely giving what we have freely received (see Matt. 10:8).

As a result, prophetic language supports and reinforces language inspired by contemplation of God. At the beginning of the Book of Job we see a proper tone to be used in speaking of the Lord's actions. But the tone weakened as Job's unjust situation was prolonged and as he listened to the criticisms of his friends. The language of mysticism restores vigor to the values of popular faith by strengthening them and enabling them to resist every attempt at manipulation. It thus prevents the distortion that turns these values into fruitless resignation and passivity in the face of injustice. But conversely the language of contemplation likewise becomes more vigorous and more community-minded to the extent that it is nourished by popular faith.

Mystical language expresses the gratuitousness of God's love; prophetic language expresses the demands this love makes. The followers of Jesus and the community they form — the church — live in the space created by this gratuitousness and these demands. Both languages are necessary and therefore inseparable; they also feed and correct each other. Jeremiah brings out the connection:

> Sing to the Lord;
> praise the Lord!
> For he has delivered the life of the needy
> from the hands of evildoers. (Jer. 20:13)

The figure and theme of the suffering servant in Isaiah show numerous and very valuable points of contact with Job. In the first of Isaiah's poems, God presents the servant and describes his mission among the nations:

> Here is my servant, whom I uphold,
>   my chosen, in whom my soul delights;
> I have put my spirit upon him:
>   he will bring forth justice to the nations.
> He will not cry or lift up his voice,
>   or make it heard in the street;
> a bruised reed he will not break,
>   and a dimly burning wick he will not quench;
>   he will faithfully bring forth justice.
> He will not grow faint or be crushed
>   until he has established justice in the earth;
>   and the coastlands wait for his teaching.
>   (Isa. 42:1–5)

Anointed with the Spirit of the Lord, the servant has as his task to promote and bring forth justice (*mishpat*) on earth, to restore the full justice of God.

Emphasis on the practice of justice and on solidarity with the poor must never become an obsession and prevent our seeing that this commitment reveals its value and ultimate meaning only within the vast and mysterious horizon of God's gratuitous love. Building a just society requires a stimulus and an enveloping atmosphere that gratuitousness alone can supply. The point here is not to assign greater importance to the element of play and gratuitousness than to justice but to ensure that the world of justice finds its full meaning and source in the freely given love of God.

The world of unmerited love is not a place dominated by the arbitrary or the superfluous. Without the prophetic dimension, the language of contemplation is in danger of having no grip on the history in which God acts and in which we meet God. Without the mystical dimension the language of prophecy can narrow its vision and weaken its perception of the God who makes all things new (Rev. 21:5). Each undergoes a distortion that isolates it and renders it inauthentic.

The journey of prophecy and the journey of contemplation are precisely that: a journey. The road must be traveled in freedom without turning from it because of its pitfalls, and without pretending ignorance of its ever new forms, for unjust human suffering continues to be heartrending and insatiable; it continually raises new questions and causes new dilemmas. It never ends; neither does protest, after the manner of Job. Although the way of talking about God has become clearer, it continues to be mysterious, as awesome and as alluring as ever.

The language of contemplation acknowledges that everything comes from the Father's unmerited love and opens up "new horizons of hope" (Puebla, no. 1165). The language of prophecy attacks the situation — and the structural causes — of injustice and deprivation in which the poor live, because it looks for "the suffering features of Christ the Lord" in the pain-ravaged faces of an oppressed people (Puebla, no. 31–39). Both languages arise, among the poor of Latin America as in Job, out of the suffering and hopes of the innocent. Poverty and unjust suffering are in fact the situation of the majority in Latin America. Our theological reflection thus starts from the experience of the cross and death as well as from the joy of the resurrection and life.

This twofold language is the language that Jesus, prefigured by Job, uses in speaking of the Father's love. The author of the Book of Job stammers out what Christ will say unhesitatingly. He starts from the experience of unjust human suffering, which Jesus in turn will share on the "two sticks" of which Gonzalo Rose speaks with such tenderness. The author of Job reminds us of the call for justice that issues from God the liberator. The Messiah will make that same call his own as a central element in the message of love that sums up "the ten commandments of God," which fit into our hands "like ten more fingers," to cite Gonzalo Rose again. The author of Job directs us toward that gratuitousness of the Father's love that will be the heart of the proclamation and witness of Jesus Christ. He seeks a way; he offers himself as "the way" (John 14:6).   — *On Job*, 94–97

CONTEMPLATION AND JUSTICE

The key to the interpretation of the Book of Job is a study of Job's second reply to God, which brings out the true relationship between justice and gratuitousness. Job's first reply to God was focused on himself. Here the point of reference is God: God's plans, God's words, God's presence. Job's attitude has changed, therefore, though there is still no acknowledgment of any sins that supposedly have brought deserved suffering upon him. His conviction of innocence is deep-seated. At no time does God accept the accusations made by Job's theologian friends. God thus implicitly confirms the integrity of Job, whose own unyielding and heartrending assertion of it has called into question an entire way of understanding God and the relationship of human beings to God.

There has been a transformation in Job. The change is due to his understanding of God's speeches, for these have given an answer to his profound anxieties. It is not indeed the kind of answer he had been looking for, and yet it brings the fulfillment of his hopes. The Lord's words have released him from the cell in which he had found himself imprisoned because of the contradiction between his experience of his own innocence and the doctrine of retribution. He had the courage to face up to the contradiction and to proclaim it for all to hear.

From the depths of the abyss and even in the cruelest suffering ("My flesh is clothed with worms and dirt; my skin hardens, then breaks out again" [7:5]), he had asserted his right to speak:

> Therefore I will not restrain my mouth;
> I will speak in the anguish of my spirit;
> I will complain in the bitterness of my soul. (7:11)

It was a difficult and even tortuous road he had to travel in order to speak of God. But was it the only road? Or perhaps the best? We must examine in some detail the following very important passage:

v. 1 Then Job answered the Lord:

v. 2 I know that you can do all things, and that no purpose of yours can be thwarted.

v. 3 [You said:] "Who is this that hides counsel without knowledge?" Therefore I have uttered what I did not understand, things too wonderful for me, which I did not know.

v. 4 [You said:] "Hear, and I will speak; I will question you, and you declare to me."

v. 5 I had heard of you by the hearing of the ear, but now my eye sees you;

v. 6 therefore I despise myself, and repent [repudiate, retract] in dust and ashes (42:1–6)

There are three steps in this response of Job: an acknowledgment that God has plans and that these are being carried out; a discovery of previously unrecognized aspects of reality; a joyous encounter with the Lord. All this has an inevitable consequence: the abandonment of his attitude of complaint and sadness.

1. Yahweh has asked Job over and over what he, Job, knows and understands about the divine works. Here Job uses the same verb "know" to express what he has just learned and now has as his deepest conviction. "I know" was also the phrase he used when he spoke of his conviction that his *gōʾēl*, the God who liberates, would defend him (see 19:25). Job thus begins here with a profession of faith in the power of God.

God reproached Job for trying to obscure the divine plans (see 38:2). God asserted that such plans do indeed exist, but they do not possess or control God; much less, then, is God controlled by those human beings who claim to know God's intentions in detail. Rather the contrary is true, for, as God said,

"Everything under heaven belongs to me" (41:11, NIV). Job
now knows that "no purpose of yours can be thwarted" (42:2)
even if the human mind cannot always comprehend the manner
of its execution. God does indeed have plans, and the world is
not a chaos as Job had pictured it in his opening monologue.
What Job was really rejecting was, first, the moral order as
presented to him by his theologian friends and, second and
consequently, the God to whom they appealed. If there is no
alternative to the doctrine of temporal retribution, then for
someone who has experienced what Job has experienced, the
conclusion is inevitable: the world is indeed a chaos. If the only
possible order is the order of justice that his friends proclaim,
then Job must become, even against his will, a defender of dis-
order, because his fate will be the same whether he is upright
and innocent (9:15–20) or not. The proof that this position into
which he has been forced never satisfied him is his ardent plea
that he might debate the matter not with his friends but with
God. In his lamentation (which is a form of prayer) Job, like
Jeremiah, was close to God, closer than were his friends with
their theology. Job has at various moments acknowledged the
greatness of God (see 9:4, 34–35; 12:19; 13:21–22; 23:4–6);
now he knows that one manifestation of divine power is that
God has plans and carries them out in an utterly free manner.

2. In his final answer Job recalls (42:3) that God spoke of
a plan or intention (ēṣāh, 38:2) in which God's gratuitous love
is the ground of all existence. Job's answer is inspired by what
God said.[1] What he has now heard from the mouth of Yahweh
has given him a glimpse of another world, an order different
from the one he rejected but for which until now there seemed

---

1. Bishop Gerardo Valencia of Buenaventura, Colombia, once described this
contemplative experience in very simple words: "Thank you, my God, for letting
me feel your nearness. Allow me to improvise this discourse, having learned of you
from you, like the children whose mother has them learn little speeches for her
birthday. Allow me, then, God, my most loving Father, to hesitate and stammer,
to put both hands over my face, to dash ahead and stop, complain, and end here"
("Los dos elementos," in his *Con Dios a la madrugada* [Bogotá: Tercer Mundo,
1965], 44).

to be no alternative. All this is still not entirely clear to him, but at least he is no longer being suffocated by the religious universe of his friends and indeed of his age.

The words of God (38:2) that Job cites in Job 42:3 have made him realize his own limits: he had been speaking of "what I did not understand," literally "without intelligence," "without discernment." Job's words here are a new and specific reference to God's speech, in which the idea of the discernment whereby Job ought to be attuned to God's plan played a key role. A change has begun, for Job now realizes that there are "things too wonderful for me." The important thing here is not Job's admiration for the magnificence of creation but rather his recognition of the plan of God. It is a plan of gratuitous love, and it is in light of this love that God's will to justice in the governance of the world reveals its full meaning.

The questions Yahweh inexorably pursued have revealed to Job the freedom and love that permeate God's plan. As a result, Job can speak of hitherto unsuspected facets of reality that he does not fully understand but that are not therefore any less real. He is not saying that he has acquired any further information from all that God has said; on the contrary, these wonders too are beyond his ability to grasp completely, but he has indeed begun to understand, to acquire the needed discernment. He still has a long road to travel. Previously, when he moved within the framework of the doctrine of retribution, he did not have any journey at all ahead of him because at bottom everything was (supposedly) understood, and he was already at the goal. This is no longer the case; he sees things differently now. God is present to him as an abiding newness.

3. Job again cites God: "Hear, and I will speak; I will question you, and you declare to me" (42:4). The salvo of questions launched by God, as well as the direct dialogue at last granted to Job have left him no choice but to acknowledge humbly and joyfully an encounter that has changed his life: "I had heard of you by the hearing of the ear, but now my eye sees you" (42:5). The verb "know" plays an important role in God's speeches,

which are a lengthy and penetrating challenge to Job's knowledge (and thereby to the theology of his three friends). Job now perceives that there is another way of knowing and speaking about God. His previous contact with God had been indirect, "by hearing" through others (his friends, for example!); now it is direct, unmediated.

Job is now beginning to savor the Pauline "face-to-face" encounter with God in which faith, hope, and love abide, "and the greatest of these is love" (1 Cor. 13:13). This encounter brings the fullness of life to the believer. Job therefore surrenders to God and can say with Jeremiah in time of crisis: "the Lord is with me" (Jer. 20:11), and with the psalmist: "I shall behold your face in righteousness; when I awake I shall be satisfied, beholding your likeness" (Ps. 17:15). He can repeat here, after this meeting with God, what he had earlier said in hope: "How my heart yearns within me" (Job 19:27, NIV).[2]

Yet the meeting has been a costly one. God had said: "Who can confront me and be safe?" (41:11). Job has learned the truth of these words, for he goes away limping from this confrontation with God, as Jacob did after his struggle with the angel (Gen. 32:24–31). Limping, but content, for he has seen his Lord, and the revelation given to him has opened up a new world to him. He had hoped for this meeting and at bottom had always been confident that it would take place. At the worst moment of crisis he had exclaimed: "I shall see God" (Job 19:26). This hope is now satisfied. Job has previously addressed God on various occasions in protest; now he does so in acceptance and a submission that is inspired not by resignation but by contemplative love. The encounter with God is a logical stage, given Job's attitude as a person of prayer.

---

2. Ordinary believers can have an intense experience of God's nearness. An Ayacuchan workman, for example, has said: "It makes no difference where we are, because we poor folk are with God our Little Father at all times; we never leave him for even a moment" (La religiosidad popular en el Perú," ed. José Luis González [mimeographed, Lima], 1984), 53.

Despite all his protests, Job has always been convinced of God's nearness and has always desired to draw close to God (see 10:8–9, 12; 14:14–15; 29:4–5). All the greater, therefore, was his affliction when he felt far from God. Nevertheless, the closeness he now experiences is beyond all his hopes: "Now my eye sees you" (42:5b).

4. The steps Job has just taken, the discoveries he has made, lead him to a conclusion ("therefore") ... "I repudiate what I have said, and repent [repudiate, retract] in dust and ashes" (42:6).

According to the majority of commentators, the general meaning of the passage seems clear: Job stands now as a creature before his God, as a child before his Father. His complaints and protests had in fact never outweighed his hope and trust. He does not now withdraw his claim of innocence, for his conviction on this count is as great as his faith in God. Nor does he have to withdraw it, for Yahweh has not repeated the accusations of the three friends. Neither does Job accept with resignation something he regards as unjust. God, however, has now made known to Job a plan and the meaning of a justice that cannot be contained in the straitjacket of the doctrine of retribution. Job, for his part, has come to see that his language had perhaps been disrespectful. He therefore repents and humbly proposes to do penance in dust and ashes.

This interpretation is basically satisfactory and is consistent with Job's stubborn assertion of his innocence as well as with what Yahweh will say in the verses that follow, namely, that Job has spoken correctly about Yahweh (42:7–8). Yet the translation of v. 6 ("I retract and repent in dust and ashes") has always left an unanswered question: What does Job retract? In point of fact, the verb translated as "retract" has no object.[3] The only alternatives, then, are to supply an object for "repudiate" as the

---

3. In Job 42:6, "retract" has no object in the Spanish translation by Luis Alonso Schökel and José Luis Sicre in *Job: Comentario teológico y literario* (Madrid: Cristiandad, 1983), 593, which is in turn based on the version of Mexican writer José Luz Ojeda, 593. See also Norman C. Habel, *The Book of Job* (Philadelphia: Westminster, 1985), 576.

translation above does, and run the risk of altering the meaning
signaled earlier, or to look for other translations of the verb, or
to settle for a degree of ineptitude in the phrase for the sake of
a general meaning that seems clear from the context.
It is of interest to note here for comparison a new translation of 42:6 that I have made use of in translating the verse.
This translation brings out the rich consistency of the verse with
greater depth and clarity.[4] The key to the new version is to be
found in the meaning of the verb *naham,* which is correctly
translated as "to repent." The translator points out, however,
that when *naham* is used with a certain preposition *'al* it means
"to change one's mind" or "to reverse an opinion" (see e.g.,
Exod. 32:12, 14; Jer. 18:8, 10; Amos 7:3, 6). The text in Job
thus means: "I repudiate and abandon [change my mind about]
dust and ashes."

The phrase "dust and ashes" is an image for groaning
and lamentation; in other words, it is an image befitting the
situation of Job as described before the dialogues began (see
2:8–12). This is the object of the retraction and change of mind
of which this key verse speaks. Job is rejecting the attitude of
lamentation that has been his until now. God has shown him
that this attitude is not justified. He does not retract or repent
of what he has hitherto said, but he now sees clearly that he
cannot go on complaining.

This translation illumines the whole of Job's final response
and makes it more coherent. The Hebrew verb *m's,* "reject,
repudiate" is no longer left hanging without an object; it refers,
as does the verb "repent" (taken in the sense of "change one's
mind"), to Job's attitude of protest and reproach: "I repudiate
dust and ashes." This means that in his final reply what Job is
expressing is not contrition but a renunciation of his lamentation and dejected outlook. Certain emphases in his protest had
been due to the doctrine of retribution, which despite everything

---

4. Dale Patrick, "The Translation of Job XLII, 6," *Vetus Testamentum* 26
(1976): 369–71.

had continued to be his point of reference. Now that the Lord has overthrown that doctrine by revealing the key to the divine plan, Job realizes that he has been speaking of God in a way that implied that God was a prisoner of a particular way of understanding justice. It is this whole outlook that Job says he is now abandoning.

Many difficulties remain, but the horizon is expanding. Job begins to see the way by which he is to go to meet God and others. This explains his gratitude and joy for what has been revealed to him in the debate with his friends and with God, and especially in the speeches "from the heart of the tempest."

Job's answer gives a better understanding and represents a high point in contemplative speech about God. Job has arrived only gradually at this way of talking about God. At one point he had even felt God to be distant and unconnected with his life; he had then confronted this God in a bitter lawsuit. Now he surrenders to Yahweh with renewed trust. Like Jeremiah in a passage to which reference must be made in any effort to understand the Book of Job, Job might have said at this point: "You seduced me, Lord, and I let myself be seduced" (Jer. 20:7). Job truly believes "for nothing"; never before has he believed in such an utterly disinterested way.   — *On Job*, 82–87

GRACE AND JUSTICE

What is it that Job has understood? That justice does not reign in the world God has created? No. The truth that he has grasped and that has lifted him to the level of contemplation is that justice alone does not have the final say about how we are to speak of God. Only when we have come to realize that God's love is freely bestowed do we enter fully and definitively into the presence of the God of faith. Grace is not opposed to the quest of justice nor does it play it down; on the contrary, it gives it its full meaning. God's love, like all true love, operates in a world not of cause and effect but of freedom and gratuitousness. That is how persons successfully encounter one another in a complete and unconditional way: without payment of any kind of charges and without externally imposed obligations that pressure them into meeting the expectations of the other.

In the debate with his friends Job came to see that he must transcend his individual experience. The dialogue brought home to him that his situation was not exceptional but was shared by the poor of this world. This new awareness in turn showed him that solidarity with the poor was required by his faith in a God who has a special love for the disinherited, the exploited of human history. This preferential love is the basis for what I call the prophetic way of speaking about God.

But the prophetic way is not the only way of drawing near to the mystery of God, nor is it sufficient by itself. Job has just experienced a second shift: from a punitive view of history to the world of grace that completely enfolds and permeates him. In the first major step Job was not required to deny his personal suffering but to open himself to the suffering of others as well and to commit himself to its elimination. In this second stage the issue is not to discover gratuitousness and forget the demands of justice, but to situate justice within the framework of God's gratuitous love. Only in the perspective of the latter is it possible to understand God's predilection for the poor. This special love does not have for its ultimate motive the virtues and merits of the poor but the goodness and freedom of God, a God who is not simply the guardian of a rigid moral order. This preference for the poor — Job now realizes — is a key factor in authentic divine justice. Consequently there is no opposition between gratuitousness and justice, but there is indeed an opposition between gratuitousness and a conception of justice that can be translated into demands made of God by human beings and that renders God prisoner of our deeds or our cultic actions. There is indeed a contradiction between the free, gratuitous, and creative love of God and the doctrine of retribution that seeks to pigeonhole God.

Inspired by the experience of his own innocence, Job bitterly criticized the theology of temporal retribution as maintained in his day and expounded by his friends. But his challenge stopped halfway and, as a result, except at moments when his deep faith and trust in God broke through, he could not escape the dilemma so cogently presented by his friends: if he was innocent, then God was guilty. God subsequently rebuked Job for remaining prisoner of this either-or mentality (see 40:8). What he should have done was to leap the fence set up around him by this sclerotic theology that is so dangerously close to idolatry, run free in the fields of God's love, and breathe an unrestricted air like the animals described in God's argument — animals that humans cannot domesticate. The world outside the fence is the world of gratuitousness; it is there that God dwells and there that God's friends find a joyous welcome.

The world of retribution — and not of temporal retribution only — is not where God dwells; at most God visits it. The Lord is not prisoner of the "give to me and I will give to you" mentality. Nothing, no human work however valuable, merits grace, for if it did, grace would cease to be grace. This is the heart of the message of the Book of Job.

There is no doubt that in the period when the Book of Job was written, vagueness about any life beyond the present made the experience of suffering more intense and the doctrine of retribution less credible. But the Christian profession of faith in a future life does not essentially alter the point the poet was trying to make. The new and unparalleled fact of Christ brings a rupture but at the same time establishes a continuity. The gratuitousness of God's love is the framework within which the requirement of practicing justice is to be located.

Human works as such do not justify; they do not save. St. Paul says, in light of the revelation given in Jesus Christ, that human works cannot tie God's hands. This is the point of his statement about "justification by faith" (Rom. 3:28). The faith that saves is itself a grace from the Lord. Entrance into the kingdom of God is not a right to be won, not even by the practice of justice; it is always a freely given gift. "By grace you have been saved," he tells the Ephesians (2:5). God is entirely independent of space and time. God acts only in accordance with the utterly free divine will: God does what God pleases to do. No love at all can be locked in.

The prophet Hosea is quite explicit about this divine love that operates independently of any human merits. When Yahweh's people ask forgiveness, Yahweh replies: "I will heal their faithlessness; I will love them freely" (Hos. 14:4). Because of this freely given love, God will always turn "the Valley of Achor" (misfortune) into "a door of hope" (see Hos. 2:15).

All this does not mean, however, that God does not look for a certain kind of behavior from human beings. Faith finds expression in works, but these works do not become a claim upon God, for if they did, they would betray their own meaning. Paul's insight into the gratuitousness of salvation and the mysterious, utterly free love of God gets to the very heart of the revelation given in Jesus Christ. Paul himself tells us that faith works through love (Gal. 5:6). The reign of God makes the ethical demand that every believer practice justice, but this demand is not in any way inconsistent with the free and unmerited initiative of God. On the contrary, it acquires its full scope and vitality only when located within this gratuitousness. That is why Paul is able to speak of salvation as unmerited and then sum up a little later by saying: "For we are what he has made us, created in Christ Jesus for good works, which God prepared beforehand to be our way of life" (Eph. 2:10).

The justice of God is a fundamental datum of the Bible, and therefore God at no time rebukes Job for having demanded justice. For God to reproach him for this would be to contradict the promise God had made to Abraham: "I have chosen him, that he may charge his children and his household after him to keep the way of the Lord by doing righteousness and justice; so that the Lord may bring about for Abraham what he has promised him" (Gen. 18:19). Nor can Yahweh contradict the act of liberation on which the covenant was based: "I am the Lord your God, who brought you out of the land of Egypt, out of the house of slavery" (Exod. 20:2). But in the just governance of the world God does not follow well-trodden paths that would limit divine action. Moving through history, God walks a path in freedom.

This freedom of God is a constant theme in the teaching of Jesus. It is, for example, the point of the parable about the laborers in the vineyard (Matt. 20:1–16). When the landowner decides to give a full day's wage to those who started work at the eleventh hour, toward the end of the day, his decision brings objections from those who had come to work early. The landowner tells one of them: "Friend, I am doing you no wrong; did you not agree with me for a denarius? Take what belongs to you, and go" (v. 14). The justice of God is not bound by the formalities of human justice. There is, then, this guileless expression of sovereign freedom and goodness: "Am I not allowed to do what I choose with what belongs to me? Or do you begrudge my generosity?" (v. 15). This is also the point of the parable of the prodigal son, in which the serious and obliging elder son cuts such a sad figure because he thinks he can confine paternal love within a narrow conception of justice.

Job has just been delivered from the envy that paralyzes reality and tries to put limits to the divine goodness that leaves no room for generosity and, even worse, tries to take God's place. Yahweh, the God of life, has restored Job to a life that refuses to be imprisoned in a narrow ethical order but rather draws inspiration at every moment from the free and unmerited love of God. This deliverance is the object of Job's contemplation.

If the process of deliverance had not reached this point, Job would have retained a bit of the theology of retribution and, with it, a myopic view of God. The irony in God's speeches is, as it were, the scalpel that cuts into Job's wounded flesh and makes it impossible for the evil to remain and put forth new shoots. This critical juncture has been difficult and painful, but the result is worth the suffering. There remains in the world perhaps an obstinate residue of the unknown; we are still far removed from a completely transparent universe. Job still has many questions, but the unknown is no longer a monster that threatens to devour everything, including his few and fragile certainties. The beast that is his ignorance has not vanished, but like Behemoth and Leviathan it is under control because of what he now knows about God and God's love.

In rejecting the theology of retribution Job has not been freed from the necessity of practicing justice, but only from the temptation of imprisoning God in a narrow conception of justice. He has been delivered, at least in principle, from the most subtle form of idolatry. God is now seen by Job as completely free, untrammeled by the narrow theological categories in which Job had been trying to enclose God's dealings with humankind. God is a presence that leads amid darkness and pain, a hand that inspires confidence. Not all ignorance is dispelled, but the route is clearly marked. Luis Espinal, a priest murdered in Bolivia, wrote these beautiful and profound words:

> Train us, Lord, to fling ourselves upon the impossible, for behind the impossible is your grace and your presence; we cannot fall into emptiness. The future is an enigma, our road is covered by mist, but we want to go on giving ourselves, because you continue hoping amid the night and weeping tears through a thousand human eyes.[5]

That is what Job did: he flung himself upon the impossible and into an enigmatic future. And in this effort he met the Lord.

—*On Job,* 87–92

---

5. "Gastar la vida," in *Oraciones a quemarropa* (Lima: CEP, 1982), 69. Søren Kierkegaard writes: "In the whole Old Testament there is no other figure one approaches with so much human confidence, boldness, and trust as Job, simply because he is so human in every way, because he resides in a *confinium* touching on poetry" (*Kierkegaard's Works*, 7:204).

JOB AND JESUS

Jesus speaks to us of the Father, and in his discourses language about God achieves its greatest expressiveness. The Son of God teaches us that talk of God must be mediated by the experience of the cross. He accepts abandonment and death precisely in order to reveal God to us as love. Universal love and preference for the poor distinguish the message of the divine reign that both purifies human history and transcends it. Sin, which is the refusal to accept the message, brings Jesus to his death; the cross is the result of the resistance of those who refuse to accept the unmerited and demanding gift of God's love.

The final words of Jesus — "My God, my God, why have you forsaken me?" (Matt. 27:46; Mark 15:34) — speak of the suffering and loneliness of one who feels abandoned by the hand of God. But when he cries out his feeling of abandonment in the opening words of Psalm 22, he also makes the rest of the psalm his own. The whole of the psalm must therefore be taken into account if we are to understand the meaning of his lament.

Psalm 22 expresses the cruel loneliness experienced by a man of deep faith. In the midst of this experience he turns to his God:

> Why are you so far from helping me, from the words of
>   my groaning?
> O my God, I cry by day, but you do not answer;
>   and by night, but find no rest.
> Yet you are holy,
>   enthroned on the praises of Israel. (Ps. 22:1–3)

In the Bible complaint does not exclude hope; in fact, they go together, as we saw in Job. The confidence of the psalmist grows as he recalls that this is a God who has delivered the people of Israel from slavery and deprivation:

> In you our ancestors trusted;
>   they trusted, and you delivered them.

> To you they cried, and were saved;
>> in you they trusted, and were not put to shame.
>>>>>> (Ps. 22:4–5)

The psalmist is referring to the deliverance from Egypt and to Exodus 3:7, the experience on which biblical faith was based. All the more reason, then, for him to describe his own pitiful situation in all its bleakness. This man who laments knows that God does not regard suffering as an ideal. His complaint is filled with a longing for life.

> But I am a worm, and not human;
>> scorned by others, and despised by the people.
> All who see me mock at me;
>> they make mouths at me, they shake their heads;
> "Commit your cause to the Lord; let him deliver —
>> let him rescue the one in whom he delights!" . . .
> I am poured out like water,
>> and all my bones are out of joint;
> my heart is like wax:
>> it is melted within my breast;
> my mouth is dried up like a potsherd,
>> and my tongue sticks to my jaws;
>> you lay me in the dust of death.
> For dogs are all round me;
>> a company of evildoers encircles me.
> My hands and feet have shriveled;
>> I can count all my bones. (Ps. 22:6–8, 14–17)

The person speaking in this psalm tells of his misfortune and abandonment, but he says not a word of personal faults that would have merited such adversity. He is an innocent man who has been treated unjustly. This fact makes it easier for the evangelists to apply the text to Jesus at various moments in their accounts of his death.

The psalmist sinks deeper into suffering and loneliness. His situation is due to those who harass him and mock his faith in a God who can deliver him. But he remains steadfast; he knows that his God is bent on justice and hears and protects the poor:

> For he did not despise or abhor
>   the affliction of the afflicted;
> he did not hide his face from me,
>   but heard when I cried to him. . . .
> The poor shall eat and be satisfied;
>   those who seek him shall praise the Lord.
> May your hearts live forever!
>   (Ps. 22:24, 26)

The God who could hear the cry of the Israelites when they were oppressed in Egypt does not disdain "the destitution of the destitute," the poverty of the poor and the least of human beings. Verse 26 is an allusion to Deuteronomy 14:29, which says that "the resident aliens, the orphans, and the widows" — the biblical triad used in referring to the poor and helpless — shall all "eat their fill."

This solidarity with the poor and the starving, which leads to an ongoing transformation of history and requires behavior to this end, is the fruit of the gratuitous love of the God in whom the psalmist believes and hopes. This accounts for his self-surrender and praise toward the end of the poem:

> I will tell of your name to my brothers and sisters;
>   in the midst of the congregation I will praise you:
> You who fear the Lord, praise him!
>   All you offspring of Jacob, glorify him;
>   stand in awe of him, all you offspring of Israel! . . .
> All the ends of the earth shall remember
>   and turn to the Lord;
> and all the families of the nations
>   shall worship before him.
> For dominion belongs to the Lord,
>   and he rules over the nations.
>   (Ps. 22:22–23, 27–28)

Jesus did not compose this psalm; he inherited it. It had its origin in the suffering of a believer, perhaps someone who in some way represented his people. The important thing is that Jesus made it his own and, while nailed to the cross, offered to the Father the suffering and abandonment of all humankind. This radical communion with the suffering of human beings brought him down to the deepest level of history at the very moment when his life was ending.

In adopting this psalm Jesus also gave expression to his hope in the liberating God who with predilection defends the poor and the dispossessed. Luke could therefore put on the lips of Jesus not the cry of abandonment but words of confident self-surrender: "Father, into your hands I commend my spirit!" (Luke 23:46; see Ps. 31:5). He who has been "abandoned" abandons himself in turn into the hands of the Father. He confronts the forces of evil and sin when, in communion with the hopes of the human race, he asserts that life, not death, has the final say. All this is part of the redemptive experience of the cross. It is there that Jesus experiences and proclaims the resurrection and true, unending life and becomes "the source of eternal salvation." The Letter to the Hebrews speaks of the value of Jesus' death for our salvation:

> In the days of his flesh, Jesus offered up prayers and supplications, with loud cries and tears, to the one who was able to save him from death, and he was heard because of his reverent submission. Although he was a Son, he learned obedience through what he suffered; and having been made perfect, he became the source of eternal salvation for all who obey him, having been designated by God a high priest according to the order of Melchizedek.
>
> (Heb. 5:7–10)

Communion in suffering and in hope, in the abandonment of loneliness and in trusting self-surrender in death as in life: this is the message of the cross, which is "foolishness to those who are perishing, but to us who are being saved it is the power of God" (1 Cor. 1:18). Because it is "foolishness" it can pass unnoticed by those who have eyes only for wonders and manifestations of might. Paradoxically, this power of God is at the same time "weakness" (1 Cor. 1:25). It inspires the language of the cross, which is a synthesis of the prophetic and the contemplative and the only appropriate way of talking about the God of Jesus Christ.

By using this language one engages in a dangerous remembrance of him who was publicly crucified and whom the Father raised to life. This kind of talk — which the wise and understanding of this world regard as madness — calls all human beings together as a church via the privileged choice of the weak and despised of human history (1 Cor. 1:26–29).

At the same time, however, if we are to use the language of the cross we must have made our own the meaning of the crucifixion. Only by following Jesus is it possible to talk of God. From the cross Jesus calls us to follow in his steps, "for," he tells us, "my yoke is easy, and my burden light" (Matt. 11:30). The invitation to follow Jesus must be set in the context of the gratuitousness that is the way of the cross.

These considerations do not eliminate the element of protest from the final words of Jesus; they are rather an attempt to situate it properly. Even in his lament Jesus "spoke correctly of God." His cry on the cross renders more audible and more penetrating the cries of all the Jobs, individual and collective, of human history. To adopt a comparison that Bonhoeffer uses in another context, the cry of Jesus is the *cantus firmus,* the leading voice to which all the voices of those who suffer unjustly are joined. — *On Job,* 97–101

THE AGONY OF JESUS
AND THE SUFFERING OF THE WORLD

Those who suffer unjustly have a right to complain and protest. Their cry expresses both their bewilderment and their faith. It is not possible to do theology in Latin America without taking into account the situation of the most downtrodden of history; this means that at some point the theologian must cry out, as Jesus did, "My God, my God, why have you forsaken me?" This cry cannot be muted.

This kind of communion in suffering demands watchfulness and solidarity. "Jesus will be in agony until the end of the world. There must be no sleeping during that time."[6] Commitment to the alleviation of human suffering, and especially to the removal of its causes as far as possible, is an obligation for the followers of Jesus, who took upon himself his own "easy yoke and light burden." Such a commitment presupposes genuine human compassion, as well as a measure of understanding of human history and the factors that condition it. It also requires a firm and stubborn determination to be present, regardless of the consequences, wherever the unjust abuse the innocent.

Human suffering, whatever its causes — social, personal, or other — is a major question for theological reflection. Human suffering is not limited to suffering caused by social injustice. It is undeniable, however, that this latter kind of suffering is found on a vast scale and marked by refined cruelty in Latin America; that many other human wants have their origin in it; that it is occasioned by a contempt for the life of the poor that has its roots in sin — that is, in the refusal to love God and other human beings; and that the responsibility for removing its cause is ours, at least in part.

In Latin America we are still experiencing every day the violation of human rights, murder, and torture. Our task here is to find the words with which to talk about God in the midst of the starvation of millions, the humiliation of races regarded as inferior, discrimination against women, especially women who are poor, systematic social injustice, a persistent high rate of infant mortality, those who simply "disappear" or are deprived of their freedom, the sufferings of peoples who are struggling

---

6. Blaise Pascal, *Pensées* (Baltimore: Penguin, 1968), no. 919 (313).

for their right to live, the exiles and the refugees, terrorism of every kind, and the corpse-filled common graves of Ayacucho. What we must deal with is not the past but, unfortunately, a cruel present and a dark tunnel with no apparent end.

In Peru, therefore — but the question is perhaps symbolic of all Latin America — we must ask: How are we to do theology while Ayacucho lasts? How are we to speak of the God of life when cruel murder on a massive scale goes on in "the corner of the dead"?[7] How are we to preach the love of God amid such profound contempt for human life? How are we to proclaim the resurrection of the Lord where death reigns, and especially the death of children, women, the poor, indigenes, and the "unimportant" members of our society?

These are our questions, and this is our challenge. Job shows us a way with his vigorous protest, his discovery of concrete commitment to the poor and all who suffer unjustly, his facing up to God, and his acknowledgment of the gratuitousness that characterizes God's plan for human history. It is for us to find our own route amid the present sufferings and hopes of the poor of Latin America, to analyze its course with the requisite historical effectiveness, and, above all, to compare it anew with the word of God. This is what has been done by those, for example, who in recent years have been murdered for their witness of faith and solidarity with the poorest and most helpless, those now known as "the Latin American martyrs."

— *On Job,* 101–2

---

7. This is the meaning of the Quechuan word *Ayacucho.*

13

Connecting to Others

The spirituality outlined in these writings is above all about the spirituality of a people. Throughout Latin American and other parts of the world, one of the ways this is experienced is through base Christian communities. In addition to being places where people share their struggles in light of the Word of God, these communities are also the place where deep friendships can be forged in the pilgrimage through life. Even as we have our moments of solitude, we are reminded that we are not totally alone, and as these writings bring out, we ultimately come to know who we are only in relationship with others.

The development of the communal dimension of faith is a characteristic of Christian life in our day. Vatican II contributed a great deal to this development. In Latin America one way this trend has found expression is in the rise of the basic ecclesial communities, which, in the judgment of Puebla, "are one of the causes for joy and hope in the church" (no. 96).[1] We are also dealing with another essential aspect of following Jesus Christ, the communal experience of our encounter with him.

---

1. Dom Hélder Câmara says of this phenomenon: "The evident disproportion between the weakness of the basic communities and the immense twofold mission entrusted to them is proof that the Lord God is still exalting the humble" (address at a meeting of CELAM in Lima, September 1975; published in *Signos de lucha y esperanza: Testimonio de la Iglesia en América Latina, 1973–1978* [Lima: CEP, 1978], 178a).

For many Latin American Christians this community dimension is not something added simply and with joy to the Christian outlook already in place. In fact, the journey toward life in community frequently takes an unexpected turn: a passage through a painful experience of profound solitude or loneliness. The experience of the solitude of the desert is a profound aspect of the encounter with God. Passage through this desert is a journey of pure faith, with the support and guidance of God alone. In solitude the Lord speaks to us "tenderly" (Hos. 2:14), calls us to fidelity, and consoles us. Being all alone with God, who enriches us with the gift of happiness in the innermost depths of our being, is an ineffable, largely incommunicable, experience.

This experience of solitude is a classic theme in the history of spirituality, but it has special features in our present situation. It leads to an urgent realization of the importance of Christian community, not as a group of which we deign to be a part (as though we might just as well have made the opposite choice), but as a basic ecclesial dimension of walking according to the Spirit.   — *We Drink from Our Own Wells*, 128–29

THE DARK NIGHT OF INJUSTICE

The passage through what has been called "the dark night" of injustice is part of the spiritual journey in Latin America. On this journey "of an entire people toward its liberation through the desert of structural and organized injustice that surrounds us...it is very important to persevere in prayer, even if we hardly do more than stammer groans and cries, while in this struggle the image of God in us is purified in an extraordinary 'dark night.'"[2]

---

2. Juan Hernández Pico, "La oración en los procesos latinoamericanos de liberación," in Alejandro Cussiánovich et al., *Espiritualidad de la liberación* (Lima: CEP, 1980), 181, 183.

Crossing of the desert takes place only in "a deep and vast wilderness," as John of the Cross said. Many of those who seek to be in solidarity with the poor Latin American masses experience this solitude. There is no authentic acceptance of that commitment that does not involve great difficulties. There are problems with those who see their privileges being challenged; there is isolation due to the new and hitherto unexperienced consequences of assuming the needs of the world of the poor from within; there is distrust and even hostility from many who share the same faith.

However, what renders these difficulties even more intense is the situation of poverty and exploitation in which the poor live. It is a situation that seems to have no end; it is like living halfway through a tunnel. The interests that the poor are challenging, both within each country and at the international level, are very powerful. There is, in addition, the great — and unwanted — human cost of an effort at liberation in which no successful outcome can even be glimpsed. It is what García Márquez calls "the immensity of our solitude."[3]

All this gives rise to moments of great suffering and deep loneliness. Juan Alsina, another murdered priest, wrote as follows on the evening before he was found dead:

> We have come to the end of the road; we cut a path but now we are among the rocks...we shall continue on, those of us who remain. How long?... "None of those who dipped their bread in the fleshpots of Egypt will see the Promised Land without passing through the experience of death...." Who is at the other end of the phone? Who is knocking on the door at this hour? The difficulty is not to know what I will do but what they will do, and the most painful question of all: Why? This is the source of

---

3. Ibid., 54.

the uncertainty and the consciousness of uncertainty, the fear.[4]

Yes, the fear, and why not? The fear not only of dying, which itself is no small matter, but also of weakening, of thinking unduly of oneself. Of beginning to consider other and less costly forms of commitment.

When they find themselves alone — and there are many kinds of solitude — many persons would like to rewrite their lives; they wish they had not done or said this or that. Not all wishes at such a moment are dictated by a healthy self-criticism; weariness plays a part, as does cowardice, and even despair at the thought of the many obstacles and misunderstandings that must be overcome. There are also moments for great decisions in which nothing is clear, but a decision must nonetheless be made. There are no fixed points of reference. All that remains is the conviction that one wants to do the Father's will and serve the people, but the moment is so filled with spiritual aridity that despite one's conviction one's tongue clings to the roof of one's mouth (Ps. 137:6).

In all these circumstances there is a new encounter with oneself and, above all, a new face-to-face encounter with the Lord, who is testing and consoling us. John of the Cross speaks of the "frightful night" through which one must pass, but he also says that the desert is "the more delightful, savory, and loving, the deeper, vaster, and more solitary it is." Such is the twofold experience of the Christian who wishes to be faithful to the Lord even in the blackest depths of "the dark night of injustice."

These are the unvarnished experiences of followers of the Lord. They are echoes, reverberating down through the history of the Christian community, of the cry of Jesus himself (Mark 15:34). But in these experiences Christians do not fail to realize that the deep and rending solitude they feel comes on the

---

4. "Ultimas reflexiones" (September 1973), in *Signos de lucha y esperanza: Testimonio de la Iglesia in América Latina, 1973–1978* (Lima: CEP, 1978), 235–36.

threshold of the most tremendous and most radical communion
possible: communion in the life and joy of the resurrection.
— *We Drink from Our Own Wells*, 129–31

LIVING TOGETHER

The passage through solitude leads to a profound community
life. The solitude of which I am speaking is something quite
different from individualism. In individualism there is a large
measure of withdrawal, at the level of thoughts and interests,
in order to ensure a life of quiet privacy. The experience of
solitude gives rise to a hunger for communion. There is an
aloneness with oneself and with God that, however hard it may
be to endure at certain times, is a requirement for authentic
community.

God does not call us to the desert to wander endlessly there,
but to pass through it, in order to reach the promised land. The
journey through the desert creates a community flowing with
the milk and honey of the fellowship of those who know God
as their Father. There we can sing with the psalmist:

> How very good and pleasant it is
> when kindred live together in unity!
> It is like the precious oil on the head,
> running down upon the beard,
> on the beard of Aaron,
> running down over the collar of his robes.
> It is like the dew of Hermon,
> which falls on the mountains of Zion.
> For there the Lord ordained his blessing,
> life forevermore. (Ps. 133)

There is, however, no question here of two stages: first solitude and *then* community. Rather it is within community that
one experiences solitude. The support of the community is

essential for crossing the desert. So true is this that only in community can one travel this road. According to basic ecclesial communities in Brazil:

> The faith and courage of the members of our communities in the face of threats, misunderstandings, and persecution for justice' sake are sustained and strengthened by the support each individual gives the others, by the support each community gives the others, by our very struggle and activity, by meditation on the word of God, and by the recollection of the witness given by those who have struggled for justice.[5]

Community life cultivates receptivity for God's reign and also proclaims it; in this reception and proclamation a community builds itself up as a community. "Only in community can we hear, accept, and proclaim the gift and grace of the Lord, the special call to overcome everything that destroys comradely communion (oppression, injustice, marginalization, discrimination, etc.) — because at the same time it destroys communion with God — and to struggle for the values of the kingdom that Jesus proclaimed."[6]

The community is also the place where we remember the death and resurrection of the Lord. Paul speaks with realism of our membership in the body of Christ. It implies liberation of our own bodies from the forces of death: sin, the root of all injustice. Against the background of the poverty and exploitation in which the majority of Latin Americans live, against the

---

5. Conclusions of the meeting at Vitoria (January 1975), in *Signos de lucha y esperanza: Testimonio de la Iglesia in América Latina, 1973–1978* (Lima: CEP, 1978), 314a.

6. Parish of Christ the Redeemer, "Celebramos nuestra fe," in RIMAC, documentation service of the Instituto Bartolomé de Las Casas. These are communities formed by the power of love for God. "Love is not weakness or false complacency. It is the power of God. It is this Christian love that must inspire us to form strong communities in which we encourage one another to fulfill our obligations, defend our rights, and demand the promulgation and observance of just laws" (Bishop Gerardo Flores of Verapaz, "En el aniversario de los trágicos acontecimientos de Panzós" [May 29, 1979], in *Páginas* 25 [October 1979]: 68).

background of their emaciated, sometimes massacred, bodies, the Spirit deepens in us the meaning of the Eucharist as an act of thanksgiving to the Father for sharing with us the body of the dead and resurrected Christ.

The breaking of the bread is at once the point of departure and the point of arrival of the Christian community. In it is expressed profound communion in human sorrow and joyous acknowledgment of the risen Savior who gives life to and raises the hope of those assembled in *ecclesia* by his words and deeds.

It is in the Eucharistic community that hope in the Lord is fed:

> The Eucharist, or the Supper of the Lord, should hold the central place in our communities, together with the sharing of the word of God. When they are celebrated among the poor and oppressed, they are both a promise and demand of justice, of the freedom and the fellowship for which the peoples of the Third World are struggling.[7]

The Eucharist celebrates a hope and expresses a confidence that the communion of life that does not yet exist among us can become a reality. This anticipation is not an evasion; rather it motivates a present commitment. It represents an acknowledgment that the gift of life given by the risen Christ concerns every moment and every area of human existence.

This celebration is carried out in community — but a community that extends beyond the confines of the near and the local, because it is both the expression and the task of the entire church. As Rutilio Grande put it:

> This morning, here in Apopa, the several parish communities here represented are not present as a sect cut off either from the local church or from the universal church. We feel ourselves part of the church, which we love and

---

7. Fourth International Congress of Theology, "Documento final," in *Páginas* 28 (March 1980): 6; Eng. trans. in *The Challenge of Basic Christian Communities,* ed. Sergio Torres and John Eagleson (Maryknoll, N.Y.: Orbis Books, 1981), 241.

want to see continually renewed by the power of the Holy Spirit...in the midst of the world and its problems. We love the church not simply in the light of what it ought to be but as it now is, with its need of continual conversion.[8]

In the church we experience moments of solitude as well as times of community sharing. We are a messianic people on pilgrimage through history and we are, of course, exposed to the vicissitudes of that process in its varied forms; nonetheless it is in and with the people that we go our way. The ecclesial outlook is one of the dominant notes of the spirituality now coming to birth in Latin America. It is in the church, the historical sacrament of the kingdom of life, that the committed Christians of Latin America are living — and dying.

— *We Drink from Our Own Wells,* 131–35

8. Homily of Rutilio Grande at Apopa, El Salvador, February 13, 1977.

14

Choosing Life

God calls us to choose life (Deut. 30:19–20), especially in light of poverty, which entails unjust and early death. The ideal is that there are no poor among us (Deut. 15:4), none who are insignificant. The presence of the poor is not an inevitable fate but a challenge to resist being hardhearted and close-fisted (Deut. 15:7). Gutiérrez recognizes that poverty is reality and urges us to choose life through openheartedness and open-handedness. The poor have need of material things, but like all people they also need gratuitous offers of friendship, welcome, and intimacy, all of which make us human.

A SPIRITUALITY OF LIFE

The struggles of the poor for liberation represent an assertion of their right to life. The poverty that the poor suffer means death: a premature and unjust death. It is on the basis of this affirmation of life that the poor of Latin America are trying to live their faith, recognize the love of God, and proclaim their hope. Within these struggles an oppressed and believing people is increasingly creating a way of Christian life, a spirituality. Latin American Christians will thus cease to be consumers of spiritualities that are doubtless valid but that nonetheless reflect other experiences and other goals, for they are carving out their own way of being faithful both to the Lord and to the experiences of the poorest.

This historical movement, with its focus in the process of liberation, is truly the terrain on which a people's spiritual experience is located as it affirms its right to life. This is the soil in which its response to the gift of faith in the God of life is taking root. The poverty that brings death to the poor is no longer a motive for resignation to the conditions of present existence, nor does it discourage Latin American Christians in their aspirations. The historical experience of liberation that they are now beginning to have is showing them, or reminding them, of something down deep in themselves: that God wants them to live.

A reading in the light of faith, then, gives us to understand that the breakthrough of the poor in Latin American society and the Latin American church is in the final analysis a breakthrough of God in our lives. This breakthrough is the point of departure and also the axis of the new spirituality. It therefore points out to us the way that leads to the God of Jesus Christ.

Some are surprised because they think of the struggle for liberation as taking place in the social and political sphere and thus in an area that has nothing to do with the spiritual. Everything depends on what one means by spiritual. For the moment, let me say that the process of liberation is a global one and it affects every dimension of the human. Moreover, the poverty in which the vast majority of Latin Americans live is not simply a social problem; it is a human situation that issues a profound challenge to the Christian conscience.

An entire people is giving rise to a spirituality, not simply an individual who stands apart and is to some extent isolated, at least initially. What is happening among us today represents a departure from the beaten path; it also forces us to realize that following Jesus is not a private matter but is part of a collective enterprise. In this way we recover the biblical understanding of people's journey in search of God.

The spirituality being born in Latin America is the spirituality of the church of the poor, to which Pope John XXIII called all of us, the spirituality of an ecclesial community that is trying to make effective its solidarity with the poorest of this world. It is a collective, ecclesial spirituality that, without losing anything of its universal perspective, is stamped with the religious outlook of an exploited and believing people. The journey is one undertaken by the entire people of God. It leaves behind it a land of oppression and, without illusions but with constancy, seeks its way in the midst of a desert. It is a new spirituality because the love of the Lord who urges us to reject inertia and inspires us to creativity is itself always new.

In following Jesus the central drama is played out in the dialectic of death followed by life. In this dialectic and in the victory of the risen Jesus, the God of our hope is revealed. This is a profound and strictly paschal spirituality. It bears in mind all the things that exploit and marginalize the poor, and it draws its nourishment from the victory against "dying before their time" (as Bartolomé de Las Casas put it) that that situation entails. It embodies the conviction that life, not death, has the final word. The following of Jesus feeds upon the witness given by the resurrection, which means the death of death, and upon the liberating efforts of the poor to assert their unquestionable right to life.

The relationship between an oppressive system and the God who liberates, between death that seems to have the upper hand and the God of life, adumbrates a way of following Jesus and being his disciples under the conditions now prevailing in Latin America. Jesus is not to be sought among the dead: he is alive (Luke 24:5). To seek him among the living is to choose life, as the Book of Deuteronomy (30:15–20) says. This choice is the basis of a spiritual experience that is pointing the way to a new path in following Jesus in Latin America.

— *We Drink from Our Own Wells*, 29–30

AN ACCEPTABLE TIME OF LIBERATION

Our increasingly clear awareness of the harsh situation in Latin America and the sufferings of the poor must not make us overlook the fact that the harshness and suffering are not what is truly new in the present age. What is new is not wretchedness and repression and premature death, for these, unfortunately, are ancient realities in these countries. What is new is that the people are beginning to grasp the causes of their situation of injustice and are seeking to release themselves from it. Likewise new and important is the role that faith in the God who liberates is playing in the process. It can be said without exaggeration that we are experiencing an exceptional time in the history of Latin America and the life of the church. Of this situation we may say with Paul: "Now is the acceptable time; see, now is the day of salvation" (2 Cor. 6:2). Such a vision does not make the journey of the poor less difficult nor does it gloss over the obstacles they encounter in their efforts to defend their most elementary rights. The demanding, cruel reality of wretchedness, exploitation, hostility, and death — our daily experience — will not allow us to forget it. The question is not of a naive optimism but rather of a deep trust in the historical power of the poor and, above all, a firm hope in the Lord.

These attitudes do not guarantee a better future; but as they draw nourishment from a present that is full of possibilities, they in turn nourish the present with promises. So true is this that if we do not respond to the demands of the present, because we do not know in advance where we may be led, we are simply refusing to hear the call of Jesus Christ. We are refusing to open to him when he knocks on the door and invites us to dine with him (Rev. 3:20).

We are experiencing a time of solidarity in Latin America. Throughout the continent there is a growing movement of solidarity in defense of human rights and, in particular, the rights of the poor: in Nicaragua, El Salvador, Guatemala, and Bolivia; also of those who have been exiled or have disappeared in Haiti, Uruguay, Chile, Argentina, Paraguay, and other countries. At the grassroots and local levels there has been a proliferation of groups and organizations dedicated to solidarity among and with the dispossessed. The ease with which the popular sectors move from the local to the Latin American scene is impressive. This is the first flowering, at the continental level, of what José María Arguedas called "the fellowship of the wretched." The anonymous heroes involved in these efforts are countless, and the generosity poured out in them is beyond measure.

The word "solidarity" has been used among the poor of the Latin American continent for the action that follows upon their new awareness of their situation of exploitation and marginalization, as well as of the role they must play in the building of a new and different society. For Christians this action is an efficacious act of charity, of love for neighbor and love for God in the poor. Christians thus realize that the question is not simply one of personal attitudes. The issue is the solidarity of the entire ecclesial community — the church — with movements of the poor in defense of their rights. This accounts for the rise of many groups whose purpose is not simply to practice solidarity themselves but also to help the church as a whole to bear witness to, and to live up to, its proclamation of the reign of God.

The present is also a time of prayer. Base-level ecclesial communities exemplify the intense and hope-filled prayer going on in Latin America. Yet the forecasters of doom and failure, those of the type who at the beginning of the Second Vatican Council John XXIII spoke of as "prophets of gloom," have been claiming that the life of prayer is vanishing from Latin America. Latin Americans at the base level have a completely different experience. This wealth and intensity of prayer is more than great milestones in the journey of a people, but above all is the daily practice of humble prayer in numberless localities. Nowhere in the Latin American church is more fervent and joyous prayer to be found amid daily suffering and struggle than in the Christian communities among the poor. It is our acts of gratitude and hope in the Lord that make us free (Gal. 5:1).

For many, a growing maturity in their solidarity with the commitment to liberation has, by a dialectical process, brought a new emphasis on prayer as a fundamental dimension of Christian life. The result has been a mighty development of prayer in popular Christian groups. Daily experience, and even the result in writings among a people for whom oral expression is the dominant kind, are proof that prayer is widespread and creative.

It is a time of solidarity and a time of prayer — but also, and in a sense synthesizing those two, a time of martyrdom as well. There are many who have devoted their lives, to the point of suffering death, in order to bear witness to the presence of the poor in the Latin American world and to the preferential love that God has for them.

What did the contemporaries of the early martyrs think about the events of their time? Perhaps the complexity of the factors in any historical situation, their own closeness to the events, and even their lack of personal courage prevented them from seeing the significance of occurrences that today seem so clearly to have been heroic testimonies to faith in the Lord. It is a fact that a consensus with regard to what is happening before our eyes is always more difficult to reach; this is because present events, unlike those of the past, are not situated in a world that we regard as idyllic and that we envelop in golden legends. Present events form part of our own universe and demand of the individual a personal decision, a rejection of every kind of complicity with executioners, a straightforward solidarity, and uncompromising denunciation of evil, a prayer of commitment.

But the poor are not fooled; they see the truth and speak out when others remain silent. They see in the surrender of these lives a profound and radical testimony of faith; they observe that in a continent where the powerful spread death in order to protect their privileges, such a testimony to God often brings

the murder of the witness; and they draw nourishment from the
hope that sustains these lives and these deaths. According to the
very earliest Christian tradition the blood of martyrs gives life
to the ecclesial community, the assembly of the disciples of Jesus
Christ; it is happening in Latin America. Fidelity unto death is
a wellspring of life. It signals a new, demanding, and fruitful
course in following Jesus.

The new way is not entirely new. The present-day Latin
American experience of martyrdom bids us all turn back to one
of the major sources of all spirituality: the blood-stained experience of the early Christian community, which was so weak in
the face of the imperial power of that day.

The questions and crises of Latin America represent a road
that must be traveled and a price that must be paid for the sake
of what is fundamental: the recognition of the time of salvation in which these countries are now living. In Psalm 42 the
psalmist's prayer is not turned nostalgically to the past, for such
nostalgia would mean attachment to our own feelings rather
than to God. The psalmist says:

> Why are you cast down, O my soul,
>   and why are you disquieted within me?
> Hope in God; for I shall again praise him,
>   my help and my God....
> O send out your light and your truth;
>   let them lead me:
> let them bring me to your holy hill
>   and to your dwelling.
> Then I will go to the altar of God,
>   to God my exceeding joy;
> and I will praise you with the harp,
>   O God, my God. (Ps. 42:11; 43:3–4)

The "I shall again give him praise" is already a present reality.
The Latin American church is passing through an unparalleled
period of its history. The concrete and efficacious commitment
of so many Christians to the poorest and most disinherited, as

well as the serious difficulties they encounter in their commitment to solidarity, are leaving a profound mark on the history of Latin America. The attitude of those who believe they can continue to rely on the support of the church for maintaining their privileges is changing, but so is the attitude of those who were beginning to look upon the church as an institution belonging to the past. We are not now in the evening of the history of the church but are beginning the new day of opportunity for evangelization that we never had before.

To some all this may smack of simplistic and naive optimism. True enough, the exhaustion produced by an unending situation of wretchedness, the tensions caused by the resistance men and women must engage in if they are to win out in their commitment to liberation, the depression felt at the abiding attitude of suspicion that greets every effort at effective solidarity with an exploited people, the resistance experienced within the people of God itself — these facts do not permit an easy optimism or allow us to forget the marginalization, the suffering, the deaths. However, we must be aware of the change that has taken place. Despite — or thanks to — the immense price that is being paid, the present situation is nourishing new life, revealing new paths to be followed, and providing reason for profound joy.

The unconditional generosity (sometimes accompanied by the giver's own blood) that has been shown in Latin America in recent years is making its nations fruitful and is confronting the ecclesial community with a demanding, but most promising moment in its history. In the faces and hands of the dispossessed the Lord is knocking, and knocking loudly, on the community's door. By feeding the hope of the poor the church will be accepting the banquet to which the Lord of the kingdom invites us. The question is, Do we know how to make use of that opportunity?

Solidarity, prayer, and martyrdom add up to a time of salvation and judgment, a time of grace and stern demand — a time, above all, of hope.

— We Drink from Our Own Wells, 23–25

TOWARD A NEW SPIRITUALITY

Latin America lives with questions and varied perspectives, with impasses and new pathways, with suffering and hope. For this reason it is also becoming the crucible in which a new and different way of following Jesus is being developed. Different means proper to Latin America and shaped by the real experiences of the Latin American countries.

In these countries the pain that is felt at the wretchedness of the poor and the atrocities to which they are subjected, but also the love of God that burns especially in those who have given their lives out of love for their brothers and sisters, have become a fire that consumes — and fuses — the disparate elements of our Latin American reality and our Latin American history. From this action — which is only apparently destructive, inasmuch as in it a basically creative work is also being accomplished — there is emerging the "gold refined by fire" (Rev. 3:18) of a new spirituality. If we reject this and if we are not willing to be thus consumed, along with our weapons and our baggage, we remain bogged down in what is secondary and anecdotal and perhaps even in the deformity and perversity that marks what is happening in Latin America. We prefer a selfish inertia to constancy, illusion to hope, the honor of worldly trappings to a profound fidelity to the church, fads to the truly new, authoritarianism to moral authority and service, a tranquilizing past to a challenging present. In short, we prefer mammon to the God of Jesus Christ.

                          — *We Drink from Our Own Wells*, 25–26

THE SONG OF THE POOR

What we are confronted with is a foreign land, a passage through a desert, testing and discernment. But in this same land, from which God is not absent, the seeds of a new spirituality can germinate. This spirituality gives rise to new songs to the

Lord, songs filled with an authentic joy because it is spirituality that is nourished by the hope of a people familiar with the suffering caused by poverty and contempt.

The present experience of Latin American Christians is one that has been given profound expression in the psalms. Trusting as he does in the Lord who is "a stronghold for the oppressed" (Ps. 9:9), the psalmist is able to proclaim:

> I will give thanks to the Lord with my whole heart;
> I will tell of all your wonderful deeds.
> I will be glad and exult in you;
> I will sing praise to your name, O Most High.
>
> (Ps. 9:1–2)

Because he is sure that the Lord "loves righteousness and justice" (Ps. 33:5), the psalmist can sing:

> Rejoice in the Lord, O you righteous.
> Praise befits the upright.
> Praise the Lord with the lyre;
> make melody to him with the harp of ten strings.
> Sing to him a new song;
> play skillfully on the strings, with loud shouts.
>
> (Ps. 33:1–3)

We are living in an acceptable time in which the Lord says: "Listen! I am standing at the door, knocking; if you hear my voice and open the door, I will come in to you and eat with you, and you with me" (Rev. 3:20). Not a violent entrance but a quiet knock that calls for an attitude of welcome and active watchfulness, of confidence and courage. Indifference, privileges, and fear make many persons spiritually deaf; as a result, the Lord passes by without stopping at their houses. But there are also many in these times who hear the Lord's call and try to open the doors of their lives. We are living in a special period of God's saving action, a time when a new route is being carved out for following Jesus.

— We Drink from Our Own Wells, 19–20

Part Three

The Challenge of
the Kingdom:
Living in the Spirit

15

Announcing the Kingdom

The following reflections come from Gustavo's book Sharing
the Word through the Liturgical Year. *They are his homily
reflections for the last Sunday in Ordinary Time, the Feast of
Christ the King, which stresses the universal rule of Jesus in
the kingdom he came to establish. This kingdom is a gift, not
simply a human achievement. It begins in history, where God is
present and active. To accept the gift of the kingdom requires
commitment to the task of justice and life-giving liberation.
Proclaiming this Gospel is integrally related to building a just
society.*

THE KINGDOM OF GOD
AND ETERNAL LIFE

Jesus' preaching, beginning in the fifth chapter of Matthew with
the beatitudes, concludes now by reminding us of what is essential in the conduct of the disciples. The Son of Man (Matt.
25:31), the king (v. 34), will come to judge the nations. His
kingdom is not a kingdom of power but of service: "The Son of
Man came not to be served but to serve" (Matt. 20:28). This
is the criterion for judgment. Entering into the kingdom, definitive life, eternal life presupposes that disciples have followed the

path of the master in serving all people and especially those with the greatest need.

Eternal life is not limited to what is beyond human history. It is not only future life, it is eternal life. That means life of all times, including the present. The demands of the kingdom lead to giving life now: giving food, something to drink, etc. These actions must express the grace that God has given us in giving his own life. The preferred addressees are the least and the most forgotten. Here Matthew uses the same term he uses to refer to Bethlehem (2:6), the insignificant city from which the Messiah comes. In this sense, all the poor and forgotten people are insignificant like Bethlehem, yet from them, the Lord comes to us. This is why the text is telling us that in serving the poor we are serving the Christ of our faith and that in solidarity with the neediest we recognize the humble kingship of the Son of Man. There is no other way to "inherit the kingdom" (25:34), that is to say, be face to face with the Lord.

— *Sharing the Word*, 265–66

THE SOCIAL AND HISTORICAL DIMENSIONS OF THE GOSPEL

God's judgment is not confined to the realm of the individual. Commenting on this text in Matthew (25:31–46), John Paul II recalled its "social dimension," stating that he was "referring to the total universal dimension of injustice and of evil." He concluded with these severe warnings: "In the light of Christ's words, the poor South will judge the opulent North. And poor people and poor nations — poor in different ways, not only lacking food but also deprived of freedom and of other rights — will be judging those who snatch away their possessions, accumulating for themselves the imperialist monopoly of economic and political predominance at the expense of others" (in Namao, Canada, September 7, 1984, no. 54). The Lord and the poor of our country have much to say about the indifference, the frivolity, and the subtle cruelty of those who accumulate for themselves the goods they take away from others.

The Son of Man is king. He is also a shepherd, and he will look after his sheep (Ezek. 34). His reign of service is here and now an expression of his victory over death (1 Cor. 15). Believing that God has communicated his own life to us does not take us out of history. On the contrary, it makes us assume it fully because what is definitive is judged by what is transitory.

—*Sharing the Word*, 266–67

THE KINGSHIP OF CHRIST

The core of Jesus' message is the kingdom of God. The God of Jesus Christ is the God of the kingdom, the one who is involved in human history from which the image of kingdom is taken. The God of the Bible cannot be separated from his plan, the kingdom. Central in the synoptic Gospels, the theme of the kingdom does not present itself in the same way in John. In his Gospel, the focus of the theme is on the kingship of Christ.

This is what we have in John 18:33–37. Echoing the accusation of Jesus, Pilate asks Jesus: "Are you the King of the Jews?" (v. 33). The accused prepares his answer with a previous question, which shakes the Roman official's ground: "Do you ask this on your own, or did others tell you about me?" (v. 34). Pilate's arrogance does not intimidate Jesus, who then gives his own answer in the well-known words: "My kingdom is not from this world" (v. 36). Jesus gives the reason: my kingdom does not use coercion, it is not imposed. The idea is repeated: "my kingdom is not from this world."

We can easily fall into the temptation of interpreting this statement as a reference to a kingdom on an exclusively religious and spiritual level, with little or no influence in the temporal realm, in concrete history. However, such an interpretation does not correspond to the Gospel as a whole. An earlier text from John can help us understand the present text. In chapter 8, in the middle of a harsh controversy with the Pharisees, Jesus tells them: "I am not of this world" (8:23). The terms in the original Greek language are exactly the same. There is a distance and even a rupture, and Jesus wants to point it out. However, it is not between what is religious and temporal but rather between domination and service. Jesus' kingdom is unlike the one that Pilate knows, a kingdom of arbitrariness, privileges, and domination. Jesus' kingdom is a kingdom of love, justice, and service.   — *Sharing the Word*, 267–68

AUTHENTIC KINGSHIP

Pilate is astute and he is not misled. He does not see in Jesus' answer a denial of his kingship. He infers and insists: "So you are a king?" (18:37). The Lord accepts without hedging: "You say that I am a king. For this I was born, and for this I came into the world": to inaugurate a world of peace and fellowship, of justice and respect for other people's rights, of love for God and for one another. This is his kingdom, which comes into human history, enhancing it and leading it beyond itself, a kingdom that will have no end, though it is present as of now; it is not only for the future, "his dominion is everlasting" (Dan. 7:14). It is not limited to the past, to the present, or to the future. In the Lord's Prayer, we ask for this kingdom to come in its fullness.

Jesus bears witness to that truth. He gives testimony of the will to love of the Father whose reign "is everlasting" as the prophet Daniel announces (7:14). If we listen to the voice of Jesus, we belong to the truth (John 18:37), we are made to "be a kingdom" (Rev. 1:6). Jesus and the kingdom he proclaims are the ultimate meaning of our lives, "the Alpha and the Omega," (v. 8), "the beginning and the end."   — *Sharing the Word*, 268

THE RULE OF LOVE AND SERVICE, NOT DOMINATION

Jesus is condemned to death for claiming he is a king. This is what his accusers are saying and Jesus himself admits it to Pilate, the representative of the king (the Roman emperor) whose armies are occupying Palestine and oppressing its inhabitants (Luke 23:1–3). Jesus' status as "the King of the Jews" is found in the inscription on the upper part of the cross (Luke 23:38). It is in stark contrast with the physical situation of the man nailed on the cross. Is this a king? Of what kingdom?

The people who had been listening to Jesus' preaching are looking at the crucified one in bewilderment and perhaps consternation. The officials (literally the leaders) who had been challenged by his teaching are scoffing at him now; they are enjoying their victory. The one who had presented himself as the Savior is not able to save himself. They were thinking that this would discredit him before the crowd (vv. 35–38). Once again, they had misunderstood. But we too run the risk of misunderstanding — affirming, for example, that Jesus admits he is the king of a purely spiritual realm without any connection with this world. The kingdom of God, which the Messiah announces, is a universal reality from which no one escapes. In a beautiful christological canticle, Paul tells us that "all things have been created through him and for him" (Col. 1:16).

Here the radical opposition is not between what is spiritual and temporal, religious and historical. Rather, it is between the power by domination and the power of service. Jesus is not a king like this world's kings who dominate and mistreat those who are under them. Jesus does not use his power for his own benefit, and this is precisely why he does not save himself. The Lord has come to teach us that all power (political, religious, or intellectual) is at the service of the oppressed and the destitute.

—Sharing the Word, 268–69

A KINGDOM OF SOLIDARITY

Service, not domination, is the great norm of the kingdom announced by the Lord. It is betrayed when we use whatever power we have received in order to impose our ideas and to preserve our privileges, for example, when as church people we take advantage of our situation in society to turn a deaf ear to the rights of people who do not share our faith. An attitude of service presupposes sensitivity to listen to others. That testimony alone will open hearts and minds to the proclamation of the kingdom of Christ. The attitude of Jesus, who never used his power to his own advantage, broke the hardness of one of the criminals with whom he was crucified (Luke 23:40–41). The Lord's testimony made him understand of what kingdom Jesus was king, of a kingdom that, from now on, in this world and in society, must change our way of perceiving things and relating with others. It must inspire us to incarnate the great values of the reign of God in our history.

In fact, we must not forget that the one in whom the Lord has made the "fullness of God" (Col. 1:19) dwell is the son of David (Mark 10:47), a man of our history, and, as Luke reminds us (23:6), a Galilean — a member, therefore, of a despised people. From that situation, the Lord is calling us to a kingdom of solidarity; he is calling us to be with him (Luke 23:43). — *Sharing the Word, 269–70*

16

Liberating the Poor

According to Luke 4, to liberate is to give life because Jesus is announcing the God of life. These selections come from Gustavo's book The God of Life, *which deals with the Lord's care for all, especially for those whose lives are most threatened. To be committed to the liberation of the poor means two things — solidarity with the poor and a protest against poverty. Real poverty means privation, or the lack of goods necessary to meet basic human needs, and early death. Above all, to be poor means to be insignificant. Poverty is an evil and always against the will of God. It is a subhuman condition in which the majority of humanity lives today, and it poses a major challenge to every Christian conscience and therefore to spirituality and theological reflection.*

THE MISSION OF THE MESSIAH

The Old Testament says that God gives life. Jesus Christ says the same in his preaching. In his Gospel, John emphasizes the point that "God so loved the world that he gave his only Son, so that everyone who believes in him may not perish but may have eternal life" (3:16). Jesus reveals himself as "the way, and the truth, and the life" (14:6). The theme of life is fundamental in the story told by John and by the New Testament as a whole. Jesus makes it the focus of his proclamation.

In a section of the Gospel of Luke that is very familiar to us (4:16–20) Jesus uses passages from the prophet Isaiah (61:1–2 and 58:6) to make a public statement of his mission. The text in question plays a role in the Gospel of Luke similar to that played by the exodus in the Old Testament. Both express God's will to set human beings free.

The Messiah states his mission as follows:

> The Spirit of the Lord is upon me,
>> because he has anointed me
>>> to bring good news to the poor.
> He has sent me to proclaim release to the captives
>> and recovery of sight to the blind,
>>> to let the oppressed go free,
> to proclaim the year of the Lord's favor.
>
> (Luke 4:18–19)

Luke takes advantage of the scene during the visit to Nazareth, which Matthew (13:53–58) and Mark (6:1–6) also report, to tell us of what the messianic work will consist; he also takes great care to show its universal scope. This work is not for the benefit solely of one nation among others; the covenant is now to be with all the nations of the earth. This is undoubtedly the reason why Luke omits from his citation of Isaiah 61 the second part of verse 2: "and the day of vengeance of our God," with its connotation of punishment for the pagans. The same universalist outlook appears a few verses later in the reference to Elijah and Elisha being sent to the gentiles (see Luke 4:25–27).

The various human situations mentioned (poverty, captivity, blindness, oppression) are manifestations of death. The preaching of Jesus, who has been anointed Messiah by the power of the Spirit, will cause death to withdraw by introducing a source of life that is meant to bring history to its fulfillment. This programmatic passage confronts us with the dilemma: death or life, which is central to biblical revelation and calls upon us to make a radical choice.

In Luke 4:18–19 the most important aspect is the proclamation of the good news to the poor, which is of primary importance in the Messiah's mission. The good news proclaimed to the poor can only be the news that they will cease to be poor and to suffer from poverty. The poor (Greek: *ptochoi*; the same word is used in Isa. 61:1 LXX) in Luke are clearly those who lack the necessities of life (see Luke 6:20; 7:22; 14:13–21; 16:20, 22; 18:22; 19:8; 21:3). It is to these that deliverance is proclaimed. The good news preached to them is given concrete form in the three statements that follow: release for captives, sight for the blind, and freedom for the oppressed. In all these instances we find one and the same proclamation, the dominant idea being freedom.

Even Luke's expression "sight to the blind" is a reference to freedom, for the literal meaning of the Hebrew text of Isaiah 61:1 is: "and to those in chains the opening of the eyes." The image the prophet uses for the emergence from the darkness of a prison clearly signifies a liberation (this is why the text of Isaiah is rightly translated: "and release to the prisoners"). But the Greek translation of the Old Testament (the Septuagint, LXX), which Luke is following, gives a figurative version; the metaphor in the Hebrew original, "opening of the eyes," is replaced by "recovery of sight," and "to those in chains" by "to the blind." The Greek translation thus drops the Hebrew text. If we go back to the latter, we recover the original meaning of the passage; "recovery of sight to the blind" must therefore likewise be understood in the perspective of liberation.

Luke replaces Isaiah's words "to bind up the brokenhearted" with "to let the oppressed go free," which is an expression taken from Isaiah 58:6. By including this promise, which in its Isaian context is accompanied by others of the same kind, Luke emphasizes the liberation aspect of the Messiah's programmatic statement.

> Is not this the fast that I choose:
> to loose the bonds of injustice,
> to undo the thongs of the yoke,
> to let the oppressed go free,
> and to break every yoke?
>
> (Isa. 58:6)

"Oppressed" translates a word derived from the Hebrew verb *rss*, which indeed means to oppress, but with the connotations of to crush, to grind down, to smash physically. The good news the Messiah proclaims to the poor is focused on liberation. This perspective is further underscored by the phrase "a year of favor from the Lord" or, in Luke, "a year acceptable to the Lord," which is also to be proclaimed. The reference is to the jubilee year, meant to be celebrated every fifty years; during this year "you shall return, every one of you, to your own property" (Lev. 25:13), because in the final analysis Yahweh alone owns the land (Lev. 25:23).

This jubilee clearly had to do with liberation: "You shall hallow the fiftieth year and you shall proclaim liberty throughout the land to all its inhabitants" (Lev. 25:10). By doing away with all unjust inequality, the year of the Lord's favor was meant to contribute to the permanent establishment of a fellowship among the members of the Jewish people and, in the final analysis, of communion with God. The list of the actions to be taken by the Messiah is thus clearly concerned with life and liberation.

The reign of God, which is a reign of life, is the ultimate meaning of human history, but its presence begins even now as a result of the concern of Jesus for the least regarded participants in this human history. The passage in Luke attests to this: "Today this scripture has been fulfilled in your hearing" (4:21). The word "today" is a key term in Lucan theology (2:11; 5:26), as it is in Deuteronomy; in Luke 4:21 the meaning is that the prophecy of Isaiah (the prophet most often cited in the Gospels) is fulfilled. This is the moment of integral liberation in Christ; therefore, in the person of Jesus the kingdom has become present in our midst (see Luke 17:21). But the life that he brings us is rejected by many.

Luke tells us that those who heard his sermon on this occasion wanted to throw him down from the top of the hill (4:28–30). The proclamation of the Gospel of liberation to the poor is not an easy task. The giving of life may bring death at the hands of those who have chosen death against life. The experience of many parts of the Latin American church in recent years bears eloquent testimony of this.

—*The God of Life*, 6–9

SPIRITUAL POVERTY
AND VOLUNTARY POVERTY

While the option for the poor is connected to material poverty, we can also understand poverty in two other senses: spiritual poverty and voluntary poverty. Spiritual poverty is not in the first instance detachment from the goods of this world; it is rather the unavoidable consequence of something more profound and significant: to place our lives in God's hands. The foremost biblical text (but not the only one) is: "Blessed are the poor in spirit" (Matt. 5:3). Spiritual poverty is a synonym for "spiritual infancy," and it is a criterion for the conduct of a disciple of Christ. There are two metaphors — the first deriving from a social situation, the other from the age of the person — which when placed in a spiritual context manifests what our relationship to God must be. Spiritual poverty feeds itself from the will of God, as Jesus does, according to the Gospel of John.

Material goods are necessary for human life, but priorities must be established. The message of the passage is qualified in a somewhat ambiguous way as abandonment to Providence (Matt. 6:25–32), but it is more a call to liberty: "But strive first for the kingdom of God and his righteousness, and all these things will be given to you as well" (Matt. 6:33). It is a vital condition of spiritual poverty.

Many people of the world live in real, material poverty and social insignificance; their situation is not simply a matter of economics. Poverty is a complex reality with many different players; in the frame of theological reflection in Latin America and the Caribbean we talk about the social insignificance and marginalization and unrecognized basic human rights as well. A person can be insignificant because of economics, race, gender, culture, ethnicity, or other reasons.

Poverty is also a condition that has numerous human causes: social structures and mental categories. Solidarity with the poor is not limited to direct assistance to the poor; it must also manifest a commitment to eliminate the root causes of poverty. This perspective was slow to make its way into the social magisterium of the Catholic Church, but it has been evident in the past few decades.

The ultimate instance of real poverty and disrespect of the human dignity of every person made in the image of God is early death; it is prevalent and unjust, and it represents a serious challenge. Archbishop Oscar Romero denounced this situation, which Medellín and Puebla called "inhumane" and "against the Gospel," and for this he was accused of advocating social conflict. This solidarity with the poor requires a denunciation of the condition in which they live, as well as its causes.

Spiritual poverty and a commitment to alleviating real poverty are profoundly related and cannot be separated. Out of spiritual poverty — a condition of the disciples who dedicate their lives to service of the kingdom and a search for God's will — is the attitude of detachment, or freedom from the material goods of the world, for the true disciples realize that where one's treasure resides is also where the heart abides (Matt. 6:21). Spiritual poverty calls us "to be poor," Romero said, "and become involved in the poverty of our people as if they were our own family."

Voluntary poverty is a way of life. Spiritual poverty and voluntary poverty are united in the expression "preferential option for the poor." The word "preferential" has, as one of its primary sources, the phrase of John XXIII: "the church for everyone and in particular the poor." "Preferential" reminds us that God loves all people, but his first love is the forgotten and oppressed, the poor. Universality and preference are both present in the Christian message. The phrase "preferential" is new, but its content is very old and requires simply opening the Bible to find it. Karl Barth, a good Gospel reader, said: "God always favors the poor and [is] against the rich."

If it is preferential, it is not, by definition, exclusive. Preference and universality are in tension, not in contradiction, as prayer and action are not contradictory, but are in tension. The preferential option says that "the poor are first." "Priority" or "privileged" could be substituted for "preferential." They are similar expressions. Most important is not to lose sight of either the universality of God's love nor that the weakest and insignificant come first. To live these two poverties implies a conversion. Each Christian, and the whole church, must convert.

A church for the poor is a church that makes its own the practice of Jesus, that makes memory of him in the Eucharist and service, that communicates through the languages of gratuity and justice, prophecy and mysticism, and that lives spiritual poverty and a commitment to the poor, two basic conditions so that the testimony we give of the coming of the kingdom is authentic.   — "Close to God, Close to the Poor," *Páginas* 220 (December 2010): 12–14

17

Walking in the Spirit

In recent decades, one of the most painful dimensions of the Latin American church has been the number of lay people, priests, nuns, and bishops who have been assassinated because of their solidarity with the poor. These assassinations have been occurring especially since the Episcopal Conference at Medellín (1968). Neither the conferences at Puebla (1979) nor Santo Domingo (1992) spoke explicitly about Latin American martyrdom, but at Aparecida (2007), the church began speaking explicitly about martyrdom. The following text from a forthcoming book by Gustavo speaks about how following Christ led, for some, to offering their lives for the people they served, loving them until the end.

The backbone of the preferential option for the poor, for the socially insignificant, is what Paul calls "walking according to the Spirit" (Rom. 8:4). Following Jesus nourishes commitment with the poor, giving it deep roots and opening it to fertile places of creativity. This does not deny that there are other reasons to take up this option; it simply locates the option in the liberating and humanizing project of the Gospel. Spirituality, with its primary place in theological reflection, has tried to illuminate the world of the poor in Latin America and the

Caribbean. This spirituality is constantly nourished by testimonies from Christian people and communities who seek to live according to the Christian message.

The gratuitous and demanding love of God expressed in the testimony of Jesus provides a model for human behavior: "Whoever says, 'I abide in him,' ought to walk just as he walked" (1 John 2:6). God's love, from which no one is excluded, at the same time gives preference to the forgotten in history, the oppressed and insignificant: "So the last will be first, and the first will be last" (Matt. 20:16). Living this double dimension of the love of God, its universality and its preference, gives substance to the option for the poor in walking with Jesus, the Messiah, and makes present the mystery hidden since the beginning of time and revealed by him (Rom. 16:25–34).

Solidarity with the least of our society takes on different forms, each with its own demands, joys, and faltering steps, and reveals a new presence of God in our lives. The option for the poor has, at its heart, a spiritual element and the mystical quality of gratuity that gives it depth and fertility. It not only reinforces the social aspect of solidarity with the poor but also it rejects injustice and oppression. Nor is it a shortsighted spiritualization that ignores the historical and human dimensions of life. It stresses the scriptural injunctions that direct all that comes into play in our commitment with others.

The Latin American and Caribbean people, predominantly poor and faithful at the same time, live in the heart of a situation that excludes them and mistreats them and from which they seek liberation in the God of life. Our late friends Victor and Irene Chero gave voice to the poor in Peru when they said to John Paul II on his 1985 visit to the country, "Our hearts break with pain as we see our wives infected with tuberculosis, our children die or grow up debilitated and without a future," to which they added, "but despite all this we believe in the God of life." This is the context and the vital reality that a reflection of faith cannot avoid; it must rather be continuously nourished by it.

THE SIGN OF MARTYRDOM

Following Jesus addresses the question of the meaning of human existence and offers criteria with which to establish priorities that correlate with the Good News (the "treasure" according to Matt. 6:21). This process calls for a permanent change of mind and heart. The option for the poor as a component of spirituality implies conversion. Conversion is a prerequisite, according to the Gospels, for embracing the kingdom by following in the footsteps of Jesus (Mark 1:15). This demand is not limited to the personal realm; it embodies the church as a whole.[1] Only a church in the humble process of permanent conversion will be able to be a sign and symbol of the kingdom in changing times.

Hostility and a lack of understanding are among the overt and subtle challenges that the path of discipleship entails. These are not sought out for their own sake, but they also should not be avoided or feared, for to fear or avoid hardships threatens personal fidelity and integrity. The challenges faced by many in the church of Latin America and the Caribbean are what Dietrich Bonhoeffer described as the "cost of discipleship."

To be on the side of the forgotten, to participate in what Pius XI called the "fight for justice," worries the world's powerful. In remote places of our country, many offer their lives daily amid intimidation and suspicion. Their commitment is reflected in those gestures toward the poor that help us find Jesus. The denunciation of injustice and oppression is anchored in faith in the God of life. In some cases this commitment has been sealed by the blood of those who sought to be in solidarity with the poor and insignificant, and, as Archbishop Romero said, they have died with "the symbol of martyrdom." Archbishop Romero is now counted among them, and there were many others. They are all privileged witnesses of the Gospel,

---

1. "We affirm the need for conversion on the part of the whole church to a preferential option for the poor, an option aimed at their integral liberation" (Puebla, no. 1134).

of hope, and, above all, of the paschal joy that comes from following Christ.

In a reflection on spirituality in Latin America and the Caribbean, we cannot avoid the cruel contradiction revealed by martyrdom on a continent that claims to be Christian. Aparecida remembers those who "though not canonized, have lived out the Gospel radically, and have offered their life for Christ, for the church, and for their people" (Aparecida, no. 98).

Martyrdom is a testimony of faith in Christ, an offering of one's life for one's deepest beliefs. In the same way, love and service to others also is a form of martyrdom.

The intent here is not to surreptitiously introduce a social or political element into the language of religion. Instead, it is to highlight a way of understanding Christian faith, faith in the Son of God, who became one of us, who took on our flesh, and whom we must encounter in history, especially among the forgotten and marginalized. This is the meaning, "for the people," which Oscar Romero affirmed with all its clarity, as did Enrique Angelelli and Juan Gerardi, bishops close to their people, and who remain close to us in memory and friendship. This is also the case of many companions who gave their lives in witness — sisters, laypeople, priests.

This spirituality — precisely because it has the option for the poor as an essential component — is not a kind of oasis amid everyday commitments or a refuge from difficulties and conflicts. "Holiness — Benedict XVI would say at Aparecida — is not a flight toward self-absorption or religious individualism, nor does it mean abandoning the enormous economic, social, and political problems of Latin America and the world, let alone is it a flight from reality toward an exclusively spiritual world" (Aparecida, no. 148). Instead, amid arduous challenges, a profound joy comes from following Jesus, a joy that radiates love that is given and received.

IMITATING JESUS CHRIST

In this spirituality, encountering the poor means encountering Christ. Following Jesus is not about a literal imitation of Jesus; it is discipleship that is permanent, creative, and inspired by his life. To follow in Jesus' footsteps without detaching ourselves from the social injustice faced by many of our brothers and sisters is to travel the sidewalks along which the poor of this world circulate, helping us to keep hope alive and maintain tranquility when storms arise.

Spirituality means conforming our lives to the life and practice of Jesus Christ. Jesus reveals the love of God in his preaching of the kingdom in both words and deeds. To continue to proclaim that the kingdom of God has come is to bring the works and words of Jesus Christ into the present. This is what the life of the Christian entails: to "do the will of the Father," as opposed to simply saying "Lord, Lord" (Matt. 7:21; Jer. 7:1–7). Spirituality does not deal with an isolated slice of human existence but rather the entirety of Christian life with all its complexity. Discipleship provides goals that lead us to walk in communion with other people, especially with the poorest and those in most need. Contemplation and solidarity are the two aspects of a life animated by an overall sense of existence that is the source of faith and joy. Both contemplation and solidarity are translated into good works, attitudes, gestures, and commitments, signs, according to the Gospel of John, that communicate an option of life.

Faith is not only an intellectual assent to a given message; it is the vital reception and the putting into practice of the Gospel message in everyday life and conduct. The Gospel in practice is not simply the application of clearly defined principles or previously elaborated doctrine; it is the terrain where we experience God and a commitment in history. It is the terrain of the discernment of faith and freedom and the innovative commitment to embark upon the path of following Jesus until the Holy Spirit "guides us into all truth" (John 16:13). This perspective has nothing to do with a reductive pragmatism but is rather a conduct moved by grace.

The term "following" implies that spirituality is a path on which people gain maturity and depth. The image of a road allows us to talk about the steps made in good time or even accelerated, but also slow steps with detours and stumbling along the way, and times of uncertainty and loneliness as one tries to find one's way. When this spiritual process is lived out in the heart of a people challenged by the suffering of the innocent, there arise painful perplexities that center on the perceived distance and even absence of the God of our faith (Jer. 15:18; Lam. 3:20–24). The spirituality of the poor of Latin America, located on a historic path that includes successes and failures, has deep roots and profound hope.

— "A Lifestyle," unpublished manuscript

18

Sharing the Table

A crucial part of sharing for Gutiérrez is recognizing "the other," acknowledging not simply differences but the equality and dignity each person has as a child of God. The story of the multiplication of the loaves and fishes is mentioned twice in both Matthew and Mark and once in both Luke and John. Though some spiritualize this narrative, here the people are not hungry for more preaching but are hungry for food, a basic, physical need. In these texts Gutiérrez brings out Jesus' concern for physical as well as spiritual needs. This story also reminds us that it is possible to give from almost nothing; physical hunger is satisfied with a few fish and a little bread, and dignity is affirmed by offering simply a seat at the meal.

SHARING FROM OUR POVERTY

The biblical story of the multiplication of the loaves and fishes reveals much about the spirituality of Jesus, and it teaches us what we must incorporate into our lives if we are to walk in his footsteps. The mission of Jesus introduces this sharing, which is part of the work of the Holy Spirit, who will "be with us forever" and is "another Advocate" (John 14:16–17). For John the truth is acted out; it is manifested in concrete works of fraternity and fellowship (John 3:21).

The story of multiplying the bread and fish has a Eucharistic tone. This story made an impression on the disciples as it is the only miracle of Jesus that appears in all four Gospels. They understood this act of Jesus to be the essence of the kingdom: communion with Christ and connection among human beings, communion and connection built through and expressed by sharing. This is evidenced in John 6:1–15 as well as in the other versions of the story.

Jesus looks at the people who have followed him and been nourished by his word for hours and expresses concern about the tired and hungry "sheep without shepherd," who are mostly slaves, poor and insignificant. He instructs the apostles to give the people something to eat. At that time he is referring to physical hunger, empty stomachs, to say it bluntly. Philip, speaking the obvious, responds by saying that they do not have money to buy food for so many people. Andrew notes that a little boy has five loaves of barley and two fish, a quantity of food absolutely insufficient for so many people.

Jesus is not hindered by monetary problems; he rejects the possibility that a lack of money will prevent them from feeding the crowd and the warning that what little they have is insufficient. The central point is not a matter of the amount of the resources; this story hinges upon Jesus' teaching that we must learn to give in our poverty. Three times in the story it is noted that the crowd is asked to sit down (vv. 10–11). The Lord takes the few loaves that are offered, gives thanks, and distributes them to the people along with the fish (v. 11). The text never mentions multiplication (this comes from an implied and understood mathematical deduction), but there is plenty for everyone. The crowd's physical hunger has been satiated. The love that inspired the act went beyond the need, even to the point of providing leftovers. This act of Jesus is recognized as a prophetic sign (v. 14).

The story highlights the importance of sharing, even from one's minimal resources; it goes beyond multiplication. The focus of the story is communion with God and among people.

The Eucharist is precisely an expression of love and creation of community with Jesus and among ourselves.

SHARING AND FRIENDSHIP

Only in a world in which everyone has already eaten will we be able to find each other completely and live in fraternity; a utopia, in the best and original sense of the term, consistent with the Gospel, able to change history. Physical hunger must be assuaged and the thirst for dignity and equality quenched. "I do not call you servants any longer.... I have called you friends," says Jesus to his followers and then the reason for this new situation: "because I have made known to you everything that I have heard from my Father" (John 15:15). Jesus has shared his message and offered his friendship; the crowd listened and accepted his word in deep communion.

Friendship is fundamental in the Gospels, particularly in John; it implies respect for the other, equality, and dignity among people. The sabbath and jubilee perspectives lead us to consider everybody brothers and sisters, particularly those who constantly experience violation of their right to life, health, and education. In a society corrupted by lies and characterized by a system that incorporates marginalization and oppression of the most vulnerable, the right to truth is also theirs. These are those whom the Pharisees call the "crowd, which does not know the law" and distinguish as "accursed" (John 7:49).

Love is always abundant, even overabundant. Twelve baskets were filled with leftover bread and fish. The number is significant (in Mark 8:19, Jesus highlights it by asking his disciples: How many baskets full of broken pieces did you collect?), and there is a general consensus that the reference is to the twelve tribes of Israel, the twelve apostles, the figure of God's people. The baskets, lying in the middle of the grass are an interpellation, a calling, to those who wish to follow in Jesus' footsteps, that they continue his works throughout history and build a community of discipleship. Those who are "part-ners" in the etymological sense of the word, "part-ake" in bread, or more precisely, eat from the same bread. It is this work that Paul references regarding the collection for the poor in the church in Jerusalem, testing "the genuineness of your love against the earnestness others" (2 Cor. 8:8). Sharing bread is the expression of God's love, it is the word of life, it is to "be guided by the Spirit" (Gal. 5:25).

Today, as the number of people who are excluded from the economy and who have nothing with which to sustain their lives continues to rise, the meaning of sharing has become particularly demanding. This situation calls for urgent actions of solidarity. The invitation to share is foundational in building a society without marginalization, where justice is established. This society must also be inclusive where no one remains outside and no one is missing. A society in which we share the table of life implies establishing justice. The table offers a welcome in which "the poor, the crippled, the blind and the lame" are all invited (Luke 14:21), the despised and dirty, the migrant, the "bad and good" (in this order, says Matt. 22:10 in the NAB). The priority of the option is directed toward all of these.

— "The Table of Life," *Páginas* 217 (March 2010): 6–10

19

Living the Beatitudes

Gutiérrez states that in Matthew the poor in spirit are the disciples. The disciple follows Jesus by loving the least and last ones. Matthew 25 brings out that the face of Jesus must be recognized in the faces of the poor. The rewards of the beatitudes will come to fullness in the kingdom but they begin now. Eternal life is not only future, it is present; it is not only after this life, but it begins in the present moment.

THE ETHICS OF THE KINGDOM

The beatitudes in Matthew are the Magna Carta of the church that is made up of the disciples of Jesus. Our following in his footsteps finds expression in actions toward our neighbor, especially the poor, in life-giving works; in these, love of God and love of neighbor are intertwined and call each for the other. We shall not be able to shed light on the question: "Where is God?" unless we are able to answer the Lord's challenge: "Where is your brother?" (Gen. 4:9). In this way we cause the kingdom to come, we cause the appointed time to arrive as the result of the free acceptance of God's gift. Acting "as free people" (1 Pet. 2:16), by our behavior we "wait for and hasten the coming of the day of God" (2 Pet. 3:12).

After Peter's first sermon, on Pentecost, with its focus on the death and resurrection of the Lord, his hearers spontaneously ask: "Brothers, what should we do?" Peter answers: "Repent" (Acts 2:37–38). The Gospels lay down this same requirement from the first moment of the proclamation of the kingdom. Conversion means a change of behavior, a different approach to life, the beginning of following Jesus.

Discipleship is a central theme of many of the actions and sayings of Jesus in the Gospel of Matthew. This characteristic of his Gospel is a key to understanding the meaning of his version of the beatitudes (Matt. 5:3–10). This difference between his version and Luke's (which is regarded by scholars as closer to the words of Jesus) is commonly attributed to his effort to "spiritualize" the beatitudes, in the sense that he allegedly takes statements that in Luke were a concrete, historical expression of the coming of the Messiah and turns them into purely interior, unincarnated dispositions.

I do not think this is the case. It is undeniable that the Gospel of Matthew is especially insistent on the need of concrete, material actions toward others and especially the poor (see Matt. 5:13–16; 7:15–23; and beyond a doubt, 25:31–46). The least that can be said is that this insistence is incompatible with an alleged Matthean spiritualism. The obvious contradiction between these two approaches would seem to be the result not of anything in Matthew but of applying to the first Gospel categories inconsistent with its real outlook.

The beatitudes open the section of the Gospel known as the Sermon on the Mount, a lengthy, polemical presentation of the new law in its relationship to the old. The sermon sets down the main ethical demands a Christian must meet. It does not limit itself to a wearisome reminder of the law in which "it was said" (see Matt. 5:21, 27, 31, 33, 38, 43), but puts the disciples on notice that they must continually seek new forms of loving others, fulfilling the new law: "I say to you." Continuity and newness. Jesus speaks with the full authority with which he is invested. An ethics that has its roots in the gratuitousness of God's love is always creative.

The righteousness in question, which "exceeds that of the scribes and Pharisees" (Matt. 5:20), is not limited to obeying precepts but draws its inspiration from an ever new and imaginative love. It leads us to the kingdom and makes the kingdom present even now in history. Kingdom and righteousness (gift and task) are the two key words that enable us to see the basic structure of the carefully constructed text that is the beatitudes. The first and last of these speak of the promise of the kingdom here and now (the other six beatitudes use the future tense). Each block of four beatitudes ends with the mention of righteousness or justice:

to the poor in spirit	belongs the *kingdom* of heaven
those who mourn	will be comforted
the meek	will inherit the earth
those who hunger and thirst for *righteousness*	will be filled
the merciful	will receive mercy
the pure in heart	will see God
the peacemakers	will be called children of God
to those who are persecuted for *righteousness*' sake	belongs the *kingdom* of heaven

The kingdom is the center of Jesus' message, the utopia that sets history in motion for Christians. Matthew speaks of the kingdom of heaven in order to avoid mentioning the name of God, out of a respect that is inborn in the Jewish mind. Righteousness or justice is a theme closely connected with that of the kingdom.

Matthew retains the richness and complexity of the term "justice" (righteousness) in the Bible. Justice is the work of God and therefore must also be the work of those who believe in God. It implies a relationship with the Lord, namely, holiness; and at the same time a relationship with human beings, namely, recognition of the rights of each person, especially of the despised and the oppressed; in other words, social justice. In a pithy summarizing statement that comes right in the middle of the sermon, Matthew says forcefully: "Strive first for the kingdom of God and his righteousness" (6:33).

The kingdom and its six specific descriptions are the reason for the happiness to which the beatitudes bear witness; in all of them this reason is clearly asserted: the people described are blessed or happy "because" the promise is fulfilled now and will be in the future. The gift of the Lord produces happiness in those who dispose themselves to receive it and who act accordingly. The beatitudes are clearly located in the dialectic of gift and demand.   — *The God of Life*, 118–20

DISCIPLESHIP AND THE BEATITUDES

A lot of ink has been lavished on the first beatitude. Matthew's addition "in spirit" has always been a subject of controversy. In both Matthew and Luke the word "poor" represents the Greek *ptochoi*. In Luke the persons referred to are — it is often said — poor in the literal, material sense. The Greek word used already points in this direction. Whom does Matthew have in mind when he adds "in spirit"?

In the biblical mind (and indeed the Semitic mind generally) the words "in spirit" are used to indicate a dynamism at work; the spirit is breath or vital force. It is something that manifests itself in knowledge, understanding, virtue, and decision-making. Spirit is the dynamic aspect of human existence. The addition of "in spirit" is often used in the Old Testament to change the original meaning of certain words, thereby giving them a figurative sense. For example, "lofty" or "high" describes a bodily condition, but the addition of "in spirit" as in "a haughty spirit" (Prov. 16:18) or "arrogance," directs our attention to a different human dimension. In like manner, "err in spirit" (Isa. 29:24) is to be understood as meaning that someone is on the wrong road; the strayer is a person who does not find the proper path.

The addition, in this context, suggests someone who does not observe the commandments of God.

"Poor in spirit" is an expression of that kind; it points to something more comprehensive than an attitude of detachment from material possessions. "In spirit" transforms an economic and social condition into a readiness to accept the word of God. This is a central theme in the biblical message: spiritual childhood. The reference is to living as people fully open to the will of God; to making God's will our food, as Jesus says in the Gospel of John. To be poor in spirit is to be a disciple of Christ.

It has been suggested that Matthew's text be translated: "Blessed are they who choose to be poor."[1] The purpose is to preclude the spiritualist interpretation. The intention is praiseworthy, but the translation is somewhat inadequate and leaves an ambiguity. The choice of poverty underscores a dynamic aspect of Christian life and of solidarity with the least important persons of history. However, spiritual poverty refers to a more comprehensive and more radical outlook than the acceptance of real poverty or the cultivation of an attitude of interior distance from material possessions.

Accepting poverty is indeed a manifestation of spiritual childhood, but discipleship is not limited to this. Discipleship means, above all, an openness to the gift of God's love and a preferential solidarity with the poor and oppressed; only in this context does it makes sense to choose a life of poverty. Real poverty is not a Christian ideal but a condition required today of those who seek to be in solidarity with the really poor, with the unimportant folk, those who lack the necessities of life that their dignity as human beings and children of God requires. Real poverty is, according to the Bible, an evil, a situation not intended by the God of life, an acceptance of means seeking to eliminate the injustice that causes the spoliation and mistreatment of the poor. This effort necessarily presupposes a

---

1. See the detailed study of Fernando Camacho, *La proclama del Reino* (Madrid: Cristiandad, 1987), who is following the lead given by Juan Mateos in his translation of the beatitudes in the Nueva Biblia Española.

solidarity with their hopes and interests, friendship with them, and sharing both their lives and their struggle for justice. This commitment and quest manifest an acceptance of God's will, and this acceptance in turn is the core of spiritual poverty or spiritual childhood; it is the essence of discipleship.

In the second beatitude ("blessed are those who mourn"; in some versions, this is the third beatitude) there is question of an affliction that causes one to weep. The suggestion is of suffering due to bereavement, catastrophe, or oppression (see 1 Macc. 1:25–27). Matthew uses a form of this verb to convey the feelings of the disciples regarding the presence of Jesus in their midst: "The wedding guests cannot mourn as long as the bridegroom is with them, can they?" (Matt. 9:15). Here it is the absence of the Lord that causes the disciples to mourn. They desire and wait for his bodily presence, as they do for the accomplishment of God's will and kingdom. Blessed, therefore, are they who do not resign themselves to having injustice and aggression prevail in the world; for, as Medellín says, "where . . . we find social, political, economic, and cultural inequalities, there will we find rejection of the peace of the Lord, and a rejection of the Lord himself" (*Peace*, no. 14).

They will be comforted. The Greek verb *parakalein*, "to console," takes us back to Second Isaiah: "The Lord has comforted his people, and will have compassion on his suffering ones" (Isa. 49:13). The comfort here connotes a liberation: the Hebrew verb translated by the Greek *parakalein* means literally that God will enable the people to give a deep sigh of relief (*naham*, to restore breathing); God will deliver them from Babylonian domination. Luke shows Jesus fulfilling the promise of consolation for Israel (see Luke 2:25). This will also be the mission of the Spirit, the Paraklete (Comforter), who "will guide" us "into all the truth" (John 16:13) and whose presence ensures our freedom (see 2 Cor. 3:17). Happy are they who have learned to share the sorrow of others, even to the point of weeping with them; for the Lord will comfort them, drying their tears and removing "the disgrace of his people . . . from all the earth" (Isa. 25:8; see Rev. 21:4).

The third beatitude ("blessed are the meek") is sometimes regarded as an elucidation of the first. The Hebrew words *'anaw* and *'ani* (both meaning "poor") are also translated by the Greek word *praeis* (used here), which means "humble, meek." The source of this Matthean beatitude seems to be Psalm 37:11: "The meek shall inherit the land." The emphasis in "meek" is on the ability to deal with others. The meek are those who are able to accept others; meekness, then, is a human quality (the Bible never speaks of the meekness of God). Even Jesus uses the term of himself: "Come to me, all you who labor and are burdened, and I will give you rest. Take my yoke upon you and learn from me, for I am meek and humble of heart" (Matt. 11:28–29, NAB). In another passage of Matthew, Jesus applies to himself the prophecy of Zechariah about the king who comes "meek and riding on an ass" (21:5, NAB). To be meek, then, is to be like the master.[2] As Romano Guardini aptly says, meekness is "not . . . weakness, but . . . strength become mild."[3]

To the meek is promised the land, which is the object of profound hope on the part of the Jewish people and conveys strong overtones of stability, of something permanently acquired. Land is the first description of the kingdom in the beatitudes, and in the Bible it clearly connotes life.[4] Even among us today, the promise of land continues to be a promise of life for so many peasants and aborigines who have for centuries been dislodged from their own land. To them the land is what Bishop Luis Dalle called "the place of communal brotherhood." In their struggle for land they find in the Bible a source of inspiration and in the kingdom a utopia that sets history in motion.

2. See Jacques Dupont, *Les Béatitudes* (Paris: Gabalda, 1973), 3:473–543. His analyses are an important source of what I say in these pages on the beatitudes.

3. Romano Guardini, *The Lord*, trans. E. C. Briefs (Chicago: Regnery, 1954), 70.

4. See Walter Brueggemann, *The Land: Place as Gift, Promise, and Challenge in Biblical Faith* (Philadelphia: Fortress, 1977).

The beatitude speaks of "inheriting" the land, and the same verb will be used in Matthew 25:34–35, where the kingdom is inherited by those who feed the hungry and give drink to the thirsty.

In the fourth beatitude appears the theme of justice or righteousness. The addition of "thirst" to "hunger" lends the statement a greater urgency. The object of this aching desire is justice or righteousness, both as a gift from God and a human task; it specifies the conduct required of those who want to be faithful to God. To be just means to recognize the rights of others, especially of those who are most destitute. To be just also supposes a relationship with God that can be described as holiness. Such is the behavior of the Lord (Isa. 11:4–5).

Justice done to the oppressed is an essential element of the messianic message. The establishment of what is right and just is the mission that God entrusts to the people and the task in which God is revealed as the God of life. Those who hunger and thirst for justice await it from God, but their waiting is not passivity; it implies a determination to bring about what they desire. Their desire — like "striving first for...righteousness" (see Matt. 6:33) — will be satisfied; this satisfaction will be an expression of the joy that the coming of the kingdom of love and justice produces.   — *The God of Life*, 120–24

THE MERCY OF GOD

The mercy of God is a favorite theme of Matthew and is a behavior required of the followers of Jesus. Matthew links this call with the Old Testament when he cites Hosea 6:6 (NIV): "I desire mercy, not sacrifice" (Matt. 9:13; 12:7). Matthew 25:31–46 describes the works of mercy and tells us that those who do these works will enter the kingdom of heaven. Those who refuse to practice solidarity with others will be rejected. The deciding point will be the practice of mercy. The beatitude in Matthew declares happy are those who will receive God's love, which is always a gift. But this gift demands that the recipients be merciful to others.

Who are the clean of heart? The common tendency to identify religion with interior and cloistered attitudes can make it difficult to understand the sixth beatitude. Psalm 51 puts us on solid ground here: "You desire truth in the inward being, therefore teach me wisdom in my secret heart.... Create in me a clean heart, O God, and put a new and right spirit within me" (vv. 6 and 10). Cleanness of heart presupposes sincerity, wisdom, and steadfastness; there is no question, therefore, of anything ritual or external. As Joel says, conversion means rending hearts, not clothing (Joel 2:12–13).

This interior attitude accounts for the disagreements between Jesus and the Pharisees. One of these has to do with cleanness of heart and ends with this clear statement: "For out of the heart come evil intentions, murder, adultery, fornication, theft, false witness, slander. These are what defile a person, but to eat with unwashed hands does not defile" (Matt. 15:19–20). In Matthew, "Pharisee" does not refer only to the historical enemies of Jesus; it also signifies misunderstanding fidelity to God and the commandments. Phariseeism consists of professing one thing and doing another, separating theory from practice, doctrine from everyday behavior. This is why Jesus calls these persons hypocrites. Matthew is trying to warn the disciples of Jesus not to succumb to a similar frame of mind.

The Letter of James twice rejects those who are "double-minded" (Greek: *dipsychos,* James 1:7–8, 4:8). Those who are of two minds cannot hope for anything from God; they are not steadfast in God's service because they have set their hearts partly on something or someone other than the Lord. The God of the Bible demands a complete surrender; to straddle the issue is to be an idolater. Matthew says: "No one can serve two masters; for a slave will...hate the one and love the other" (Matt. 6:24). If we are to draw near to God, we must cleanse our heart, unify our lives, and be single-minded. "You shall love the Lord your God with all your heart, and with all your soul, and with all your might," commands Deuteronomy (6:5), a text that Matthew repeats (Matt. 22:37). To be clean of heart, then, means not being double minded, not being a hypocrite. In the indigenous language of Peru the word for hypocrite is a person "of two hearts" (*iskat sonkko*). The reference is to a person who tries to do justice simultaneously to two loves, each of which because of its comprehensiveness and radicalness excludes the other. If we are to be disciples of the Lord, we must be consistent, like the master. Therefore the clean of heart, those who are whole, will see God "face to face," as Paul says (1 Cor. 13:12). This promise is a source of joy to the followers of Jesus.

Peacemaking is an essential task of Christians. But if we are to grasp the scope of "peacemaking" we must set aside a narrow view of peace as simply the absence of war or conflict. This is what the seventh beatitude calls upon us to do. The familiar Hebrew word *shalom* has a rich content.[5] The word refers to a state of wholeness and integrity, a condition of life that is in harmony with God, other people, and nature. *Shalom* is opposed to all that militates against the well-being and rights of persons and nations. In a denunciation of those who act unjustly, Jeremiah says: "For from the least to the greatest of them, everyone is greedy for unjust gain; and from prophet to priest, everyone deals falsely. They have treated the wound of my people carelessly, saying, 'Peace, peace' [*shalom, shalom*], when there is no peace [*shalom*]" (Jer. 6:13–14).

The real meaning of peace is the establishment of authentic justice and salvation, in this case for an entire people, and not the issuance of formal proclamations. The word "wound" translates a Hebrew word (see Jer. 8:10; Ezek. 22:27; Prov. 1:19) which signifies a life spent in quest of profit by means of oppression and theft. When Isaiah describes the Messiah as

---

5. The Septuagint reveals this rich complexity by using, without distinction, twenty-five words to translate *shalom*. On the wealth of meaning that the word has in the Bible as a whole, see Walter Brueggemann, *Living Toward a Vision* (New York: United Church Press, 1976).

"Prince of peace," the words he uses are "Prince of *shalom*"; the Messiah brings wholeness of life.

Justice and peace are closely linked in the Bible. "Righteousness and peace [*shalom*] will kiss" (Ps. 85:10). Both are denied to the poor and oppressed; therefore they are meant especially for those robbed of life and well-being (Ps. 72). Peace must be actively sought and established; the text refers to *makers* of peace and not to what is usually meant by "peaceful" and "pacifists."

Medellín points out quite aptly that peace is not found; it is built. All Christians, and especially those in Latin America, must resist personal and collective injustice with unselfish courage and fearlessness. The peaceful can fight for life and justice. Those who build this peace — which implies being attuned to God and God's will in history, as well as a wholeness of life, both personal (health) and social (justice) — "will be called children of God"; such is the title of the followers of him who has sent the Spirit to enable us to say: "Abba! Father" (Gal. 4:6). Children of God is the "new name" that, according to one of the letters to the seven churches, is inscribed on the "white stone" that those faithful to the Lord will receive as an identification (see Rev. 2:12–17).

The eighth beatitude brings together the two key terms: kingdom and justice (or righteousness). Those who live by, and establish, justice (have a hunger and thirst for it) bring upon themselves the opposition of the powerful, as is attested to by the prophets and the life of Jesus himself. Those who have made the decision to be his disciples cannot be above their teacher (see Matt. 10:24). Matthew is very aware of this risk that disciples run; consequently, the theme of persecution appears at various points in his Gospel (5:44; 10:23; 23:34).

Luke's fourth beatitude takes into account the difficulties that disciples face: "Blessed are you when people hate you, and when they exclude you, revile you, and defame you on account of the Son of Man" (Luke 6:22). Matthew adopts this focus of discipleship in all his beatitudes. Matthew lends greater force to his statement about persecution "for righteousness' sake" by adding a promise of happiness for those who are insulted "because of me." Matthew 5:11 is therefore quite close to Luke 6:22, which speaks of persecution "on account of the Son of Man," while at the same time he establishes an equivalence between justice and Jesus as motives for the hostility experienced. In this way Matthew prepares the way for the surprising identification in chapter 25 between love-inspired actions done for the poor and actions done for the Son of Man who has come to judge all the nations. To give one's life for the sake of justice is to give it for Christ himself. The christological perspective at work in the beatitudes is clear.

The kingdom is promised to those who suffer for justice. By repeating the term "kingdom" Matthew seeks to round off and lend force to his text by means of the literary device known as inclusion. The promises in the six beatitudes enclosed between the first and the last are specifications that help us grasp the meaning of the kingdom. Land, comfort, satisfaction, mercy, the vision of God, and divine sonship or daughterhood spell out the life, love, and justice produced by the reign of God. These promises are gifts of the Lord, fruits of his gratuitous love, and call for a certain kind of behavior. The beatitudes tell us of the attitudes proper to the followers of Jesus, to whom they are addressed. The attitudes prescribed in this teaching must be translated into acts of solidarity with others, especially the poor and helpless, so that the Father may be glorified (see Matt. 5:16).

Matthew is not offering us a spiritualized version of the original beatitudes. His perspective is quite different; his interest is in discipleship. The followers of Jesus must feed the hungry and visit those in prison. Such actions are expressions of their longing for justice; therefore they will be misunderstood and persecuted (see also Luke 6:22–23). On the part of the disciples, the need is for concrete, material acts of solidarity, which are important to Matthew throughout his Gospel.

— *The God of Life*, 124–28

WITNESSING THROUGH WORKS

The beatitudes pinpoint the attitudes proper to disciples. The verses that follow the beatitudes in the Gospel of Matthew are completely attuned to them and thus form with them a single text that ought to be interpreted as a whole:

> You are the salt of the earth; but if salt has lost its taste, how can its saltiness be restored? It is no longer good for anything, but is thrown out and trampled underfoot. You are the light of the world. A city built on a hill cannot be hid. No one after lighting a lamp puts it under the bushel basket, but on the lampstand, and it gives light to all in the house. In the same way, let your light shine before others, so that they may see your good works, and give glory to your Father in heaven. (Matt. 5:13–16)

Jesus said the disciples are to be the salt of the earth and the light of the world; the images embody a call for an identity and a visibility. Salt gives flavor and must do this permanently; if it becomes itself tasteless, it loses its specific function and can only be thrown out. The task of the disciples is to make known the message of Jesus; this is knowledge that must be made flavorful, for then people will appreciate the teaching and want to grasp it more fully. If the followers of Jesus do not put the commandments of their master into practice, they lose their identity and betray their mission; they become fools.

The visibility that light creates is confirmed by the images of the city on a mountain and the lamp that cannot be hidden. The phrase "light of the world," which is parallel to "salt of the earth," brings out the universal scope of the responsibility disciples have. The followers of Jesus cannot hide or conceal the message they bring. Only a personal and Christian identity will allow a genuine dialogue with others ("the earth," "the world").

Disciples are therefore called upon to bear witness through concrete actions. The entire opening section of Matthew 5 is

directed toward verse 16, and the evangelist emphasizes the
movement by connecting the verse with what has gone before:
"In the same way" — marked by the identity and visibility of
true disciples — their conduct is to shine before others. "Good
works" refer to concrete behavior that is in accord with God's
will; they refer especially to works of mercy, a classical list of
which is given in Matthew 25:31–46.

Witness in Matthew is not in the service of self-glorification
but is to be given for the glory of God. This is the ultimate
purpose of the commitment of disciples, that through it human
beings may be led to the Father. To glorify the Father means to
acknowledge the primacy of love for him, to adhere to his will,
and to be faithful to his plan for the human race.

The works of the disciples are a way to the Father; by doing
them, the disciples make the way of Christ their own. Matthew
5:1–16, the introduction to the Sermon on the Mount, shows
us the part played by deeds in the attitudes befitting a disciple.
"Blessed are the poor in spirit," and so on, means "blessed are
the disciples." Disciples are those who practice justice or righteousness through life-giving works of love and thereby glorify
the Father.

The focus seen here makes it possible to connect Matthew 5,
with which the preaching of Jesus begins, and chapter 25, with
which this preaching concludes. The proclamation of the kingdom begins with the promise made to the poor in spirit and
ends with the gift of the kingdom to those who come to the aid
of the materially poor. The disciples are said to be blessed, or
happy, because they give life by giving food to the hungry and
drink to the thirsty, by clothing the naked and visiting prisoners, by concrete actions; in this way they proclaim the kingdom
and enter into it. This is what James calls "the royal law" (2:8);
it is the law of the kingdom.

A fruitful relationship between Matthew and Luke may now
be established. The beatitudes of Luke emphasize the gratuitous
character of the love shown by the God who has a preferential love for the materially poor. The beatitudes in Matthew

complement those in Luke by bringing out the ethical demands made of the followers of Jesus, demands that flow from the loving initiative taken by God. The difference between the two evangelists is thus one of emphasis since both aspects are present in each version; their approaches are complementary. Matthew is not spiritualizing the beatitudes, he is "discipleizing," to coin a word. The followers of Jesus are those who translate the grace they have received — a grace that makes them witnesses to the kingdom of life — into works done for the neighbor and especially for the poor; disciples are those who enter into solidarity, even at the material level, with those for whom the Lord has a preferential love. That is why they are declared "blessed" and suited for entrance into the kingdom that has been "prepared...from the foundation of the world" (Matt. 25:34). Matthew's beatitudes emphasize the need of behavior oriented to others. This is a requirement that flows from the gift of the kingdom. Nothing makes greater demands for solidarity with others than the gratuitousness of God's love.

— *The God of Life*, 130–32

20

Witnessing to the Ends of the Earth

*In his writings Gutiérrez holds up a number of people as wit-
nesses to the God of Life. Some are well known, others less so.
Some lived centuries ago, others recently. The following selections are some examples of those who have inspired Gutiérrez
because of their fidelity to the Gospel. Each brings out different
dimensions of discipleship and an undying commitment to the
reign of God.*

BARTOLOMÉ DE LAS CASAS:
DEFENDER OF THE POOR

*Bartolomé de Las Casas (1484–1566) was a Dominican mis-
sionary and bishop of Chiapas in Mexico. He was a staunch
defender of the poor, indigenous people during the Spanish
Conquest.*

Fray Bartolomé, reminding us that those who exploit and murder the Indian, who "have gold as their actual, principal end,"
will deny them the name of Christian stating, "Christ did not
come into the world to die for gold."[1] No, it will be ambition
for riches and capital that will kill Christ, in the murder of the

---

1. *Octavo remedio,* 1542, *Obras escogidas,* 5:88b.

Indians. Indeed, the Dominican friar will identify these "Indian oppressed" with Christ himself.

In his *History of the Indies*, Las Casas recounts how, in his endeavor to "protect these miserable people and prevent their perishing," he embarked on the difficult — and actually questionable — enterprise of a peaceful colony in the lands of today's Venezuela. To this purpose, he offered the king a sum of money in exchange for the concession of these lands. A raw realism induced him, at that moment, "in virtue of the great experience he has had, to establish upon this negotiation all of the Indians' good, freedom, and conversion — on the purely temporal interest of those whose help was necessary to attain this."[2]

This manner of "negotiation" scandalized a certain individual who held cleric Las Casas in high esteem and who now expressed his perplexity and disapproval. Bartolomé favored this personal friend with an explanation. In that reply he has given us one of the most impressive passages anywhere in his works, and it will be worthwhile to transcribe it in its entirety:

> The cleric learned of this, and said: "Supposing, Sir, that you were to see Our Lord Jesus Christ abused — someone laying hands on him, afflicting him, and insulting him with all manner of vituperation — would you not beg with the greatest urgency and with all your strength that he be handed over to you instead, that you might worship and serve and please him and do everything with him that, as a true Christian, you ought to do?"
>
> "I surely would," replied the other.
>
> "And supposing they would not simply give him to you, would you not purchase him?"
>
> "That I would do indeed," said the other. "Of course I would purchase him."
>
> Then the cleric added: "Indeed, Sir, I have but acted in that very manner. For *I leave, in the Indies, Jesus Christ,*

---

2. *Historia de las Indias*, bk. 3, ch. 131, *Obras escogidas*, 2:490a, b.

our God, scourged and afflicted and buffeted and crucified, *not once but millions of times,* on the part of all the
Spaniards who ruin and destroy these people and deprive
them of the space they require for their conversion and
repentance, *depriving them of life before their time.*"[3]

After this paradoxical sale of the Gospel and of Christ and
his own ambivalent, reformist attempt at peaceful colonization
in Venezuela, Las Casas is seized with a passion: his love for the
living Jesus Christ, scourged, buffeted, crucified, and murdered
in the "captive poor" of the Indies "not once, but thousands of
times." He assimilates the conviction that a love of Christ must
necessarily impel a person to try to achieve the liberation of the
Indians and to prevent the "untimely" looting of their lives by
way of the regime of the *encomienda.* Once more, and in this
case he identifies Christ and the poor, we find a fine perception
of the poor and their material, concrete, and temporal lives. The
spoliation, exploitation, and murder is "blasphemy of the name
of Christ."

There are echoes of this central text in another work by Fray
Bartolomé de Las Casas. Apropos of the link between the love
of God and the love of neighbor, Las Casas writes: "The one
who loves God does not hate the brethren, does not prefer
material to spiritual wealth, but always behaves generously."
As usual, Las Casas will prove his proposition with an appeal
to "authorities": Augustine and Chrysostom will be among his
favorites. But the definitive argument is to be found in the
Gospel: among the numerous texts he cites, the first will be
from Matthew 25, ever suggestive, that reminds us of the one
who has said, " 'Whoever helps one of the helpless, helps me'
(Matt. 25:40). That one thinks that his ministry makes him a
servant alongside God," and knows that God regards a service
rendered a fellow servant as rendered to God.[4]

---

3. *Historia de las Indias,* bk. 3, ch. 138, *Obras escogidas,* 2:511b; emphasis
added.
4. *De Único,* 167v; *Bartolomé de Las Casas: The Only Way* (Mahwah, N.J.:
Paulist Press, 1992), 136.

God is at the center of any relationship of charity and justice and is absent from any contempt for neighbor. In a concrete relationship with the other, the final destiny of all human existence is at stake: God "regards as done to Himself" any deed addressed to our neighbor. An act addressed to the poor always reaches the God present in the poor.

Two annotations regarding the same Matthean text show what a constraint this has become for him. In a commentary on the expressions, "You fed me nothing.... You gave me no water" (Matt. 25:41–42), Bartolomé insists: "They are damned, not for doing evil, but for not doing good."[5] Abstention from acting is impossible. To neglect to do something for a person in need is to fail to do one's duty of helping that person. It constitutes a sin of omission. Concretely, in the Indies, neutrality is impossible.

Bartolomé returns to this Gospel passage, recalling a penetrating question posed by Augustine of Hippo: "If someone is damned to hellfire by Christ saying to him or her, 'I was naked and you did not clothe me,' to what hellfire will they be damned to whom he says, 'I was clothed and you stripped me!' "[6] That is what is actually going on in the Indies. Not only are the naked not clothed, but, perversely, the poor of those lands are violently unclothed: the Indians are despoiled of their legitimate possessions. The poor are robbed and, in them, Christ himself. A keen biblical sense enables a believer to read what is at stake for those who genuinely believe in Christ and see him present in the suffering of the Indians.

It is impossible to arrive at this outlook if one regards the Indians as a naturally inferior race. Nor can one come to this conclusion merely in a defense of the Indians as human beings with rights formally equal to those of all others. One reaches this pinnacle of spirituality only if one perceives in the Indian, as did Bartolomé de Las Casas, the poor of the Gospel. Lassègue

---

5. *De Único*, 169; *The Only Way*, 138.
6. *De Único*, 196; *The Only Way*, 162.

is correct: "This admirable text, in all its simplicity, expresses a high point in the spirituality of the sixteenth century, as of all the Christian centuries — the identification of Christ with the martyred Indian."[7]

Surely the dwellers of the Indies are persons, with all of the rights appertaining to them as such. But more than anything else they are "our siblings, and Christ has given his life for them" (*Apología* 252v), to the point of identifying himself with these "Indian oppressed." This will be a capital point in the theological thought of Bartolomé de Las Casas, which has such deep evangelical and spiritual roots. It is a point to which the practice of solidarity with the poor invariably leads. The Lascasian contribution took shape in the light of the Gospel and in the face of a reality contrary to the demands of that Gospel.

— *Las Casas,* 61–66

JOHN OF THE CROSS:
THE DANGERS OF IDOLATRY

John of the Cross (1542–91) was a Spanish mystic and poet whose spiritual writings speak about the path to union with God, which in part necessitates the need for purification from all idols.

What interest could John of the Cross, the saint of the "Ascent of Mount Carmel," be to so many in Latin America who suffer extreme poverty, destitution, and violence? Do not the dark nights, the purifications, the betrothals with God seem very far from daily life? This saint, for whom themes such as social justice seem foreign, who never commented on nor even cited Luke 4:16 or Matthew 25:31–46, of what interest can he be for us? These are important texts in the lived experience of Christians in Latin America and in my own reflections.

7. Jean-Baptiste Lassègue, *La larga marcha de Las Casas* (Lima: CEP, 1974), 157, n. 1.

There are persons who are universal because of the intensity of their lives and their thought. More than traversing the world with their ideas, they go to the very center of it and thus find themselves equidistant from everything that happens on the surface. John of the Cross is one of them, universal because of his singularity. If John of the Cross is a universal man he would not be alien to what is happening in Latin America.

On our continent we pose for ourselves a lacerating question: How to say to the poor person, to the oppressed person, to the insignificant person, God loves you? Indeed, the daily life of the poor seems to be the result of the denial of love. The absence of love is, in the final analysis of faith, the cause of social injustice. The question of how to tell the poor person "God loves you" is much greater than our capacity to answer it. The breadth of this unavoidable, demanding, challenging question, to use a phrase very dear to John of the Cross, makes our answers very small. Is not the work of John of the Cross a titanic effort to tell us that God loves us? Is our interest (as Latin Americans) in his witness and work not to be found in the very heart of Christian revelation?

We Christians in Latin America are convinced that what is at stake in our people's efforts to achieve an all-encompassing and multifaceted liberation is our way of being Christians, our very faith, our hope, and our love. This commitment is not to be limited to the field of social justice, though this is of primary importance, but we do not see a different way of being followers of the Lord, of being disciples of Jesus. John of the Cross reappears because for him too what is at stake is a way of being Christian. In Latin America we try to live the option for the poor, the preferential option for the poor person, as a spiritual experience, that is, as an experience of the Lord. This is very clear in the Christian communities throughout the continent. The witness of John of the Cross becomes relevant and important for us in our spiritual experience.

John of the Cross has reminded us that to be a believer is to think that God is enough. The night of the senses and the spiritual night ought to strip us, and finally liberate us, from idolatries. In the Bible idolatry is a danger to every believer. Idolatry means trusting in something or someone other than God, giving our lives over to what we have made with our own hands. We frequently offer victims to such an idol, which is why the prophets link idolatry and murder so often.

We in Latin America are also convinced — and John of the Cross helps us to understand this — that in the liberation process we are capable of creating our own idols for ourselves. For example, the idol of justice. Justice can become an idol if it is not placed in the context of gratuity, if there is no real friendship with the poor person nor daily commitment with him or her. Gratuity is the framework for justice and gives it meaning in history. Social justice can also be an idol, and we have to purify ourselves of this to affirm very clearly that only God suffices and to give justice itself the fullness of its meaning.

In the same way the poor person to whom we wish to commit ourselves and with whom we wish to live in solidarity can become an idol. An example of this is the idealization of the poor person by some in Latin America as if they had to demonstrate to themselves and to others that every poor person is good, generous, religious, and for that reason we have to be committed to him or her.

Another idol can be our own theology, the theology we are trying to formulate in Latin America, beginning with the reality of suffering and of hope found in our people. John of the Cross reminds us of a fundamental biblical datum: our love for God grows to the degree that our love of neighbor grows.

We in Latin America are seeking to understand the liberation process as a journey not only to social freedom but equally and above all toward full friendship with God and among ourselves. This is what we understand by the formula "preferential option for the poor." This is the journey, and we believe that it implies time. The option for the poor is a theocentric option, a life centered on God — just as John of the Cross desired.

John of the Cross affirms that he is trying to approach the themes mentioned here by beginning with experience, science, and equally — as he nicely puts it — by "cuddling up with Scripture." The result is poetry in verse or in prose. And poetry is doubtless the greatest human gift a person can receive. How can we speak of love without poetry? Love is the thing that has always given rise to poetry. From this continent marked by unjust and premature death, we also think that experience is the necessary condition to be able to speak about God and to say to the poor person "God loves you." Experience of the mystery of God.

I have always admired those philosophers and theologians who speak about what God thinks and wants as if they had breakfast with God every day. John of the Cross reminds us, however, that this is impossible, that we can speak of God and the love of God only with great respect, aware of what his master Thomas Aquinas said: "What we don't know about God is much greater than what we know."

Although I come from a continent marked by death, I also want to say that I come from a continent in which a people is undergoing an exceedingly profound experience of life. This is expressed when people organize so that their most elementary rights will be respected; it is also expressed in their rich religious life. From this experience the poor of our continent — without using the word "mystical" — express a profound sense of God. This lived experience does not contradict their poverty or their suffering. I come from a continent where there is great holiness and generous and anonymous self-giving. There are many people who live in extremely difficult areas, who risk their physical life between the two kinds of gunfire that today kill people in my country — hunger and cruel, brutal terrorism.

— *The Density of the Present,* 138–45

DOM HÉLDER CÂMARA:
A PROPHETIC TESTIMONY

*Dom Hélder Câmara (1909–99) was a courageous archbishop
from Olinda and Recife, Brazil, well known for his commitment
to the urban poor and his fight against poverty and injustice in
Latin America.*

Dom Hélder was a mystic and a witness of hope amid realities
that seemed hopeless. Union with God was the heart of his life;
like Jesus, he did not know rest, but he did know the peace that
comes with placing one's life in God's hands. This contemplative dimension was expressed not only in his words but in a
presence that permeated all aspects of his life. To say that he
was a mystic does not mean that he was distant from people
and their daily troubles. Rather it highlights why people were
so important to him: in them he found a specific and demanding
approach to his faith in God.

Dom Hélder tells a story to illustrate this. Soon after he was
named archbishop of Recife, an incident took place that impacted
the city. A thief broke into a church, took consecrated hosts from
the tabernacle, and scattered them on the ground. A Mass of
reparation was requested, and Dom Hélder agreed. During the
Eucharistic celebration he spoke with his people: "Finding the
consecrated hosts on the muddy ground has profoundly moved
us, but, brothers and sisters, open your eyes, Christ lives also
in the mud amongst us every day; in the inhuman huts of the
poor, in the midst of the swamp, our faith must find Jesus Christ
alive." He had worked before in the slums of Rio de Janeiro.
He concluded, inspired by the Gospel of Matthew, that the face
of Christ reveals to us the face of the most poor: "Even though
for some, this may seem strange, I am convinced that in the
Northeast of Brazil, Christ is called José, Antônio, or Severino."

Dom Hélder never abandoned this perspective, despite the
enormous problems it caused. Like Jesus of Nazareth, he knew
misunderstandings and violent attacks. On one occasion his

house was shot at, a bullet visible in the façade. This occurred shortly before Henrique Pereira Neto, a young and committed black priest and a close collaborator of Dom Hélder, was assassinated. This unprecedented act of violence was followed by a relentless campaign of defamation. Marginalized and silenced in his home country during the military dictatorship, Dom Hélder lived through all this with great fidelity to the Gospel, the church, and the people.

In his pastoral work in the slums of Rio de Janeiro, Dom Hélder, as bishop, found an incompatibility between this situation and the Gospel. He did not hesitate to speak out about poverty and urgently solicited immediate help to eliminate the economic and social structures that produced it. In 1964 in his first message as archbishop of Recife he would write to his dioceses: "If we want to remove the root of our social ills it is necessary to break the vicious cycle of underdevelopment and misery."

In 1959 John XXIII convened the Second Vatican Council. Dom Hélder was present from the beginning, among those who, overcoming some limitations in the initial stages, were faithful to the first intuitions of Pope John. Dom Hélder was part of a very dynamic group of bishops and theologians known as the "church of the poor," a name proposed by John XXIII to the Council. His presence was congenial and welcoming, a discreet presence that did not seek a place of honor, but was decisive in many of the issues discussed.

With his long history and already the archbishop of Recife, Dom Hélder arrived in Medellín, Colombia, in 1968. At Vatican II John XXIII recalled the biblical theme of the signs of the times, and Medellín also took this up with helpful clarity. The poverty in most of Latin America and the Caribbean made the proclamation of the Gospel there a great challenge. The inhumane social causes and mental categories of these situations came to the forefront. The fact that this situation was not accepted as an inevitable certainty changed the focus and consequently how to address the problems. John Paul II later recalled this breakthrough in his opening discourse at Puebla in

1979 and during his visit to Cuba in January 1998. Dom Hélder said, in an often quoted phrase: "When I help a poor person, it is said I am a saint. When I ask why he is hungry, I am labeled a communist."

Dom Hélder would call poverty the primary instigator of all violence, namely, armed counterviolence and domination by authority, a perverse process which he would call "the spiral of violence." There is no intention here to justify violent options no matter what forms they take; instead we try to explain why violent options arise and what can be done to diminish and finally eradicate them. For Dom Hélder and others the predicament of nonviolence is that it is misunderstood as weakness and passiveness when in reality, humanely speaking, it is the most adequate and least costly option for obtaining the necessary changes. We must not avoid facing the reality of violence and its roots, but we must face it with courage. Dom Hélder's witness was exemplary and manifested an integrity that cost him misunderstanding and hostility even in Christian circles.

As John Paul II would recall: "The secret of true peace resides in its respect for human rights" (January 1, 1999). There is no peace without justice, and this implies the recognition of everyone's rights. Regardless of the difficulties, the growing awareness of the importance of human rights is one of the most positive developments in recent years in Latin America and the Caribbean. The number of people, facing slander and mistreatment, engaged in defense of human rights also keeps growing. This is a change filled with promises.

Poetry is the language of mysticism and of the best prophecy. Dom Hélder was a poet who never lost the childlike capacity to be amazed and permanently open to the new and unimaginable, to believe that something different that our eyes see and our hands touch is truly possible, to be sensitive to the beauty of life and to see in it the presence of a God that calls us to a plenitude of love and hope.

— "Dom Hélder, un testimonio profético,"
Páginas, no. 214 (June 2009): 46–53

PEDRO ARRUPE: A FREE MAN

Pedro Arrupe (1907–91) was the superior general of the Jesuits (1965–83) and was instrumental in articulating the mission for the Society of Jesus through advocacy for the poor and marginalized and by living out a faith that does justice.

From time to time there are people whose profound witness, prophetic word, and creative fidelity to the church send our faith and hope down a new course. Fr. Pedro Arrupe was one of these people. The stroke that disabled him in 1981 could only but slowly pierce his Basque temperament. First his ability to write vanished, and with courage he tried to learn again how to do so. Then his oral expression failed, and little by little he drowned in silence until he almost lost contact with the outside world. Finally he witnessed, as he had always lived, God's presence. He is no doubt one of the greatest men of our church and our time, a man who, according to John XXIII's beautiful expression, had a deep vision.

A double trait of true innovators is that they can be at once traditional and innovative. Pedro Arrupe left his mark not only on the Society of Jesus, of which he was superior general for eighteen years, but also on religious life and the Christian church. Soon after being ordained he left for Japan, which he made profoundly his own. There he learned the humility and respect characteristic of any genuine missionary in a world foreign to explicit Christian faith. He was in Hiroshima in August 1945 when the first atomic bomb fell over its inhabitants, an effective and deadly weapon. Those who have seen the pictures of the terrified faces and the mutilated bodies of Hiroshima can imagine the mark that this event left on a man who was a witness and shared the suffering of the people.

The missionary experience of Don Pedro (what he was lovingly called) inspired him to write years later, to those who work in evangelization in Africa: it is necessary to "receive before being able to give; learn first." A simple pastoral norm, this has enormous practical consequences and was also a guideline in his own behavior. Fr. Arrupe knew how to listen. The great responsibilities, the many insightful things he had to say, and the authority he had did not make him forget that every person had something important to say and must be heard. His strong personality did not overwhelm; it upheld. His timid yet friendly gaze peeked out of the frame of his sharp profile. In conversation would come an encouraging word, not just the classic pat on the back of someone who has to move on to other matters. It was the opinion and advice of someone who had shared in the truth and the difficulties, which were always overcome by faith, of living in the moment with hope and joy. There are many of us who were witness to his welcome.

Arrupe was named superior general of the Society of Jesus in 1965. In 1966 and 1968, he sent letters to the provincials in Latin America reminding them that justice is "intrinsic to the Bible." These texts were milestones in the march toward the Episcopal Conference in Medellín (1968). Fr. Arrupe participated, always willing to listen, and offered wisdom in the option for an integral liberation taken up by the church in Latin America in response to the inhumane poverty in which most of its inhabitants live.

On the eve of the decisive Thirty-Second General Assembly of the Society of Jesus (1974–75), Fr. Arrupe would say: "The church has insisted numerous times that there is no true love of God but to love your neighbor, and that there is no love for your neighbor if there is no justice. Our apostolic mission and our social mission are not two distinct missions but rather two complementary aspects of our sole and identical mission: aspects mutually necessary."

This assembly established a deep connection between faith and justice, which has marked the life of the Jesuit order in our time and was once a fertile word throughout our church. At its heart this recovers an eminently biblical and traditional stance which, in the history of the church, the Fathers offered in the first centuries to their congregations. This perspective was again affirmed in the concrete conditions of today's world and in the notion of "to feel with the church," characteristic of the spirituality of Ignatius of Loyola.

Fr. Arrupe's love for Christ and the church propelled him to engage in the greatest challenges of our day: the signs of the times. Poverty around the world and the renewal of religious life; discernment between Marxist analysis and the catechism; commitment to justice and the contemplative dimension of all Christian life; inculturation and apostolic availability; the values of the modern world and the responsibility of Christians in contemporary atheism — these were among the vast and diverse themes that he was able to tackle as a citizen of this world and as member of the universal church. It is not unexpected that his evangelizing passion, which knew no borders or limitations, was sometimes misunderstood. This difficulty did not daunt him but rather stimulated him; he suffered but he did not succumb to resentment and bitterness. "Our commitment to the poor will lead us, not surprisingly, to suffer with them and like them." A man of prayer, he lived this commitment in profound fidelity to the Lord and in rich ecclesiastical communion.

Fr. Arrupe went numerous times to Latin America, including Peru. The church on this continent was one of his preoccupations. He was in Medellín and later in Puebla. He saw in these conferences a creative continuity with Vatican II. He was particularly attached to the region of Central America. He kept close to his heart the Jesuits who worked there. He never tired of hearing about the circumstances of the death of Archbishop Oscar Romero. He was bound to him by a strong friendship and had numerous opportunities to support him during the visits that the archbishop of San Salvador made to Rome. Don Pedro strongly supported the labor of peace based in justice of the Christians of that country and of the members of his order. Some accused him of weakness, but what would they say now that the stamp of martyrdom has marked these dear and admired friends and made evident the evangelical implications of their cooperation in the option for the poor?

His health did not allow Arrupe to know about the assassination of the Jesuits in El Salvador; nevertheless he always knew of their inspiration for the contemplation of love and for the poor. He once wrote: "One thing is certain: the true joy of Christ is born out of love, and the way to achieve it is the Cross." Today, at the side of the Father, the happiness of being united with his friends and brothers who were assassinated in El Salvador must be another cause for consolation that confirms the choice they made together.

— *Páginas* 108 (April 1991): 88–90

SISTER MARÍA AGUSTINA: A TESTIMONY OF MERCY

Sister María Agustina was a religious sister murdered by the Shining Path terrorist group in Peru. She was killed in her late seventies after having lived her life close to the poor and suffering.

Many people (farmers, settlers, women, students) whom we commonly think of as ordinary, have been victims of inhumane and cruel violence that drains and shames our country. One of them was Sister María Agustina, "Aguchita," a religious of the Congregation of Our Lady of Charity of the Good Shepherd. Only her family, her sisters in religious life, and her friends knew of her. Today her face is clearly sketched in the midst of the anonymity of a town, one victim among many of different types of violence, all unjustifiable and all cruel.

This simple woman, born in the "corner of the dead" in Ayucucho, is a testimony of a life that manifests the God of Jesus Christ, who loves every person and in particular the marginalized and the poor, in whose service she dedicated all her strength. She died precisely because she lived out the will of God. The anonymous testimony from witnesses said that her treacherous assassination was due to the work that the Sisters of the Good Shepherd were doing among the poor of La Florida. Evangelization and organization among women and the marginalized of that small and humble place in our country is work that gives life. Those who seek to dominate or manipulate the poor to serve their interest cannot accept it. A village that receives the liberating word of the Gospel and then organizes becomes, little by little, independent, autonomous. The proponents of death see their privileges questioned and their politics rejected. This is what happened to Jesus. His announcement of life brought him death. Sister Aguchita died as a result of that which granted her life. A disciple of the Good Shepherd who gave his life for his sheep, she could do only what he had done.

We must understand without a doubt that those who assassinated her are the same ones who mistreat the poor; they will always find more "Aguchitas" who will get in their way. There is no conjecture, only faithfulness to the kingdom of life. She did not seek martyrdom, says a person who knew her well; she found it in her simple and faithful path. Her dream since she became a religious, writes her provincial, was "to work in the jungle," a region particularly abandoned in our country. There, she said, "The lord has brought me to give me joy before growing old and dying; I am clay in his hands." She abandoned herself to the will of a God who wants us present and active in the midst of human history.

In the same letter Aguchita said: "It seems that these were the last days of my life; therefore I must make the most of the time that flies away; otherwise I will present myself with empty hands in eternity." If her hands were full, as we all think, it is because she believed with all humility that they were empty. She was not one of the great ones of this world that the Lord brings low, nor one of the rich whom he has sent away empty; rather she was one of the hungry whom he has filled with good things (see Luke 1:52–53). Her hands were filled with the affliction and hope of the poor, the humiliations that they suffer, their efforts to affirm their dignity as human beings, their search for Christ and finding joy among their brothers and sisters. This is the same life experience of many people in our country. There is great dedication and generosity across this land that seems to vanish from our hands. Many holy people, humble and anonymous, are never seen on the front page of the newspapers; they are not important, they do not incite intense debate, they do not seek honor. Their lives are like fragrant flowers, fresh, healthy, cultivated without arrogance to make the God of life present through their beauty. From time to time this emerges rapidly and surprisingly, filling us with hope, like in La Florida. The Good Shepherd said: "No one takes it [life] from me, but I lay it down of my own accord" (John 10:18), and Sister María Agustina can say the same. The bullets that assassinated her did not take away her life; she offered it when she decided to serve God and the poor, her privileged ones. Giving her life, she gave life to all.

— "Con las manos llenas," in *María Agustina Rivas,*
testigo de la misericordia (Lima: CEP, 1991), 79–82

VICENTE HONDARZA:
THE GREATNESS OF THE ORDINARY

Vicente Hondarza was a diocesan priest killed in Peru. He was murdered by landowners because of his commitment to the poor and his solidarity with them in their struggle for land reform.

In a world in which Christianity forms part of the social fabric and provides guides for adequate and decent behavior for living together, we can become accustomed to a domestication of the Gospel. The Word of the Lord is both a lasting and new demand that becomes window dressing and a distraction for those who rule their lives according to other principles. Authentic evangelical demands are considered somewhat exaggerated and old fashioned, or they are seen as simply an overwhelming set of customs, weak precepts, or bland motivations.

All this eventually becomes the accepted form of being a Christian. An attempt to recover the message of Him who was executed for giving a witness, in word and acts, of the love of the Father for every person, and in particular for the poor, is considered offensive and hostile, if not actually dangerously dissident.

Archbishop Romero was an evangelical voice that emerged on behalf of and in defense of the poor in his country and was silenced by the forces of death. A Salvadoran and a Latin American voice, he knew how to speak of God by articulating the painful life of a country with a profound theological reflection; his voice emerged from a churchman's heart that took seriously the admonition of Peter: "Like good stewards of the manifold grace of God, serve one another with whatever gift each of you has received" (1 Pet. 4:10). His was an evangelical witness that the Lord wished to be so pure that nobody could doubt the reasons for the assassination of this humble and courageous man. What happened to Romero sheds light upon similar situations, even though some may try to skew the truth so that we become blind to the facts. Such an instance is the death of another priest, Vicente Hondarza, whose life appeared more ordinary, but was filled with unexpected courage and grace.

Paradoxical as it may seem, what is extraordinary in Vicente's story is the ordinary. Originally a farmer, he found in his priestly vocation a missionary calling and a healthy curiosity about other places. He was supportive of the poorest and loved by his people, especially by people of the countryside and the youth of the city. He was a loyal and fraternal friend, extraordinary joke-teller, and companion of all. Then one day he was dead.

His burial was accompanied by the pain and bewilderment of a whole town. Like the person to whom he dedicated his life, Vicente's life can slip from our consciousness as time goes by. I suspect this is what he most would have liked, but out of respect for him those who knew and loved him are not willing to accept it, and by a rereading of his simple life they receive a message from the Lord and better comprehend the sufferings and everyday hopes of our poor people.

The deaths of some cannot be understood apart from the life they undertook and what their lives provoked. The lives of others are understood only in their death. The doubts that emerged as soon as news about Vicente's death circulated have dissipated. Everything points to the fact that Vicente did not die in an accident. In his life everything was ordinary except his death. His assassination makes us reread the life of a good man, a generous priest, a loyal and happy companion. The ordinariness of his life appears to us with all its Christian greatness; that of the loyal and humble disciple of the Lord who told us that his "yoke is easy" and his "burden is light" (Matt. 11:30). Following Jesus revealed the kingdom, solidarity with the poor, full forgetfulness of one's self, and permanent joy. Vicente loved to serve. He did it with joy, without effort, without melodramatic gestures, almost without merit. His service was undertaken not as a duty, but as a pleasure, undoubtedly a test of profound love.

Loyal obedience made Vicente a defendant of the life of the poor, oppressed, and mistreated. His fidelity, just like in the case of his Teacher, provoked the reaction of the powerful and sowers of death. Vicente was accused of being subversive and dangerous; he could care less, not because he was brave or courageous — though he was certainly that by example — but because he did not consider himself a Christian with the privileges of the kingdom and a priest without concrete gestures of love and solidarity, without building the church of Jesus Christ.

The personal mystery of every life is in the hands of the Lord. He knows the depths of the fears, sorrows, and sins that might be limiting it. But for us, it is definitely the witness of a joyous and simple offering without compromise. How can we know that God loves us without the witness in history of men and women like Vicente? How can the men and women of Chancay perceive all the sense of the resurrection of Jesus if they do not know of existences like that of Vicente, marked by the vitality of a faithful life? How do we convince ourselves that we can all be authentic disciples of the Lord without simple examples like those of Vicente, which make near that which seems impossible and unobtainable?

The greatness of the witness of Vicente is in reminding us that the path of Christianity is not heroism but holiness. Vicente and his joy for life give us an understanding of Paul: "Consider your own call, brothers and sisters: not many of you were wise by human standards, not many were powerful, not many were of noble birth. But God chose what is foolish in the world to shame the wise; God chose what is weak in the world to shame the strong" (1 Cor. 1:26–27).

The significance of Vicente's example is in revealing to us the God who sent him among us to be another of our people, vulnerable like them. The ordinariness of Vicente is an expression of the Christian law of the incarnation, the life of God in the veins of humanity. Vicente's testimony, sealed by his generous blood, makes us take up again his ordinary life and see in it the greatness of the Lord.

— *Vicente Hondarza: Vivir y morir por los pobres*
(Lima: CEP, 1984): 85–88

OSCAR ROMERO: THE VICTORY OF LIFE

Archbishop Oscar Romero (1917–80) was the leader of the church in El Salvador. Gutiérrez offered this homily at the University of Central America (UCA) in El Salvador on the eve of the fifteenth anniversary of Romero's assassination.

We have been brought together by the physical absence of someone who has flooded our hearts and minds with his presence; someone whose presence has reached the length and breadth of this continent and beyond; someone who knew fully how to give up his life; someone who was the pastor of this diocese, whose death and resurrection have made him into a pastor of the universal church.

We have just heard the text of the Gospel of John (10:7–18) in which Jesus himself is presented as a shepherd, the Good Shepherd. This image, as so often occurs in the Gospels, is a rural image taken from Jesus' world. Those who heard these words immediately understood the central idea: the shepherd cares for his sheep and gives his life for them. He gave us his life; it was not taken from him.

Solitary, but in solidarity, Monseñor Romero made his way toward his death. Solitary, not because his friends were not nearby or did not express their affection and friendship, but because in the face of death we are all, in some way, alone. Because he was concerned about other people, those whom he pastored, those with whom he reflected, and many others, this bond of solidarity with them led him to walk with a sure step. He did not seek martyrdom; martyrdom cannot be sought, only encountered.

Nor did Jesus want to be killed, but he was convinced that his proclamation of the kingdom, of the universal love expressed preferentially for the poor, challenged those who heard it just as the final homily of Monseñor Romero — when he addressed each of the soldiers and made them see that conscience must be above any military order — challenged those who heard it.

Monseñor Romero knew what fate awaited him, and he was afraid, as any human being would be. Nevertheless, he did not turn back. Instead, he affirmed, in a phrase that we have recalled many times since, "If they kill me, I will be resurrected in my people."

We are gathered here this afternoon because we truly believe that he has been resurrected with Jesus. We could also say that he is being resurrected. This means that the resurrection is in some way a process; each day he is more alive.

If March 24, 1980, the day of his death, was bad news, his life continues to be good news: the years that he lived among us, the message that he left us, the living word that he spoke that was always attentive to what happened each day. He said, "We cannot segregate the Word of God from the present reality of a people." We cannot separate the two.

By bringing together the Word of God and the Salvadoran reality, Monseñor Romero reminded us of what is in effect good news. His martyrdom, the martyrdom of his Jesuit friends at this university and of so many more — the list in El Salvador and throughout Latin America is very long — reminds us of this good news of God's love.

"Martyr," as we know, means witness, and the witness is someone who sees something and bears witness to it, communicates it, shares it. What they shared, these martyred friends of ours, these witnesses, is God's love; this is what they bore witness to. For that reason, despite the terrible theme of unjust death — a death we still encounter among our "crucified peoples," as Ignacio Ellacuría called them — we are here to give thanks.

This is a Eucharist, we recall Jesus' death, but we also know that for a Christian — and Monseñor Romero and so many others have told us with great clarity — death is not the last word of human existence: life has the last word!

We are here because we are celebrating life. If we are gathered within these walls and beneath this roof, it is because someone told us at least once in our lives, "Christ is risen!" That is why we are here; we believed it and that is why we became Christians.

The martyrs remind us of this resurrection; they recall for us the center of our faith and of our hope. For a people like ours, as Latin Americans, it is important to remember and to repeat — always in communion with them — that death does not put an end to their hopes and joys; life is the heart of the Christian message. We are here at this Eucharist to give thanks for Monseñor Romero and for so many who have been resurrected with Jesus, who will continue to be resurrected.

The Eucharist, as thanksgiving, is always a moment of joy. It seems strange to speak of joy when we are referring to blood that has been shed, an unjust death, an assassin's bullet. Yet beyond that pain, beyond that death is the affirmation of their life, of all those we have mentioned and many more. It is on account of their lives and because they continue to live, that we give thanks, and no one can take that away from us, no one.

We feel grief, certainly, our hearts are oppressed, and yet we breathe deeply with the hope of a people that never ceases to struggle for life. They can silence our voices, but — and here I am thinking of other words of Monseñor Romero — "they cannot silence the voice of hope and joy." This is paschal joy that overcomes death.

The resurrection of Jesus is never called, in the Bible, a miracle; it is so much more. The resurrection of Jesus, if I may be permitted to express it this way, is the death of death, and that is what we are celebrating this afternoon: the death of the death of Monseñor Romero, the death of the death of so many others, the victory of life. That is why we are here today, to give thanks.

— Homily on Oscar Romero,
University of Central America, March 23, 1995

LIKE FIREFLIES:
CHRIST AND COMMUNITY

During the worst years of violence in Peru in the late 1980s and early 1990s, when it was difficult to see any end in sight, Gutiérrez offered these reflections on hope and witness in the midst of darkness and despair.

In the midst of cruel and never-ending violence that makes it more difficult than ever to find a stable job, amid alarming searches and national shortsightedness, we welcome Christmas despite the difficulties of the year. The hearts of many are prepared even as they approach Christmas with real anxiety and a disenchantment that comes from the commercialism that tries to rob the celebration from the simple and the poor.

Isaiah, the great prophet we turn to at Christmas, reminds us regarding the coming of Christ that "the people who walked in darkness have seen a great light" (9:2). The first half of the phrase is a concrete reality in Peru; is the second half only a hoped-for illusion?

To an ancient and deeply rooted poverty, the worst and most persistent pandemic that strikes the Peruvian people, aggravating factors are added that have heightened its capacity to cut short lives. In the last few years, millions of Peruvians have been cast into abysmal forms of previously unknown misery and to a bloody and unjustifiable terrorism that has ripped through lives with an unimaginable cruelty. This has created an intrinsic situation of disrespect for human rights to which neither society at large, nor uninterested politicians with only a minimum respect for the truth, have been able to respond.

Many inhabitants of the world live in a state of not being grounded; they begin to see their country as surreal and foreign. The cloak of anguishing everyday problems, the violence that can emerge at any time, and the lies of those who promise to defend but are concerned only with their own shady interests do not allow these inhabitants to come face to face with reality. Furthermore the political apathy eats away — sometimes clandestinely like the *uta*[8] — the vital organs of a nation. If this continues, the result will be atrocious and irreversible.

When darkness prevails, even a matchstick, a spark, a firefly all have uncommon reach and offer hope. At times they allow us to see our faces and acknowledge our presence; sometimes we perceive faces that are less depressed and weary than what the fog made us think and feel; sometimes we see gazes that invite dialogue and collaboration. This allows us to light other lights and break the silence. This is what these terrible years have done; they have awakened (or allowed us to see) the

---

8. Also known as "Espundia." A cutaneous condition that occurs at the site of a fly bite and is characterized by an ulceration of the skin.

enormous reserves of solidarity and anger that exist among our people.

Countless anonymous people, mostly women, have created organizations in order to survive: soup kitchens, food banks, medical centers, associations for the sick, milk for infants and children, among others. These people have confronted forces that threaten their security, kill, and violate human rights without having to look at the front page of the newspaper or view television images; they create committees and offices of solidarity. These are those who continue to remember their country, reclaiming the respect for freedoms without which there would not be human coexistence and democracy, and who remember that the human being should be of primary importance in all political and economic spheres; those who have lost their lives in this task show us a country quite different from the image drawn from an analysis that merely skims the surface of the facts.

These people are the small but contagious lights that illuminate with their dedication and generosity a dark night. The light is not at the end of the tunnel, but is rather inside the tunnel in the people who travel through it. These people illuminate the tunnel and furthermore they break down its wall and its ceiling so that it stops being a rigid and mandatory passageway and instead becomes a wide, strong, shiny avenue that leads us into "judgment and justice" and prepares us to receive the "Prince of Peace" (Isa. 9:5–6), Jesus of Nazareth.

If the coming of Christ lights our hearts, if we respond with commitment and solidarity to the gift of a loving God who gave us his only Son, we will become fireflies that form with the Holy Spirit a "vast multitude" (Ezek. 37:10) that will turn the threatening fog into a humane and peaceful night, and this will become another Christmas in which our faith will grow. If we resist out of selfishness or fear this will be one less Christmas in our lives.   —Published in *Signos* 13, no. 11–12 (December 11, 1992)

THE TWO MEMORIES OF JESUS

Jesus left us with two memories at the Last Supper. The first is to remember him in the Eucharist; the second is to wash each other's feet. As a summation of the entire Christian message, the Eucharist is a living memory of the life, teachings, death, and resurrection of Jesus and a living memory of his preference for the least ones of society.

The Gospels give us two clues for incorporating ourselves into Jesus' practice. There are in fact two memories capable of bringing us close to God. In the Bible, memory does not have a primary or exclusive relationship with the past; it points more to a present that projects itself forward. The past is there, it gives density to the actual moment, but in the precise terms of St. Augustine, "memory is the present of things past." The reminiscence of something past is done in proportion to the validity it has in the present. Memory in both testaments goes beyond just a concept; it culminates in a practice, a practice destined to transform reality. To remember is a manifestation of love, to be close to someone today. Memory is also not primarily identified with history if we understand history as simply stories of events in the past. Memory goes directly to the profound sense of history and not the details. The Gospels are reminiscences of Jesus' testament; they agree on the most substantial themes and differ little in the details. Any effort of equating all the biblical books diminishes the message.

At the Last Supper, when establishing the Eucharist, Jesus tells his friends, "Do this in memory of me." The prescription grasps the totality of Jesus' existence: his life, death, and resurrection, as well as everything he taught through his works and words, in a way that his testimony is the permanent guideline, the inspirational source for the behavior of believers. The Eucharist goes beyond ritual and formalities. To be more precise, it gives the ritual power and scope, situating it in the horizon of meaning that worship has in the Bible, namely, conversion of heart and practice of justice constantly addressed by the prophets: "I do not want sacrifices, I want contrite hearts," are Old Testament warnings that Jesus cites. To maintain this memory fresh and demanding will be the task of the Advocate, which Jesus sends: to "remind you of all that I have said to you" (John 14:26). The supper is recalled, and in it all the content of Jesus' testament when he was present in our history.

There is also a second form of memory in the Gospels. The institution of the Eucharist is not found in the narration that John makes of the Last Supper. In its place John recounts how Jesus washed the feet of the disciples, a symbolic gesture that expresses hospitality, enacted by the host's servants or by the host himself.

In the liturgies of Holy Thursday we remember a humble act of service and hospitality, but we must recover its full meaning. At the end of the washing of the feet Jesus tells the disciples, "Do you know what I have done to you? ... So if I, your Lord and Teacher, have washed your feet, you also ought to wash one another's feet. For I have set you an example, that you should also do as I have done to you" (John 13:12, 14–15). The phrase is synonymous with "do this in memory of me" — on both occasions we come face to face with "to do," which disallows simple formal repetition. The washing of the feet is a demanding symbolic gesture that puts us on the path to follow Jesus. This service also concerns the church. Oscar Romero put it this way: "The authority of the church is not command, it is service ... I want to be a servant for God and for you." [9]

By the actualization of these two memories — gratitude for its offering, service to others — we make Jesus' practice our own. The two are inseparable; if we leave one aside, we lose both. In its core they are really just one memory. A cultural memory and memory of existence have been called two ways

---

9. Oscar Romero, homily, October 9, 1978.

to "Remember Jesus Christ" (2 Tim. 2:8). They form a permanent and lasting requirement that continuously revitalizes our journey as followers of Jesus. They form the Christian community as symbols of the presence of the kingdom in history. They make present him who so loved the world that he sent his only son. — "Close to God, Close to the Poor," *Páginas* 220 (December 2010): 7–9

21

Opting for the Poor

For Gutiérrez what matters most in the end is not liberation theology per se but the liberation of people. More important now than ever, the preferential option for the poor constitutes a part of following Jesus that gives ultimate meaning to human existence and gives believers "reason to hope," a message that must be constantly enacted and reenacted throughout our lives and human history.

In May 2007 at the Fifth General Conference of the bishops of Latin America and the Caribbean in Aparecida, Brazil, Pope Benedict XVI stated: "The preferential option for the poor is implicit in the christological faith in the God who became poor for us, so as to enrich us with his poverty" (2 Cor. 8:9) (Aparecida, no. 3). Its root is faith in Christ, which Aparecida lucidly reiterates: "This commitment is born out of our faith in Jesus Christ, the God who became human" (Aparecida, no. 392). The vision of Christian life manifested in this statement and in the practice of this commitment is the most substantial part of the contribution to the universal church from the life and theological reflection of the church in Latin America. The option for the poor took its first steps in the years before Medellín, was affirmed in the period after that conference, and was invoked in subsequent episcopal conferences and in the recent teachings of Benedict XVI and Aparecida, which have given it an impact and a place it would not have had without them.

The option for the poor is not limited to the assignment of pastoral workers to areas where the poor are found. While it is good to see greater pastoral investment in areas of poverty, the option for the poor is more global and demanding. Some years ago Gregory Baum described it as "the contemporary form of discipleship."[1] The option for the poor is deployed in three arenas: following Jesus, theological work, and the proclamation of the Gospel. These three dimensions give the preferential option for the poor vitality and shape.

This option involves a commitment that implies leaving the road one is on, as the parable of the Good Samaritan teaches, and entering the world of the other, of the "insignificant" person, of the one excluded from dominant social sectors, communities, viewpoints, and ideas. It is a long and difficult, but necessary, process and a precondition for authenticity. The priority of the other is a distinguishing mark of a Gospel ethic, and nobody embodies this priority more clearly than the poor and the excluded.

FOLLOWING JESUS

To be a Christian is to walk, moved by the Spirit, in the footsteps of Jesus. Traditionally known as *la sequela Christi,* this kind of discipleship is the root and the ultimate meaning of the preferential option for the poor. (The expression "preferential option for the poor" is recent, but its content is biblical.) This commitment is an essential component of discipleship. At its core is a spiritual experience of the mystery of God who is, according to Meister Eckhart, both the "unnamable" and the "omni-namable" one. Eckhart had to reach this point in order

1. Gregory Baum, *Essays in Critical Theology* (Kansas City, Mo.: Sheed & Ward, 1994), 67.

to capture the deeper meaning of this commitment to the absent and anonymous of history. The free and demanding love of God is expressed in the commandment of Jesus, "Just as I have loved you, you also should love one another" (John 13:34). This implies a universal love that excludes no one, and at the same time a priority for the least ones of history, the oppressed and the insignificant. Simultaneously living out universality and preference reveals the God of love and makes present the mystery hidden for all time but now unveiled: as Paul says, the proclamation of Jesus as the Christ (see Rom. 16:25–26). This is what the preferential option for the poor points to: walking with Jesus the Messiah.

Puebla reminds us that "the service of the poor is the privileged, though not exclusive, means for following Christ" (see Puebla, no. 1146). The lived experiences of many Christians undertaking different journeys in solidarity with the marginalized and insignificant of history have revealed that the irruption of the poor — their new presence on the historical scene — signifies a true irruption of God into our lives.

Saying this does not deprive the poor of the historical flesh of their suffering. Nor does it deprive them of the human, social, and cultural substance of their cry for justice. It is not a shortsighted spiritualization that forgets their human dimensions. Rather, it makes us truly see what is at stake, according to the Bible, in the commitment to one's neighbor. Precisely because we so value and respect the density of the historical event of the irruption of the poor, we are positioned to make a faith-based interpretation of this event. We understand the irruption of the poor as a sign of the times, which we must scrutinize in the light of faith in order to discern the challenge of the God who has pitched his tent among us (see John 1:14). Solidarity with the poor is the source of a spirituality, of a collective — or communal — journey toward God. This journey takes place in a history that the inhuman situation of the poor exposes in all its cruelty, but that also allows its possibilities and hopes to be discovered.

Following Jesus is a response to the question about the meaning of human existence; it is a global vision of our life, but it also affects life's small and everyday aspects. Discipleship allows us to see our lives in relation to the will of God and sets goals for us to strive for and realize through a daily relationship with the Lord, which implies relationships with other persons. Spirituality comes into being on the terrain of Christian practice: thanksgiving, prayer, and a commitment in history to solidarity, especially with the poorest. Contemplation and solidarity are two sides of a practice inspired by a global sense of human existence that is a source of hope and joy.

The deepest meaning of the commitment to the poor is the encounter with Christ. Echoing Matthew's pericope of the last judgment, Puebla invites us to recognize in the face of the poor "the suffering features of the face of Christ the Lord who questions and implores us" (Puebla, no. 31). This discovery calls us to personal and ecclesial conversion. Matthew's text is, without a doubt, central to Christian spirituality and provides us with a fundamental principle for discerning and finding the road of fidelity to Jesus.

In one of his homilies Archbishop Romero observed: "There is a criterion for knowing whether God is close to us or far away: all those who are concerned with the hungry, the naked, the poor, the disappeared, the tortured, the imprisoned — with any suffering human being — are close to God" (February 5, 1978).[2] The gesture made toward the other determines the proximity to or distance from God and makes us understand the "why" of this judgment and the meaning of the term "spiritual" in a Gospel context. "Love of God and love of neighbor have become one," says Pope Benedict in his encyclical *Deus Caritas Est* (no. 15). The identification of Christ with the poor leads us to see the fundamental unity of these two loves and

---

2. Archbishop Oscar Romero, "La Iglesia cuya debilidad se apoya en Cristo: Quinto domingo del tiempo ordinario, 5 de febrero de 1978. Isaías 58:7–10; 1 Corintios 1:1–5; Mateo 5:13–16," *Homilías* (San Salvador: UCA Editores, 2005), 2:257.

makes demands on his followers. The rejection of injustice and the oppression it presupposes is anchored in faith in the God of life. This commitment has been sealed by the blood of those who, as Archbishop Romero said, died under "the sign of martyrdom" (and this was true in his own case). Aparecida has movingly recognized the testimony of these Christians, referring to "the courageous witness of our men and women saints, and of those who, though not yet canonized, have radically lived the Gospel and have offered their lives for Christ, for the church, and for their people" (Aparecida, no. 98).

The option for the poor is a key part of a spirituality that refuses to be a kind of oasis or, still less, an escape or a refuge in difficult times. It involves walking with Jesus without being disconnected from reality and without distancing itself from the narrow paths trod by the poor, and it helps us keep alive our trust in the Lord and preserve our serenity when the storm gets worse.

A HERMENEUTICS OF HOPE

If following Jesus is marked by the preferential option for the poor, so is the understanding of the faith that unfolds from these experiences and emergencies. Faith is a grace; theology is an understanding of this gift. Theology tries to say a word about the mysterious and ineffable reality that we believers call God. It is a *logos* about *theos*. Faith is the ultimate source of theological reflection, giving theology its specificity and delimiting its territory. Its purpose is — or should be — to contribute to making the Gospel present in human history through Christian testimony. A theology that is not nourished by walking Jesus' own path loses its bearings. The Fathers of the Church understood all theology as spiritual theology.

Neither the faith nor the reflection about how the faith is being lived in community is simply an individual task. This fact makes discourse on faith a labor related to the preaching of the

Gospel, a task that gives this community its raison d'être. Every discourse on faith is born at a precise time and place and tries to respond to historical situations and questions amid which Christians live and proclaim the Gospel. For that reason it is tautological, strictly speaking, to say that a theology is contextual, for all theology is contextual in one way or another. Some theologies, however, take their context seriously and recognize it; others do not.

Like other reflections on the Christian message that arise from the world of those considered socially insignificant, the theology of liberation postulates that discourse on faith must recognize and emphasize its relationship with human history and people's everyday lives, especially the challenge of poverty manifested there. This relationship with history and the challenge of poverty implies an important change in the task of theology. While we have long pigeonholed poverty as a social issue, our perception of poverty is now deeper and more complex and no longer limited to its economic dimension. Instead, we now understand that being poor means being rendered socially insignificant due to ethnic, cultural, gender, and/or economic factors. Its inhumane and antievangelical character and its final outcome of early and unjust death make it totally clear that poverty goes beyond the socioeconomic sphere to become a global human problem and therefore a challenge to living and preaching the Gospel. Poverty thereby becomes a theological question, and the option for the poor makes us aware of it and provides a way to think about the issue.

The condition of the poor questions and interrogates and at the same time provides principles and categories that open up new approaches to understanding and deepening the Christian message. Theological work consists of confronting challenges face-to-face, no matter how radical they may be, recognizing the signs of the times that contain them and discerning in them, by the light of faith, the new field of faith interpretation being presented; thus will our thinking about the faith and our speech about God speak to the people of our age.

The preferential option for the poor plays an important role in theological reflection. As is stated in the classic formula *fides quaerens intellectum,* theology is faith seeking understanding. Given that faith "works through love" (Gal. 5:6), theology is a reflection that tries to accompany a people in their sufferings and joys, their commitments, frustrations, and hopes, both in becoming aware of the social universe in which they live and in their determination to understand better their own cultural tradition. A theological language that neglects unjust suffering and does not loudly proclaim the rights of each and every person's happiness remains shallow and betrays the God of whom it speaks, the God of the beatitudes.

In the end, theology — all theology — is a hermeneutics of hope, an understanding of the reasons we have to hope. Hope is, in the first place, a gift from God. Accepting that gift opens followers of Jesus to the future and to trust. Seeing theological work as an attempt to understand the reasons for hope becomes more demanding when it begins with the situation of the poor and continues in solidarity with them. God's gift is not an easy hope. But as fragile as it may seem, it is capable of planting roots in the world of social insignificance, in the world of the poor, and of breaking out and remaining creative and alive even in the midst of difficult situations. Nonetheless, hoping is not waiting; rather it should lead us actively to resolve to forge reasons for hope.

Paul Ricoeur says that theology is born at the intersection of "a space of experience" and "a horizon of hope." It is a space where Jesus invites us to follow him in encountering the other, especially the "smallest" of his brothers and sisters, and to follow him in the hope that in this encounter, which is open to every person, believer or unbeliever, we will stand within the horizon of service to the other and in communion with the Lord.

A PROPHETIC ANNOUNCEMENT
OF THE GOOD NEWS

The preferential option for the poor that grounds theological attempts to forge reasons for hope is also an essential component of the prophetic proclamation of the Gospel, a proclamation that includes the connection between justice and God's gratuitous love. Working so that the excluded might become agents of their own destiny is an important part of this proclamation.

We cannot enter into the world of the poor, who live in an inhumane situation of exclusion, without becoming aware of the liberating and humanizing dimension of the good news. And for that very reason we cannot fail to hear the Gospel's cry for justice as well as for equality among all human beings. This is a core theme in the prophetic tradition of the First Testament, which we meet again in the middle of the Sermon on the Mount as a command summarizing and giving meaning to the life of the believer: "strive first for the kingdom of God and his righteousness" (Matt. 6:33).

The heart of Jesus' message is the proclamation of the love of God expressed in the proclamation of his kingdom. The kingdom is the final meaning of history; its total fulfillment takes place beyond history, and at the same time it is present from this moment on. The Gospels speak to us precisely of its closeness to us today. The parables of the kingdom point to a kingdom that is "already" present but "not yet" fully realized. For this reason the kingdom of God manifests itself as a gift, a grace, but also as a task, a responsibility.

The life of the disciple of Jesus is situated within the framework of the sometimes tense but always fertile relationship between free gift and historical commitment; thus our talk about the kingdom we accept in faith is situated within the same framework. The passage from the beatitudes of Matthew contains a promise of the kingdom to all who, upon accepting in their daily lives the free gift offered to them, become

Jesus' disciples. In the Gospels the kingdom is discussed through expressions and images of great biblical richness: land, consolation, thirst, mercy, the vision of God, and divine filiation. The dominant theme of these images is life, life in all its aspects. As for the requirements of discipleship, they are stated fundamentally in the first and most critical blessing: being poor in spirit. The other blessings offer variations and shades of the first. Disciples are those who make the promise of the kingdom their own, placing their lives in God's hands. Recognizing the gift of the kingdom sets them free vis-à-vis all other goods. And it opens them up to the mission of evangelization, which is linked to "remembering the poor" (Gal. 2:10), according to the advice Paul received in Jerusalem.

Theological thinking in recent decades, as well as various texts of the magisterium, has insisted upon the relationship between evangelization and the promotion of justice. Examples include the Medellín conference, the Roman Synod of 1971, *Evangelii nuntiandi* by Paul VI, and a number of speeches by John Paul II. One can see in these documents an orientation toward these two aspects that is increasingly global and unitary. The promotion of justice is seen more and more as an essential part of proclaiming the Gospel. Such promotion is, of course, not all there is to evangelization, but it constitutes an essential part of the proclamation of the kingdom, even though it does not exhaust its content. Benedict XVI, in a text cited by the Aparecida conference, stated that "evangelization has always been joined to human promotion and authentic Christian liberation" (Aparecida, no. 3, 26).

Solidarity with the poor also sets forth a fundamental demand: the recognition of the full human dignity of the poor and their situation as daughters and sons of God. In fact, the conviction grows amid the poor that, like all human beings, they have the right to take control of the reins of their lives. This conviction is not a theoretical proposition or a rhetorical appeal, but rather a truly difficult and costly, but obligatory, lifestyle. And it is urgent, if we take into account the fact that today in Latin

America and the Caribbean there are those who attempt to sow skepticism about the capacity of the poor to achieve the transformation of society by promoting what they call "the only way to think." They try to persuade the poor that in the face of the new and inescapable realities of globalization, the international economic situation, and political and military unipolarity, they have no choice but to accept the vision those realities express and to radically change the direction of their demands.

There is no true commitment to solidarity with the poor if one sees them merely as people passively waiting for help. Respecting their status as those who control their own destiny is an indispensable condition for genuine solidarity. The goal is not to become, except in cases of extreme urgency or short duration, the "voice of the voiceless," but rather in some way to help ensure that those without a voice find one. Being an agent of one's own history is for all people an expression of freedom and dignity, the starting point and a source of authentic human development. The historically insignificant were — and still are in large part — the silent in history.

The option for the poor is not something that should be made only by those who are not poor. The poor themselves are called to make an option that gives priority to the "insignificant" and oppressed. Many do so, but it must be recognized that not all commit themselves to their sisters and brothers by race, gender, social class, or culture. The path the poor must take to identify with the least of society will be different from that of people belonging to other social strata, but it is a necessary and important step toward becoming subjects of their own destiny.

The preferential option for the poor, if it aims at the promotion of justice, equally implies friendship with the poor and among the poor. Without friendship there is neither authentic solidarity nor a true sharing. In fact, it is a commitment to specific people. Aparecida says in this regard, "Only the closeness that makes us friends allows us to profoundly appreciate the values of the poor today, their legitimate desires, and their own way of living the faith. The option for the poor should lead us to friendship with the poor" (Aparecida, no. 398).

   The preferential option for the poor has three dimensions — spiritual, theological, and evangelical. It is clear that if we separate them, we distort and impoverish them. They are interwoven and nourish each other; when they are treated as watertight compartments, they lose their meaning and power. The preferential option for the poor constitutes a part of following Jesus that gives ultimate meaning to human existence, and that gives us as believers "reason to hope" (1 Pet. 3:15, NAB). It helps us see the understanding of faith as a hermeneutics of hope, an interpretation that must be constantly enacted and reenacted throughout our lives and human history, building up reasons for hope. Finally, the option for the poor propels us to discover appropriate paths for a prophetic proclamation of the kingdom of God, a communication that respects and creates social justice, communion, fraternity, and equality among people.   — *Theological Studies* (June 2009)

This article by Gustavo Gutiérrez was first published as "The Option for the Poor Arises from Faith in Christ," trans. Robert Lassalle-Klein with James Nickoloff and Susan Sullivan, *Theological Studies* 70, no. 2 (June 2009): 317–29. Reprinted with permission.